Treason and the State

This study traces the transition of treason from a personal crime against the monarch to a modern crime against the impersonal state. It consists of four highly detailed case studies of major state treason trials in England beginning with that of Thomas Wentworth, First Earl of Strafford, in the spring of 1641 and ending with that of Charles Stuart, King of England, in January 1649.

The book examines how these trials constituted practical contexts in which ideas of statehood and public authority legitimated courses of political action that might ordinarily be considered unlawful – or at least not within the compass of the foundational statute of 25 Edward III. The ensuing narrative reveals how the events of the 1640s in England challenged existing conceptions of treason as a personal crime against the king, his family and his servants, and pushed the ascendant parliamentarian faction toward embracing an impersonal conception of the state that perceived public authority as completely independent of any individual or group.

D. ALAN ORR was educated at Queen's University at Kingston, the University of Glasgow and the University of Cambridge, where he received his Ph.D. in 1997. He has taught subsequently at Carleton University in Ottawa and Queen's University at Kingston.

Well it's not flowers...but I love you anyway
—Al

Cambridge Studies in Early Modern British History

Series editors

This is a series of monographs and studies covering many aspects of the history of the British Isles between the late fifteenth century and the early eighteenth century. It includes the work of established scholars and pioneering work by a new generation of scholars. It includes both reviews and revisions of major topics and books, which open up new historical terrain or which reveal startling new perspectives on familiar subjects. All the volumes set detailed research into our broader perspectives and the books are intended for the use of students as well as of their teachers.

For a list of titles in the series, see end of book.

TREASON AND THE STATE

Law, Politics, and Ideology in the English Civil War

D. ALAN ORR

CAMBRIDGE
UNIVERSITY PRESS

CAMBRIDGE UNIVERSITY PRESS
Cambridge, New York, Melbourne, Madrid, Cape Town, Singapore, São Paulo

Cambridge University Press
The Edinburgh Building, Cambridge CB2 8RU, UK

Published in the United States of America by Cambridge University Press, New York

www.cambridge.org
Information on this title: www.cambridge.org/9780521771023

First published 2002
This digitally printed version 2007

A catalogue record for this publication is available from the British Library

ISBN 978-0-521-77102-3 hardback
ISBN 978-0-521-03733-4 paperback

CONTENTS

ACKNOWLEDGMENTS

An older and wiser friend once remarked to me that many projects of historical research begin serendipitously – a chance curiosity growing into something larger, more involved, and more substantive over a lengthy period of time. At the time I greeted this statement with great skepticism; however, I now realize that it is usually true more often than not. This book is a result of one of those chance curiosities demanding further exploration.

In this process of exploration there are many people who have helped along the way. John Morrill supervised the Cambridge doctoral dissertation from which this book derives and continued to believe in it even when I was not sure that I did. My examiners Glenn Burgess and Conrad Russell made a potentially difficult and intimidating process not only enjoyable but also highly instructive and stimulating. William Davies at Cambridge University Press has been an exemplar of patience with yet another late manuscript. Wallace MacCaffrey, Alan Cromartie, David Smith, Paul Bradbury, and Phil Withington read and commented on the manuscript at various stages of its evolution and provided invaluable input. During my time at Cambridge I was fortunate to be surrounded by a lively and supportive circle working in the early modern period including Oleg Roslak, Geoff Baldwin, Tony Nuspl, Craig Muldrew, Patrick Carter, Jurgen Overhoff, Mark Perrott, Phil Baker, Elliot Vernon, Phil West, Mary Morrissey, Nicola Perkins, Katie Craik, Neil Reynolds, Eamonn O'Ciardha, Doron Zimmerman, and Neel Mukherjee. A special thankyou goes also to Adam Slater, Steve Hudson, Hugo Azerad, and Larry Small.

I would like also to thank the staff of the Cambridge University Library Rare Books and Manuscripts Rooms as well as David De Lorenzo of the Harvard Law School Library, who was extremely helpful during a short visit in 1997. I am also grateful to the Social Sciences and Humanities Research Council of Canada, the Cambridge Commonwealth Trust, and Selwyn College Cambridge for providing generous financial assistance at various stages. Most of chapter 5 of this book appeared as part of a slightly lengthier article in the *Journal of British Studies* 39 (2000) titled "England,

Ireland, Magna Carta, and the Common Law: The Case of Connor Lord Maguire, 2nd Baron of Enniskillen." I would like to extend my gratitude to the University of Chicago Press for granting permission to reprint a revised version of that article as part of this study.

My final thankyou goes to my parents, Don and Carrole Orr, for patiently indulging these serendipitous curiosities that have preoccupied me so much in recent years. Without them all this would be impossible.

ABBREVIATIONS

AHR	*American Historical Review*
AJLH	*American Journal of Legal History*
Anderson	Named Reporter contained in the *English Reports*
BL Harl.	British Library, Harleian MSS
BL Sloane	British Library, Sloane MSS
BL TT	British Library, Thomason Tracts
Bodl. Lib. Tanner	Bodleian Library, Tanner MSS
CJ	*Journal of the House of Commons*
Coke, *Reports*	*The Reports of Sir Edward Coke, knt. In thirteen parts*. 6 vols. John Henry Thomas and John Farquhar Fraser, eds. London, 1826
DNB	*Dictionary of National Biography*
Dyer	Named Reporter contained in the *English Reports*
EHR	*English Historical Review*
Eng. Rep.	*English Reports*. London, serial
HJ	*Historical Journal*
HLQ	*Huntingdon Library Quarterly*
HLS	Harvard Law School MSS
HMC Lords XI	HMC House of Lords, *The Manuscripts of The House of Lords, Addenda 1514–1714*. vol. XI, new series, ed. Maurice F. Bond, London, 1962
HPT	*History of Political Thought*
IHS	*Irish Historical Studies*
Irish Statutes	W. Ball ed., *The Statutes at Large passed in the Parliaments held in Ireland*, 20 vols. Dublin 1784–1801.
IT Petyt	Inner Temple, Petyt MSS
JBS	*Journal of British Studies*
JEH	*Journal of Ecclesiastical History*

JLH	*Journal of Legal History*
LJ	*Journal of the House of Lords*
LQR	*Law Quarterly Review*
MM	Manuscript Minutes of the House of Lords
New DNB	*New Dictionary of National Biography*
P&P	*Past and Present*
PRO SP	Public Record Office, State Papers
SL	*The Statutes at Large*, 18 vols. London 1763–1800
SR	*The Statutes of the Realm*, 11 vols. Reprinted London, 1963
State Trials	Cobbett W. and Howell T. B. et al., eds., *A Complete Collection of State Trials*. 33 vols. London, 1809–1826
WC Clarke	Worcester College Oxford, Clarke MSS
Works	*The Works of the most reverend father in God William Laud, D.D. sometime Lord Archbishop of Canterbury*, ed. J. Bliss and W. Scott, 7 vols. Oxford, 1847–1860

Introduction

Today we frequently presume that treason is first and foremost a crime against "the state." This was not always the case. The law of treason in England was at the time of its statutory declaration in 1352 as much a personal crime against the monarch as the unlawful usurpation of his sovereign authority. Compassing the death of the monarch and his heir apparent was arguably more heinously treasonable than forging his seal and issuing false charters in his name. However, during the late medieval and early modern periods new demands emerged. The English law of treason became the principal means of enforcing not only new religious policies in England and Wales but also self-consciously "imperial" policies in the newly created Kingdom of Ireland. In the century before Britain's civil wars of the mid-seventeenth century, developments including the Reformation under Henry VIII, the extension of English control over the whole of Ireland, and the spread of the Counter-Reformation had already imposed unprecedented demands on the law of treason. However, the dramatic events of the civil wars of the 1640s culminating in the trial and execution of King Charles I for high treason in 1649 and the establishment of a "Commonwealth or Free State" in place of the monarchy constituted, unquestionably, the greatest challenge to the existing English law of treason.

Debate on the English law of treason in the early modern period has focused primarily on questions of legality: what actions constituted treason under the existing statute law? However, a failure to interpret the key treason statutes in their ideological contexts has given rise to an unfortunate tendency of "retrying" treason trials according to anachronistic standards of construction.[1] In a modern court of law no crime is deemed to have occurred unless the actions of the accused fall strictly within the relevant statute. When there is doubt whether the relevant statute applies, the case is always to be decided in favor of the accused. Relying on this kind of thinking, some scholars

[1] T. G. Barnes, review of *Tudor Law of Treason: An Introduction*, by J. G. Bellamy, *AHR* 85 (1980): 1190–1191.

have made pronouncements as to the "guilt" or "innocence" of particular persons accused of treason without adequate examination of the role played by commonly held political ideas in the events of these trials.[2] Concomitantly, the law of treason's broader roles in not only the formation of a centralized English state but also in the English imperial enterprise in Ireland and the beginnings of empire have received short shrift. State treason trials provide the opportunity to examine not only the historical evolution of a particular body of law, but also the usage and deployment of a broader range of political and juristic concepts relating to kingship and statehood. Historically speaking, questions of "legality" are not fruitfully discussed or answered without some explanation as to how the law of treason related to the history of political ideas and the often haphazard process of early modern state building.

The failure to give adequate consideration to the role of "constructive" treasons is symptomatic of this unfortunate tendency. The foundational statute of 1352 defined treason as crimes against the king, his family and his servants; however, this did not necessarily entail an allegiance-derived understanding of the English polity based only on oaths of fealty to a single individual. As J. H. Baker has noted: "In early societies there is no concept of the 'state'. Both compensation and retribution for wrongdoing are exacted at the instance of the wronged individual and his kin."[3] England on the eve of the first Civil War was no longer such a society and had not been for some time. The law of treason was inextricably bound up with contemporary ideological debates concerning the nature of sovereignty and what was increasingly denoted as "the state."[4] Treason was not simply a crime against the king's natural person or a breach of allegiance but had increasingly become the unlawful seizure of sovereign or state power.[5] It was a crime against the king not merely in respect of his person but in his role as the lawful wielder and guardian of sovereign power.

[2] An example of this failing is W. R. Stacy's treatment of the attainder of the Earl of Strafford. Stacy condemns the theory of treason in the trial of Strafford as "an unprecedented theory of accumulative treason" without having seriously examined the arguments presented with regard to their relationship to the available political vocabularies. Instead his conclusions derive from a narrow and ultimately anachronistic legalism: W. R. Stacy, "Matter of Fact, Matter of Law, and the Attainder of the Earl of Strafford," *AJLH* 29 (1985): 324.

[3] J. H. Baker, *An Introduction to English Legal History*, 3rd edn. (London, 1990), p. 571.

[4] Quentin Skinner, "The State," in Terence Ball et al., eds., *Political Innovation and Conceptual Change* (Cambridge, 1989), pp. 90–131; Quentin Skinner, *Foundations of Modern Political Thought*, vol. I: *The Renaissance* (Cambridge, 1977), Preface, pp. ix–x; Quentin Skinner, *Liberty Before Liberalism* (Cambridge, 1998), pp. 4–5.

[5] J. A. C. Thomas has made this argument with respect to the Roman law of treason, albeit it should be emphasized here that the concepts of "state" and "sovereignty" as they are discussed here are very much products of the late sixteenth and early seventeenth century: J. A. C. Thomas, ed. and trans., *The Institutes of Justinian: Text, Translation and Commentary* (Cape Town, Wynberg and Johannesburg, 1975), p. 335.

The notion of sovereignty was itself problematic. Early modern jurists and political thinkers were still struggling with the concept. "Sovereignty" in common usage was not necessarily a single arbitrary power of command, but a cluster of powers relating to the practical governance of the realm. These commonly encompassed, for example, the power to give law, levy war, make peace, appoint magistrates, and mint coin. However, the concept was, when carried into the realm of political practice, heavily contested. For example, did it include power to determine the doctrine and discipline of the established church? If so, how was this power exercised: through the king-in-parliament, through the king and the clerical estate assembled in convocation, or through the king alone in a purely personal capacity? At issue was not simply the relationship between subject and sovereign, ruler and ruled, but the very definition of the concept itself.

The English law of treason on the eve of the Civil War was a body of principles as much in keeping with Roman law notions of treason as with feudal or Germanic conceptions of treason. While the latter conceived of treason as a breach of faith or fidelity to one's feudal superior, the former saw *crimen maiestatis* – crimes of majesty or sovereignty in the lexicon of the period[6] – as, in the words of S. H. Cuttler, "an act or plot the goal of which was to diminish the greatness or security of the sovereign power" that was also "tinged with sacrilege."[7] This did not entail the discarding of existing treason legislation but simply the reinterpretation of treason statutes according to more current ideological assumptions and political realities. In 1641 the concept of kingship could mean either the office or public capacity of the monarch as head of state *or* their private person. Indeed, the received constitutional orthodoxy in the years after the accession of James VI of Scotland to the English throne in 1603 was that the two were inseparable. Accordingly, treason was a crime against both the monarch and his or her regal estate by virtue of their lawful possession of sovereign power. The actions of a traitor encompassed those that tended toward the unlawful appropriation of the authority of the state to their own private use. Only when viewed in this context will questions concerning the "legality" and legitimacy of key English state treason trials during the Civil War receive adequate consideration.

This study contends that in public law terms the early modern state was essentially a corporate body – a juristic person consisting of ruler and ruled bound together by the rule of law. This rule of law was "fundamental" to the constitution of the polity as a corporate body. In this particular instance

6 "Maiestas" was translated as both "sovereignty" and "majesty" in the early modern period.

7 S. H. Cuttler, *The Law of Treason and Treason Trials in Later Medieval France* (Cambridge, 1981), p. 6.

that law was the municipal law of England, the common law. The common law was in this sense "fundamental" to the constitution of the English and by extension the Irish polities.[8] However, within this corporation the relationship of ruler and ruled, church and polity, was becoming problematic with the traditional framework of the king's two bodies coming increasingly under strain.[9] According to the commonplace notion of the king's two bodies advanced in the writings of jurists such as Plowden and Coke the state was not a fully impersonal political entity. When the king acted in his political capacity he acted as a corporation yet his political body, his "state," remained inextricably bound up with his body natural and the heirs of his body. As Marie Axton has noted, late Tudor and early Stuart jurists "were formulating an idea of the state as a perpetual corporation, yet they were unable or unwilling to separate state and monarch."[10] The kingdom was more of the nature of a corporation entailed to a particular family than a purely abstract or impersonal entity.

However, the potential for such a separation did exist. For example, the Huguenot author of the *Vindiciae Contra Tyrannos* had, as early as the 1570s, argued that it was the people not the king that formed a perpetual corporate body.[11] Furthermore, while not calling for the supplanting of monarchy with a popular corporate republic, this author also suggested that a monarch who committed a felony against the people could be adjudged guilty of high treason.[12] In 1641 the English law of treason, statutorily defined as compassing or imagining the death of the king, depended on the inseparability of the king's corporate public authority from his or her natural person. Crimes against the political body of the whole state were also necessarily crimes against the king's natural body. The events of the civil wars of the 1640s and ultimately in 1649 the ideological demands of regicide led to the appropriation of a fully impersonal conception of the state in which the king, acting beyond his commission as an inferior magistrate, had derogated from the sovereign authority of the people.

[8] The concept of "*leges imperii*," or "fundamental laws" in late medieval and early modern usage pertains to the received laws of a particular realm as opposed to natural law (*lex naturalis*) or the law of nations (*ius gentium*), both of which applied to all peoples and all realms; I would like to extend my thanks to Mr. Robert Moody for clarifying this point. See also chapter 2, below.

[9] Michael Mendle, "Politics and Political Thought, 1640–42," in Conrad Russell, ed., *The Origins of the English Civil War* (London, 1973), p. 221.

[10] Marie Axton, *The Queen's Two Bodies: Drama and the Elizabethan Succession* (London, 1977), p. 12.

[11] Stephanus Junius Brutus [Philippe Mornay? Hubert Languet?], *Vindiciae, Contra Tyrannos: or concerning the legitimate power of a prince over the people, and of the people over a prince*, ed. and trans. George Garnett (Cambridge, 1994), pp. xxiii, 90; see also chapter 6, below.

[12] Brutus, *Vindiciae, Contra Tyrannos*, p. 156.

In the 1640s and 50s events drove ideas. Although republican modes of civic consciousness undoubtedly had some presence before the conflagrations of the 1640s England was, at least in theory, a monarchical state.[13] "Revolutionary" political thinking, such as one might attribute to the likes of Hobbes, Milton, Sidney, or Harrington, was the fruit of this era not its cause.[14] By contrast the ideas deployed in the context of state treason trials were of necessity familiar, commonplace, sometimes even disappointingly banal. They were, after all, explicitly "ideological" – political actors used them to redescribe a particular set of actions as "good," "legal," and "moral" with an eye to convincing the faint-hearted, the undecided, and the uncommitted. In order for them to have purchase with their intended audiences they were of necessity familiar and appealed to shared values and shared authorities. Nevertheless, they are very important because they demonstrate that the link between political thought and political practice was far from seamless in early modern Britain.

Quentin Skinner has emphasized the inseparable relationship of political thought to political action.[15] This study does not dispute this contention but rather accepts it as given. It does, however, offer qualification and refinement. The context of a trial and the setting of a court of law, like any institutional context, privilege certain sources, texts, ideas, and rhetorics over others. For example, even before the Long Parliament ordered that the remaining writings of Sir Edward Coke be published, his writings already enjoyed something of a quasi-canonical status. Sir John Davies was a former Chief Justice of England (however briefly) and his writings were accordingly afforded a similar status, particularly with respect to Ireland where he served as Attorney-General. In the absence of official reporting the good reputation

[13] J. G. A. Pocock has argued that before the 1640s the predominant mode of civic consciousness in England was that of territorial and jurisdictional monarchy and that civic humanism with its attendant values of active citizenship became a force only after that period: J. G. A. Pocock, *The Machiavellian Moment: Florentine Political Thought and the Atlantic Republican Tradition* (Princeton, 1975), chapter 10. This thesis has been challenged by Patrick Collinson and more recently Markku Peltonen: Markku Peltonen, *Classical Humanism and Republicanism in English Political Thought, 1570–1640* (Cambridge, 1995); Patrick Collinson, "The Monarchical Republic of Elizabeth I," *Bulletin of the John Rylands Library* 69 (1987): 394–424.

[14] Jonathan Scott, "The English Republican Imagination," in J. S. Morrill, ed., *Revolution and Restoration: England in the 1650s* (London, 1992), pp. 35–54; Blair Worden, "English Republicanism," in J. H. Burns and M. Goldie, eds., *The Cambridge History of Political Thought, 1450–1700* (Cambridge, 1991), pp. 443–475; Blair Worden, "Classical Republicanism and the Puritan Revolution," in Hugh Lloyd-Jones, Valerie Pearl, and Blair Worden, eds., *History and Imagination: Essays in Honour of H. R. Trevor-Roper* (London, 1981), pp. 182–200.

[15] Quentin Skinner, "The Principles and Practice of Opposition: The Case of Bolingbroke versus Walpole," in Neil McKendrick, ed., *Historical Perspectives: Studies in English Thought and Society in Honour of J. H. Plumb* (London, 1974), pp. 93–128.

of the author or the antiquity of a source became crucial in determining its relative *validity* and the forensic rhetoric of the day placed a premium on this. For example, the king's two bodies was an important political concept not simply because it was omnipresently *there* among an amorphous common stock of concepts, but because it received authoritative definition in Coke's report of *Calvin's Case* in the seventh part of his *Reports*. Citation of a prominent and recognized authority was an accepted, effective strategy in achieving practical political objectives. As a consequence, attempts to liberate us from the grip of law-centered political thought in the analysis of seventeenth-century political language and culture require careful reconsideration.[16]

This book is structured in two parts of two and four chapters respectively. The first chapter will discuss the growth of English treason legislation in the early modern period and its response to the demands of the Reformation, the extension of English control over the whole of Ireland, and the rise of Jesuit and missionary priest activity in the last quarter of the sixteenth century. In broader terms the law responded to three pressures: Protestant Reformation, Catholic Reformation, and the beginnings of British imperialism in Ireland. The second chapter will establish the ideological context in which the law of treason operated at the opening of the Civil War by establishing working definitions of the terms "sovereignty" and "state." Key themes here will be the development of the theory of the king's two bodies, the growth of the idea of an impersonal or abstract "state" in early modern political thought, and their respective roles in the interpretation of English treason law. The chapter will offer a concept of sovereignty as a practical cluster of positive or "state" powers that political actors contested with competing and alternately shared rhetorics. While the revisionism of the 1970s threatened to banish the concept of sovereignty from the debate on the origins of the English Civil War, the goal here is to reposition the concept of sovereignty at the center of that debate without recourse to older whiggish narratives of absolutism versus constutionalism.[17] The English Civil War *was* a struggle for sovereignty but it was not a struggle driven by rival accounts of the locus of sovereign power, king or people, ascending or descending – it was a struggle for definition. Deep ideological polarities were the legacy not the cause of these events.

The four chapters of part II consist of four detailed case studies of major English state treason trials. The first is that of Thomas Wentworth, First Earl

[16] Alan Cromartie has emphasized this point in his recent discussion of Harrington: Alan Cromartie, "Harringtonian Virtue: Harrington, Machiavelli, and the Method of the Moment," *HJ* 41 (1998): 1008–1009.

[17] The work of Johann Sommerville springs to mind here: Johann Sommerville, *Politics and Ideology in England, 1603–1640* (London, 1986); for a contrasting view see Kevin Sharpe, *Politics and Ideas in Early Stuart England: Essays and Studies* (London, 1989), pp. 286–287.

of Strafford, in March, April, and May 1641, followed by those of William Laud, Archbishop of Canterbury, over the course of 1644, Connor Maguire, Second Baron of Enniskillen, in early 1645, and concluding with that of Charles Stuart, King of England, in January 1649. The trial of Wentworth for his role in Charles I's personal rule of the 1630s in both England and Ireland was arguably the most controversial English state treason trial of the Stuart era. No study of the law of treason in the Civil War can go forward without giving it adequate consideration. Laud's trial, while receiving less attention from historians, concerned the disputed relationship of church and state and, more particularly, competing conceptions of the supremacy, Erastian and clerical. The trial of Maguire, an Irish peer tried in England for treason committed in Ireland, raised questions involving sovereignty and allegiance in a composite state or multiple monarchy. More specifically, it also raised questions concerning the constitutional relationship of England and Ireland: separate kingdoms united by a shared personal allegiance and rule of law yet divided by departures in the practice of government and the need for a shared sense of antiquity. If the trial of the king in January 1649 and his concomitant reduction from the lawful holder of sovereign power to the role of inferior magistrate in a popular state was less controversial than that of Strafford, it was only because it was so much more clearly illegal. It was an unprecedented event that no study of this kind can afford to ignore.

Treason and the State is not, therefore, an attempt at comprehensively retelling the story of the English law of treason during the middle of the seventeenth century. It is rather an examination of four occasions of state as ideological events in which both competing and alternately shared conceptions of public authority found expression as political practice. While the selection of only four trials may seem limiting, it must be remembered that two of these trials have already formed the basis of monographs.[18] Indeed, a full consideration of all aspects of any one of these trials could on its own easily form the foundation for a book-length study. The criteria by which the four trials were selected are their relative significance in constitutional terms and the availability of source material, the latter making them something of a self-selecting sample.

[18] J. H. Timmis III, *Thine is the Kingdom: The Trial for Treason of Thomas Lord Wentworth, Earl of Strafford, First Minister to King Charles I and Last Hope of the English Crown* (Tuscaloosa, Ala., 1974), and C. V. Wedgwood, *The Trial of Charles I* (Glasgow, 1964; reprinted Harmondsworth, 1983).

Part I

CONCEPTS

1

The statutory basis of English treason law

I

On the eve of the English Civil War the statutory basis of English treason was fraught with ambiguity. This was the case even though in England, unlike France, statute had authoritatively defined the law of treason during the late medieval period. In the case of late-medieval France the law of treason developed from a combination of judicial practice and the study and exegesis of Roman law texts, most notably the *Digest* of Justinian. In England treason was set out in statutes – authoritative declarations of law enacted by king, lords and commons assembled in parliament.[1] However, at the outbreak of the English Civil War the statutory basis of treason was not clearly established. How was this so? Confusion arose from two sources. First, it was unclear which statutes and which particular provisions contained in statutes were actually in force; second, even when there was agreement that a statute was in force, there were disputes over the meaning of the text. Medieval and Tudor statutes were often the product of particular political circumstances that no longer applied, yet early Stuart jurists were not averse to appropriating them to serve their arguments. Furthermore, the unscrupulous exploitation of textual ambiguities could give statutes a far more generous application than their framers had originally intended.

Since 1352 the English law of treason has been based on Edward III's statute of treasons (25 Edward III, st. 5, c. 2). Much of it is still in force. This statute was the principal statutory foundation of English treason law throughout the seventeenth century and much of the controversy that arose flowed from disputes over the meaning and scope of this brief and seemingly straightforward document.[2] Held as treasonable under this statute

[1] S. H. Cuttler, *The Law of Treason and Treason Trials in Later Medieval France* (Cambridge, 1981), pp. 8–9 and ch. 1.

[2] My thinking here has been somewhat influenced by Roger Chartier's article "Texts, Printing, Readings," in Lynn Hunt, ed., *The New Cultural History* (Berkeley, Calif., 1989), pp. 154–175.

were (1) compassing or imagining the death of the king, queen, or eldest male heir to the throne; (2) violating the king's "companion," his eldest unmarried daughter or the eldest male heir's wife; (3) levying war on "the king in his realm"; (4) adhering to the king's enemies in his own realm "or elsewhere"; (5) counterfeiting the great or privy seal, the king's coin, or bringing counterfeit coin into the realm; and (6) killing the chancellor, treasurer, or any of the king's justices in the execution of their offices.[3] The traitor's lands held in fee simple and "holden of others as of himself" were escheat to the crown.[4] The statute was careful to distinguish high treason – crimes against the king, his family and servants – from petty treason – crimes of servant against master, wife against husband, father against son, or cleric against superior.

According to J. G. Bellamy, the treason of levying war against the king originated in the latter thirteenth century when Edward I made his conquest of Wales. Bellamy has noted that Edward was undoubtedly "influenced by the Roman theory that the right of levying war belonged only to princes without a secular superior" and, while such conclusions are difficult to draw, this probably reflected the penetration of Roman law into northern Europe at this time.[5] Its inclusion in the statute of 1352 is highly significant as were the sections decreeing it treason to kill a magistrate in the execution of his office or to counterfeit coin, all of which corresponded with the Roman law of treason.[6] Early modern legal writers seem to have been fully aware of the points of convergence between their own law and Roman civil-law sources. For example, the presence of counterfeiting in both bodies of law was noted by the late Tudor writer William Fulbecke as being "for the most part consonant to the Common Law of this Realme."[7] Indeed, the great sixteenth-century French jurist Jean Bodin himself noted the similarity of the English law of treason to the Roman law of treason: "As by the laws of England, to aid the enemie in any sort whatsoeuer, is accounted high treason. Which points of treason I see not to be distinguished by these interpreto[r]s of the Roman law."[8]

[3] *SL* I: 261–262. [4] *SL* I: 262.

[5] J. G. Bellamy, *The Law of Treason in England in the Later Middle Ages* (Cambridge, 1970), p. 14.

[6] Theodor Mommsen, Paul Kreuger, and Alan Watson, eds., *The Digest of Justinian*, vol. IV, trans. Alan Watson (Philadelphia, 1985), pp. 802–804; see also Floyd Seyward Lear, *Treason in Roman and Germanic Law* (Austin, Tex., 1965), pp. 28–29.

[7] William Fulbecke, *A Parallele or Conference of The Civil Law, the Canon Law and the Common Law of this Realme of England. Wherin the agreement and disagreement of these three Lawes, and the causes and reasons of the said disagreement, are opened and discussed* (London, 1602; reprinted London, 1618), fol. 88a.

[8] Jean Bodin, *Six Bookes of a Commonweale*, trans. Richard Knolles and ed. Kenneth D. McRae (Cambridge, Mass., 1962), p. 26.

In the first of his two major studies of the English law of treason Bellamy argued that the 1352 statute was actually an attempt to narrow the scope and compass of the English law of treason. During the 1340s, while Edward III had been at war in France, his judges adjudged as treasonable such actions as common banditry and the taking of hostages for ransom by knights wearing "cote armure" with drawn sword in full war harness.[9] Bellamy has argued further that this was an obvious attempt to enforce fully the claims of Roman law that the prince possessed sole power of war and peace: "Since according to late mediaeval theory the sovereign prince alone had the right to levy open war only he could allow the holding of men to ransom. To do so without his permission in a 'war' not of his authorization was therefore lese-majesty since the taking of the ransom was the arrogation of royal power."[10] Bellamy's argument would seem to suggest the view that the treason of levying war against the king as defined by 25 Edward III did not constitute a claim by the crown to the sole power to levy war. Thus, the great magnates of the land were free to conduct their business without fear of royal reproach. While this of course may have been true of 1352, it became readily apparent that this was not how succeeding generations of Tudor and Stuart jurists interpreted the claims of the statute.

Another crucial feature of 25 Edward III was the inclusion of what became known as the "salvo" clause.[11] This section of the statute accorded

> That if any other Case, supposed Treason, which is not above specified, doth happen before any Justices, the Justices shall tarry without going to judgement of the Treason, till this Cause be shewed and declared before the King and his Parliament whether it ought to be judged Treason or other felony.[12]

The intent behind the clause may have been to keep the power to define treason in the hands of the magnates who had engineered 25 Edward III. However, it inadvertently left the door open for two key developments.

The first of these, parliamentary attainder, was both procedural and substantive in nature. Attainder was the rather extreme expedient whereby parliament passed an act declaring the accused to be guilty of the crime charged in the bill. While it was most commonly combined with a charge of high treason, a conviction of felony could also be obtained in this fashion.[13] Acts of attainder could also serve to augment the existing body of treason law

[9] Bellamy, *Law of Treason*, p. 62. [10] Bellamy, *Law of Treason*, pp. 62–63.

[11] This was the label applied by Richard Lane, the Earl of Strafford's counsel at his trial for treason in the spring of 1641: John Rushworth, *The Tryal of Thomas Earl of Strafford upon an impeachment of high treason* (London 1680; 2nd edn. 1700), p. 671.

[12] *SL* I: 262.

[13] W. R. Stacy, "Richard Roose and the Use of Parliamentary Attainder in the Reign of Henry VIII," *HJ* 29 (1986): 1–15.

by the legislation of new treasons. For example, W. R. Stacy has argued that the attainder of Richard Roose in 1531 created the additional treason of poisoning.[14] In short, attainder brought the full force of the law-making power of the sovereign to bear directly on the accused.

In the fifteenth century acts of attainder were originally used to supplement previous convictions for treason at common law and martial law and to provide for the punishment of traitors who were unavailable for trial at common law.[15] Convictions for treason under martial law or under the law of arms provided only for the forfeiture of the traitors' goods and chattels because only the common-law courts or an act of parliament could decide issues of title. Such convictions needed to be supplemented with acts of attainder in order to give the crown access to the traitors' lands.[16] Acts of attainder had also proved useful in cases where traitors had been killed in the act of rebellion or had otherwise expired (e.g. taken their own life, died of plague, etc.) before they could be brought to trial.[17] Such posthumous proceedings could be aimed either at gaining access to the deceased's lands or simply at assuring the populace that the traitor had received their condign punishment and was surely burning for his or her sins. Acts of attainder initially[18] had the further advantage that they could potentially give access to the traitor's entailed estates as well as their lands held in fee simple.[19] Finally, bills of attainder could circumvent potentially messy proceedings at common law.[20] Customarily cases of treason were determined by jury trial in the neighborhoods where they had been committed before special commissions of *oyer* and *terminer* but a statute of 1541 (33 Henry VIII, c. 23) later empowered the king to name particular shires or places of his own choosing in the commissions in cases of suspected traitors examined before king and council.[21] Additional controversial statutes of Henry VIII

14 Stacy, "Roose": 2. 15 Bellamy, *Law of Treason*, pp. 177–205.

16 J. G. Bellamy, *The Tudor Law of Treason: An Introduction* (Toronto, 1979), pp. 234–235.

17 Cade is an example of this: Bellamy, *Law of Treason*, pp. 191–192.

18 From the time of Richard II lands held in fee tail were also potentially forfeit: Bellamy, *Law of Treason*, p. 115.

19 Depending on the wording of the particular bill attainder could and usually did give access to *all* the landed estates of the traitor. For the impact of the increased use of attainder on the greater nobility of England in the fifteenth century see J. R. Lander, "Attainder and Forfeiture, 1453–1509," *HJ* 6 (1961): 119–151. The lands of dowagers were generally untouched by attainders. This combined with frequent restitutions enabled many noble families to rebuild their landed fortunes within less than a generation.

20 Bellamy dates the first use of attainder without prior proceedings from 1459 while the first such attainder in Henry VIII's reign was that of Roose: Bellamy, *Law of Treason*, p. 177; Stacy, "Roose": 2. Stacy rebuts the contention of S. E. Lehmberg that the first such attainder of Henry VIII's reign was that of Elizabeth Barton, "the nun of Kent," and her followers in 1534: S. E. Lehmberg, "Parliamentary Attainder in the Reign of Henry VIII," *HJ* 18 (1975): 681–682.

21 *SL* II: 320.

(26 Henry VIII, c. 13 and 35 Henry VIII, c. 2) had further decreed that treasons committed outside of the realm of England were to be tried by an ordinary jury in a shire of the king's choosing.[22] In spite of this, W. R. Stacy has argued, early modern juries could prove intractable and parliamentary attainder provided a swifter and more reliable alternative.[23]

The second development was that of "common-law treasons." While succeeding generations of lawyers generally accepted that everything contained in 25 Edward III was treasonable, by the sixteenth century there were divisions of opinion over whether the statute of treasons was exhaustive.[24] Could there be custom-derived, "common-law treasons" that had existed before 25 Edward III and still existed wanting but for statutory confirmation or judicial invocation? For example, Sergeant Stamford, acting as prosecution at the trial of Sir Nicholas Throckmorton in 1554, warned the accused: "You are deceived, to conclude all Treasons [are] by the statute of the 25th of Edward the third; for that Statute is but a Declaration of certain Treasons, which were Treasons before at the common law. Even so there doth remain divers other treasons at this day which cannot be expressed by that statute, as the Judges can declare."[25] Stamford lost and Throckmorton was, much to the government's consternation, acquitted, with the jurors being fined in Star Chamber for their verdict. However, the notion of common-law treasons remained in the prosecutor's arsenal. Oliver St. John invoked it during the debates over the Earl of Strafford's attainder in April 1641 and Samuel Browne made much the same argument to the House of Lords in calling for Archbishop Laud's attainder by ordinance in early January 1645.[26]

Aside from providing a legal basis for extra-statutory treasons, the idea of common-law treasons also provided a foundation for additional treason statutes. According to the "common-law mind" or mind-set under which

22 This was a key statute at issue in the trial of Maguire: see chapter 5, below.

23 Stacy has taken issue with G. R. Elton's assertion that, for the most part, treason trials held during Thomas Cromwell's ascendancy in the early English Reformation were conducted with deference to the forms of the common law: Stacy, "Roose," and G. R. Elton, *Policy and Police: The Enforcement of the Reformation in the Age of Thomas Cromwell* (Cambridge, 1972), pp. 263–326.

24 Elton and Bellamy are divided on the question of 25 Edward III's exhaustiveness in the fifteenth century: G. R. Elton, *The Tudor Constitution: Documents and Commentary*, 2nd edn. (Cambridge, 1982), p. 60.

25 *State Trials* I: 889; the text in *State Trials* is taken from Raphael Holinshed, *The Chronicles of Ireland*, in *Holinshed's Chronicles: England, Scotland and Ireland with a New Introduction by Vernon F. Snow*, 6 vols. (New York, 1965; reprinted New York, 1976). For a discussion of the use of common-law treasons by Tudor prosecutors see Bellamy, *Tudor Law of Treason*, pp. 46–47, 57.

26 BL TT E.208(7), Oliver St. John, *An Argument of Law concerning the Bill of Attainder of High Treason of Thomas Earle of Strafford: At a Conference in the Committee of both Houses of Parliament* (London, 1641), p. 8; BL Harl. MS 164, fol. 993r; *LJ* VII: 125.

many (but by no means all) late Tudor and early Stuart jurists formulated their arguments, statutes were seen as simply affirmations of a body of pre-existing, unwritten, customary, fundamental law – part of what J. G. A. Pocock has referred to as "the ancient constitution."[27] Thus, the possibility of common-law treasons left the door open for additional augmentative treason statutes – a potential that Tudor monarchs were quick to exploit.

II

The Tudor period saw a dramatic growth not only in the amount of new treason legislation but also in the scope of the law of treason. While the sheer volume of Tudor treason legislation and the limited space here prohibit the individual consideration of each new treason statute under the Tudors, certain key statutory developments must be addressed in order to provide adequate context for this study. Scholars such as J. G. Bellamy and G. R. Elton have discussed at length the development of treason legislation under the Tudors.[28] Bellamy has identified a pattern in Tudor treason legislation: after an initial phase of contraction early in the monarch's reign, usually in the form of a statute of repeal or the introduction of stronger evidentiary requirements, the scope of treason would gradually expand as new threats to the reigning monarch and the stability of the Tudor polity emerged.[29] For example, the greatest period of expansion under Henry VIII came in the last third of his reign from 1534 onwards, when the need emerged for the law of treason to serve as an instrument of state in enforcing the Reformation. Similarly, the latter two thirds of Elizabeth's reign saw a dramatic growth in treason legislation as the Counter-Reformation threatened to destabilize the embattled Tudor regime. Specific developments included the northern rebellion of 1569, Elizabeth's excommunication in 1570, increased Jesuit and seminary priest activity after 1577, and the accompanying threat of Spanish invasion.[30] This last development led in the 1580s to a series of new treason statutes aimed specifically at seminary priests and those who harbored them.

The sixteenth century also saw the extension of English sovereignty over the whole of Ireland. This created new demands on the law of treason as

[27] J. G. A. Pocock, *The Ancient Constitution and the Feudal Law*, 2nd edn. (Cambridge, 1987), chs. 2, 3; for a more recent discussion see J. W. Tubbs, "Custom, Time and Reason: Early Seventeenth-Century Conceptions of the Common Law," *HPT* 19 (1998): 363–406.

[28] Bellamy, *Tudor Law of Treason*, *passim*; Elton, *Policy and Police*, pp. 263–326 and *Tudor Constitution*, pp. 59–88.

[29] Bellamy, *Tudor Law of Treason*, ch. 2. This can also be seen in the reign of Richard II, whose attempts to bolster 25 Edward III with augmentative treason legislation were effectively reversed by the repeal statute of 1 Henry IV, c. 10: *SL* I: 428.

[30] Elton, *Tudor Constitution*, pp. 420–421.

the claims of English monarchs to suzerainty over all of Ireland required enforcement. The task was complicated by the fact that no English king or queen set foot in Ireland between 1399 and 1689, making the likelihood of war being levied directly against the monarch's person in Ireland slim indeed.[31] While an act of Poynings' Parliament (1494–5) had brought 25 Edward III and numerous other English statutes into force in Ireland,[32] the constitutional relationship between the two kingdoms remained unclear throughout the early modern period. In 1541, in response to papal pretensions of suzerainty, the Irish parliament declared Henry VIII king, thus raising Ireland from the status of a lordship of the English crown to that of a separate kingdom dependent on and subordinate to the English crown. This, however, still left many jurisdictional issues unresolved with regard to the judicial and legislative powers of the two kingdoms. For example, when the Earl of Strafford went on trial in the spring of 1641 it remained ambiguous whether Irish treason statutes made prior to Poynings' Parliament remained in force along with 25 Edward III or whether the English statute had completely supplanted them. The judicial powers of the Irish House of Lords were also poorly defined: while it was accepted that the Irish Lords had *a* judicial role, the English judges affirmed on the eve of the 1641 revolt that this role did not extend to the trying of high treason.[33] Furthermore, there was the question of the manner of trial for Irish peers: while it was established by the end of Elizabeth's reign that both Irishmen and crown servants in Ireland could be tried in England in King's Bench for crimes committed in Ireland,[34] there remained questions raised by the revival of parliamentary

[31] Steven G. Ellis, *Tudor Ireland: Crown Community and the Conflict of Cultures, 1470–1603* (London, 1985), p. 25.

[32] 10 Henry VII, c. 22 in *Irish Statutes* I: 56.

[33] Michael Perceval-Maxwell, *The Outbreak of the Irish Rebellion of 1641* (Montreal and Kingston, 1994), ch. 7.

[34] Coke states explicitly that according to 35 Henry VIII, c. 2 "which yet remains in force," treasons committed outside of the realm were to be tried "either in the kings Bench or before Commissioners in such Shire as shall be assigned by the King." In arguing that the importation of debased coin from Ireland was not treason under 25 Edward III he wrote further that coin "... must be brought from a forraine Nation, and not from Ireland, or other place belonging to the Crown of England, and so it hath been resolved, so wary are Judges to expound this statute concerning Treason, and that in most benigne sense: for albeit Ireland be a distinct kingdome, and out of the Realme of England to some purposes, as to Protections and fines levied etc. as hath been said: yet to some intent it is accounted as a member of or belonging to the Crown of this Realme. And therefore a Writ of Error is maintainable here in the Kings Bench of a judgement given in the Kings Bench in Ireland, so as the Judges did construe this statute not to extend to false money brought out of Ireland." Sir Edward Coke, *The Third Part of The Institutes of the Laws of England concerning High Treason, and other Pleas of the Crown, and Criminall causes* (London, 1644), pp. 11, 18. For the trial of Irishmen and crown servants in Ireland by King's Bench in England see Hiram Morgan, "Extradition and Treason-trial of a Gaelic Lord: The Case of Brian O'Rourke," *Irish Jurist* 22 (1987): 285–301; D. Alan Orr, "England, Ireland, Magna Carta and the Common

judicature in the 1620s and the legal status of the Irish peerage. Did Irish peers have the right to demand trial by the English House of Lords, the Irish House of Lords, some Irish version of the Lord High Steward's Court, or were they to be tried "on the country" in England?[35] In the case of Scotland the picture was somewhat clearer. With the exception of a brief period under the Protectorate, the Scottish law of treason remained an independent body of law until 1707 when it was specifically exempted from the provisions of the Treaty of Union that guaranteed the preservation of Scots law. Thereafter, the English law of treason came into force and remains so today.[36]

Another key issue that emerged in the sixteenth century was that of whether "bare words" could constitute treason. The act of printing treasonable words was sufficient to constitute an "overt act," but it remained controversial up to the outbreak of the first Civil War whether the mere speaking of treasonable words constituted treason. Elton has argued that even before Henry VIII's notorious treasonable-words statute of 1534, the king's courts had construed words as treasonable and that Henry VII's council "could entertain a charge of alleged treasonable words."[37] However, by the early 1530s and Henry VIII's break with Rome, there was the perceived need for a stronger statutory justification for treasonable words and a clearer definition of what manner of words were to be accounted treasonable. The result was the passage in 1534 of Henry VIII's aforementioned treasonable-words statute, 26 Henry VIII, c. 13.[38] In the words of Professor Elton, this statute represented "the first comprehensive statement since 1352."[39] This statute declared it treasonable,

> if any Person or Persons, after the first Day of *February* next coming, do maliciously by Words or Writing, or by Craft imagine, invent, practise or attempt any bodily Harm to be done or committed to the King's most Royall Person, the Queen's or

Law: The Case of Connor Lord Maguire, Second Baron of Enniskillen," *JBS* 39 (2000): 389–421.

35 Coke's position on this was that only "Lords of Parliament" had the right to demand trial by the House of Lords. Scottish, Irish, French and, interestingly, ecclesiastical peers, were they to stand accused of treason in England, were to be tried "on the country" as commoners by a jury of freeholders. By contrast St. John, citing Crompton and Dyer, argued, "It's true, a Scotish or French Nobleman is triable here as a common person: the Law takes no notice of their Nobility, because those Countries are not governed by the Lawes of England; but Ireland being governed by the same Laws the Peers there are triable according to the Law of England, only *per pares*": Coke, *The Third Part of the Institutes*, pp. 24–26, 30; St. John, *Argument*, p. 63; 3 Dyer 360b, 73 *Eng. Rep.* 807 (KB); and chapter 5, below.

36 William K. Dickson, "The Scots Law of Treason," *Juridical Review* 10 (1898): 251–254.

37 *SL* II: 215–216; Elton, *Tudor Constitution*, pp. 59–62 and *Policy and Police*, pp. 263–264; Bellamy, *Law of Treason*, pp. 116–123; and Isobel D. Thornley, "Treason by Words in the Fifteenth Century," *EHR* 32 (1917): 556–558 (commentary only).

38 For the drafting of this statute see Elton, *Policy and Police*, pp. 263–265.

39 Elton, *Policy and Police*, p. 265.

their Heirs apparent, or to deprive them or their Dignity, Title or Name of their Royal Estates, or slanderously and maliciously publish and pronounce, by express Writing or Words, that the King our Sovereign Lord should be Heretick, Schismatic, Tyrant, Infidel or Usurper of the Crown . . .[40]

The act's provisions against calling the king a schismatic, heretic, infidel or usurper, most likely aimed at enforcing Henry's break from Rome, did not address questions of ecclesiastical organization and practice. Other treasons discussed included the detention of royal fortifications and munitions against the entry of the king and his servants. These provisions simply gave clearer definition of what acts constituted "levying war" under 25 Edward III. The act also provided for the trial in England at common law for treasons committed outside the realm by commissions of *oyer* and *terminer* whose proceedings would then be certified into King's Bench.[41]

The most obvious point of comparison with 25 Edward III is the notion of treason as a crime of usurpation or deprivation. This idea was present in 25 Edward III but not always explicitly. For example, the counterfeiting of the great seal as stipulated under 25 Edward III was clearly an offense of usurping the king's role or, as Bellamy has argued, "accroachment." Indeed, as early as the twelfth century Glanvill defined the falsifying of royal charters as *lèse majesté* – an act that of necessity required either the unauthorized use of the king's seal or the use of a counterfeit seal.[42] However, where 25 Edward III was, perhaps not unintentionally, ambiguous, 26 Henry VIII is explicit. "Personal" treasons against the king and his family remained but it also became treasonable to deprive the king and his heirs of their kingship or to aver by words or deeds that their continued possession of the kingship is usurped. The statute reveals that by the early sixteenth century kingship was no longer solely of a network of personal allegiances but a kingly office or public capacity in which the king acted *as king*.[43]

The treasonable-words statute of 26 Henry VIII remains to this day a candidate for the most unpopular act ever passed by a parliament in England. Nevertheless, Professor Elton has made a very strong argument that the statute's demand that accused traitors be tried "according to the Laws and Customs of this Realm" received, for the most part, scrupulous observation during the ascendancy of Thomas Cromwell.[44] For example, although there

40 *SL* II: 216.
41 *SL* II: 216. A more detailed statute providing for the trial of treasons committed outside the realm was made in 1543. 35 Henry VIII, c. 2: SL II: 361.
42 G. D. G. Hall, ed. and trans., *The Treatise on The Laws and Customs of The Realm of England Commonly Called Glanvill* (Oxford, 1993), p. 177.
43 For the doctrine of capacities and the idea of the king's two bodies in relationship to 25 Edward III see chapter 2, below.
44 Elton, *Policy and Police*, pp. 293–326; for an alternate view see Stacy, "Roose."

was no hard and fast rule stipulating the necessity of two witnesses, traitors were seldom convicted on the testimony of a single witness and even then only in exceptional cases like that of More, "pursued to death by a vengeful King."[45]

Elton's arguments aside, subsequent treason legislation after Henry VIII's death was quick to mitigate the severity of Henrician treason law. The statute of 1 Edward VI, c. 12 stipulated, in consonance with previous practice, that the printing of treasonable words was treasonable but changed the law so that those making treasonable utterances became subject to the following punishments: (1) on the first conviction to imprisonment and loss of goods and chattels; (2) on the second to perpetual imprisonment, loss of goods and chattels, and "the whole Issues and Profit of all [their] . . . Lands, Tenements and other Hereditaments, Benefices, Prebends and other Spiritual Promotions for Term of Life of such Offender or Offenders . . ." Only on the third offense would treasonable words make the accused subject to the penalties of high treason.[46] Furthermore, the statute also included a number of important procedural codicils. These included the requirements that a complaint of treasonable words must be made to a member of the king's council, a justice of assize, or a justice of the peace within a span of thirty days and, in a subsequently oft-cited passage, that the offender must "be accused by two sufficient and lawful Witnesses or shall willingly without Violence confess the same."[47] The further proviso was added by 5 & 6 Edward VI, c. 11 that the two witnesses must be brought to face the accused at arraignment unless the accused had already previously confessed. The net effect of these two statutes was to bring a full Roman law standard of proof to bear in cases of high treason – only a free confession or the direct testimony of two witnesses would be acceptable.[48]

Early Marian legislation was even more ambitious in attempting to roll back the growth of English treason legislation. The statute of 1 Mary, st. 1, c. 1 made undoubtedly the most grandiloquent attempt at repeal:

> from henceforth no Act, Deed or Offence, being by Act of Parliament or Statute made Treason, Pety Treason or Misprision of Treason, by Words, Writing, Ciphering, Deeds or otherwise whatsoever, shall be taken, had deemed or adjudged to be High Treason, Pety Treason or Misprision of Treason, but only such as be declared and expressed to be Treason, Pety Treason or Misprision of Treason in or by the Act of Parliament or

[45] Furthermore, Elton has noted that More was in fact not tried under 26 Henry VIII, c. 13 but for refusing to take the oath of supremacy: Elton, *Policy and Police*, p. 307.

[46] *SL* II: 394. [47] *SL* II: 396.

[48] *SL* II: 450; according to John Langbein the two-witness rule had its origins in the Roman and canon law which specified as a standard of proof either two witnesses with direct knowledge of the crime or a confession: John Langbein, *Torture and the Law of Proof: Europe and England in the Ancien Regime* (Chicago, 1977).

Statute made in the XXV Year of the Reign of . . . King *Edward* the Third, touching or concerning Treason or the Declarations of Treasons, and none other . . .[49]

This statute was clearly intended to do away with the statutory innovations of Henry VIII's reign and in particular the treasonable-words statute of 26 Henry VIII. Unfortunately, this statute also had the unintended effect of throwing into question the procedural codicils of Edward VI's treason legislation. In discussing the two-witness rule, L. M. Hill has argued that the Marian treason reforms intended to leave procedural law intact while repealing the substantive additions of previous monarchs, most notably Henry VIII; however, because of vague and seemingly contradictory phrasing, the repeal left "a heritage of procedural confusion."[50] Indeed, Bellamy has gone so far to argue that the continued use of 25 Edward III in the later Tudor period was due to the fact that, unlike more recent treason legislation, it contained no provisions specifying procedure and standard of proof.[51]

In *The Third Part of the Institutes*, published on the order of the Long Parliament in 1644, Coke asserted that not only were the procedural codicils of 1 Edward VI, c. 12 and 5 & 6 Edward VI, c. 11 in force but that they applied to petty treason as well.[52] However, Coke's authority on the issue was hardly clear and simple. For example, his position in the *Institutes* was markedly inconsistent with his earlier role as Attorney-General in Sir Walter Ralegh's trial earlier in the century, where the accused was convicted on the testimony of a single witness, Lord Cobham, who was not brought to face the accused.[53] Coke's authority on matters of law in the 1640s was undoubtedly great but it was not without ambiguity on the law of treason. The earlier Coke, the Coke who prosecuted traitors for Elizabeth I and James I, was not the same man who wrote *The Third Part of the Institutes*, most likely in the aftermath of the parliaments of the 1620s and in fear of retribution from a vengeful king. For the former, the law of treason was a net that could not be cast broadly enough, but for the latter the law of treason was a net he was seeking most industriously to avoid.

Another important development of the Tudor period was the increasing conflation of treason with the lesser offense of praemunire. This development

49 *SL*, II: 457.

50 L. M. Hill, "The Two Witness Rule in English Treason Trials: Some Comments on the Emergence of Procedural Law," *AJLH* 12 (1968): 104–106.

51 Bellamy, *Tudor Law of Treason*, pp. 47–50 and ch. 4; an alternative view has been suggested by Lesley J. Ward in her 1985 Cambridge doctoral thesis "The Law of Treason in the Reign of Elizabeth I." Ward has argued that 25 Edward III was used in a failed attempt to prevent trials such as that of Edmund Campion in 1581 from acquiring religious overtones – this especially with the religious persecutions of the 1550s still on the edge of living memory: Lesley J. Ward, "The Law of Treason in the Reign of Elizabeth I," unpublished Ph.D. dissertation (Cambridge, 1985), pp. 247–251.

52 Coke, *The Third Part of the Institutes*, p. 26.

53 Hill, "Two Witness Rule": 106–111.

sprang from the establishment of the royal supremacy in ecclesiastical affairs and will be a recurring concern throughout this study. Professor Elton has described praemunire as a crime intended to punish invasions of "the king's regality."[54] Praemunire received definition in the two fourteenth-century statutes of 27 Edward III, c.1 and the more famous (or infamous) 16 Richard II, c. 5. The former forbade the pursuit of suits that normally fell within the jurisdiction of the king's courts, both equity and common-law, in jurisdictions outside of the realm (i.e. Rome). The statute described the removal of causes outside the realm as "in Prejudice and Dishersion of our Lord the King, and of his Crown, and of all the People of his said Realm and [tending] to the undoing and Destruction of the Common Law of the same Realm at all Times used."[55] The offense was to be punished by imprisonment and loss of both lands and goods and chattels.

The praemunire statute of 16 Richard II, c. 5, referred to as the Great Statute of Praemunire, has received more attention than its precursor, probably because of Henry VIII's ruthless deployment of it in bringing the clergy to heel.[56] This statute reaffirmed the provisions protecting the forensic jurisdiction of the king's courts and made it punishable to "purchase or pursue, or cause to be purchased or pursued in the Court of Rome, or elsewhere, by any such Translations, Processes, and Sentences of Excommunications, Bulls, Instruments, or any other Things whatsoever which touch the King, against him, his Crown, and his Regality, or his Realm."[57] Conceived over a century before the Reformation, the statute attempted to restrict both the forensic and legislative jurisdiction of the Papacy on English soil. Praemunire, furthermore, became a crime "against the King in Derogation of his Regality" tending towards the "Destruction of the Soveraignty of the King or Lord, his Crown, his Regality, and or all his Realm, which God defend."[58] The statutes of praemunire, therefore, defined a crime that was (1) a crime of encroachment on the powers of the king; (2) a crime against the sovereign authority of the king; and (3) an offense that was destructive to the very law of the land, the common law, itself. The availability of these ideas became crucial in the impeachments of both Strafford and especially Laud, when the distinction between treason and praemunire became irrevocably blurred.

However, this blurring was evident well before these trials commenced. For example, statutory developments early in Elizabeth's reign illustrated the tendency to conflate the two causes of action. The statute of 5 Elizabeth I, c. 1 against the maintaining and defending of the authority and power of the Bishop of Rome in print, writing, words or deeds stipulated that the offender

[54] Elton, *Tudor Constitution*, p. 339. [55] *SL* I: 272.
[56] W. T. Waugh, "The Great Statute of Praemunire," *EHR* 37 (1922): 173–205.
[57] *SL* I: 407. [58] *SL* I: 406–407.

was subject to "the Dangers, Penalties, Pains and Forfeitures" declared in the statute of 16 Richard II c. 5.[59] However, on the second offense the penalty was to be that of high treason.[60] Not surprisingly, treason and praemunire are discussed in close succession in Michael Dalton's *The Countrey Iustice*, first published in 1618.[61]

Other key Elizabethan statutes reflected an enlargement of the scope of English treason law in response to the growing forces of the Counter-Reformation and in particular to the 1570 papal bull *Regnans in Excelsis* against Elizabeth.[62] This bull had (1) excommunicated the English Queen; (2) declared "her to be deprived of her pretended title . . . and of all lordship, dignity and privilege whatsoever"; and (3) absolved her subjects from their oaths of "fealty and obedience."[63] The legislative response of the English parliament was swift with two statutes being passed in 1571, 13 Elizabeth, c. 1 and c. 2. The language of the statute of 13 Elizabeth, c. 1 reflected a clear propensity to see treason not only as a crime of regicide but also of usurpation:

> . . . if any persons or persons . . . during the natural life of our most gracious sovereign lady Queen Elizabeth (whom Almighty God preserve and bless with long and prosperous reign over this realm), shall, within the realm or without, compass, imagine, invent, devise or intend the death or destruction, or any bodily harm tending to death, destruction, maim or wounding of the royal person of the same our sovereign lady Queen Elizabeth; or to deprive or depose her of or from the style, honour or kingly name of the imperial crown of this realm or of any other realm or dominion to her Majesty belonging . . .[64]

Elizabeth as a queen regnant was deemed to have the office and the dignity of a king, if not the literal name, and to deprive her of them was deemed treason.[65]

Conspiracy to levy war during the queen's lifetime and new treasonable-words provisions similarly limited to the queen's lifespan also appeared with 13 Elizabeth I, c. 1.[66] The statute made it treasonable to:

> maliciously, advisedly and directly publish, declare, hold opinion, affirm or say by any speech express words or sayings, that our said sovereign lady Queen Elizabeth during her life is not or ought not to be Queen of this realm of England and also of the realms of France and Ireland; or that any other person or persons ought of right to be King or Queen of the said being under her Majesty's obeisance . . .[67]

The statute, modeled in part on the defunct statute of 26 Henry VIII, also revived during the queen's lifetime the treason of calling the monarch a

[59] *SL* I: 531–532. [60] *SL* I: 533.
[61] Michael Dalton, *The Countrey Iustice* (London, 1618), pp. 198–202.
[62] Elton, *Tudor Constitution*, pp. 423–428. [63] Elton, *Tudor Constitution*, p. 427.
[64] Elton, *Tudor Constitution*, p. 73. [65] Coke, *The Third Part of the Institutes*, pp. 6–7.
[66] Elton, *Tudor Constitution*, pp. 73–74. [67] Elton, *Tudor Constitution*, p. 74.

heretic, schismatic, infidel or usurper that had made the Henrician statute a particularly nasty piece of legal piano wire.[68]

Other statutes had even more explicitly religious overtones both reflecting attempts to deal with the growing influx of seminary priests and Jesuits into England and demonstrating the growing trend towards the conflation of treason and praemunire. For example, 13 Elizabeth I, c. 2 made it treason to bring into the realm papal bulls, to possess them, or to attempt to promulgate them. Significantly, this crime would have been considered merely a praemunire before the Reformation, and even then only if the bull was deemed prejudicial to the king, his crown, and his realm.[69] *An Act to retain the Queen's Majesty's Subjects in their due Obedience* (23 Elizabeth I, c. 1) decreed further as a general statement of principle:

> That all persons whatsoever, which have or shall have, or shall pretend to have Power, or shall by any Ways or Means put in Practice to absolve, perswade or withdraw any of the Queen's Majesty's Subjects, or any within her Highness Realms and Dominions, from their Natural Obedience to her Majesty: (2), Or to withdraw them for that Intent from the Religion now by her Highness Authority established within her Highness Dominions, to the *Romish* Religion, (3) or to move them or any of them to promise any Obedience to any pretended Authority of the See of *Rome*, or to any other Prince, State or Potentate, to be had or used within her Dominions, (4) or shall do any overt Act to that Intent or Purpose; and every of them shall be to all Intents adjudged to be Traytors, and being thereof lawfully convicted shall have Judgement, suffer and forfeit, as in Case of High Treason.[70]

The papacy was portrayed as a usurper not only of the queen's role as supreme governor of the English Church but also of her sovereignty in general in attempting to withdraw her subjects from their natural and lawful allegiance.[71] The crime was the aiding in the appropriation of the queen's government both temporal and spiritual.

This statute and the subsequent "Jesuit Act" of 1585 (27 Elizabeth I, c. 2) also offered clarification of 25 Edward III's provisions against adhering to the enemies of the king. This latter statute most notably (1) decreed that no Jesuit or seminary priest could enter the realm without it being treason; (2) commanded all such priests present to depart within forty days; (3) made

[68] Elton, *Tudor Constitution*, p. 74; John Guy has noted that this statute was actually modeled in part on 26 Henry VIII, c. 13: John Guy, *Tudor England* (Oxford, 1988), p. 298.

[69] *SL* II: 583–584; Elton, *Tudor Constitution*, pp. 428–431. Of course the problem with this statute was that not all seminary priests, Jesuits and recusants just happened to have papal bulls on them when they were apprehended.

[70] *SL* II: 624.

[71] See chapter 2, below: after the Reformation when the king became head of the English Church the question of legal sovereignty – the power to make and repeal law – became inevitably bound up with the power to alter the established religion. In the English context this constituted a mark of sovereignty.

the receiving, comforting, or maintaining of any seminary priest or Jesuit a capital felony (without benefit of clergy); and (4) commanded all Englishmen currently studying in seminaries and Jesuit colleges abroad to return home and take the oath prescribed by the statute 1 Elizabeth I, c. 1 for ecclesiastical persons.[72] Evidence suggests that Elizabethan prosecutors interpreted this statute in continuity with 25 Edward III. The construction was simple: the Pope was the enemy of the queen regnant and, since seminary priests and Jesuits had sworn allegiance to him, they were necessarily adhering to the queen's enemies.[73] These two statutes had the distinction of remaining in force throughout the Interregnum, being explicitly continued in Cromwell's controversial treason ordinance of 19 January 1654.[74]

Jacobean prosecutors, lacking the expanded statutory basis provided by 13 Elizabeth I, c. 1, still enjoyed recourse to a more generous interpretation of 25 Edward III in pursuing traitors. Furthermore, there is ample evidence from the printed accounts in the *State Trials* that this continued use of 25 Edward III owed as much to the rich potential for construction on the statute's first head as to procedural considerations. Their approach was what Conrad Russell has termed the constructive compassing of the king's death.[75] This was not new. For example, at John Story's trial in 1571 the court equated conspiring to deprive and depose the queen with a constructive compassing of her death.[76] Similarly, the Jesuit Henry Garnett, tried in the wake of the Gunpowder Plot in 1606, stood indicted not under the Jesuit Act of 1585 but under the first head 25 Edward III.[77] Sir Francis Bacon, acting as Attorney-General in *Peacham's Case* (1615), argued that the prosecution should proceed under 25 Edward III "because other temporary statutes were gone" – clearly an allusion to the statute of 13 Elizabeth, c. 1.[78] Peacham had composed a treasonous sermon "which was never preached, nor intended to be preached, but only set down in writings, and was found in his study."[79] Accordingly the indictment was to read "*Imaginatus est et commpassivie mortem et finalem destructionem domini regis.*"[80] While the judges were divided on whether Peacham had indeed committed treason, Bacon's definition of "compassing" remained significant:

72 *SL* II, p. 633; and for the oath in question: *SL* II, p. 519.

73 Ward, "Law of Treason," pp. 288–289.

74 C. H. Firth and R. S. Rait, eds., *Acts and Ordinances of the Interregnum* (London, 1911), vol. II, pp. 834–835.

75 Conrad Russell, "The Theory of Treason in the Trial of Strafford," *EHR* 80 (1965): 30–50.

76 *State Trials* I: 1090; 3 Dyer 298b, 73 *Eng. Rep.* 670 (KB).

77 Garnett, having illegally entered England in 1586, would have been able to claim benefit from James's general pardon of 1603: *State Trials* II: 222–225, 228–229.

78 *State Trials* II: 873. 79 *State Trials* II: 869. 80 *State Trials* II: 873.

there be four means or manners whereby the death of the king is compassed and imagined. The first is some particular fact or plot. The second by disabling his title; as by affirming that he is not lawful king; or that another ought to be king; or that he is an usurper; or a bastard; or the like. The third, by subjecting his title to the pope; and therby making him of an absolute king a conditional king. The fourth, by disabling his regiment, and making him appear incapable or indign to reign.[81]

Bacon argued that Peacham's actions fell under the fourth of these heads.[82] More importantly, holding that the king was not a lawful sovereign and affirming the sovereignty of another came clearly under the first head of 25 Edward III. Prosecutors continued to effect an expansion in the law of treason without the aid of additional legislation. This expansion was based on the exploitation of ambiguities in the text of the principal statute and in particular the first head.

This idea of treason as a crime of usurpation or denial of the king's powers was also perfectly compatible with the notion of common-law treasons. For example, in *R. v. Williams* (1619),[83] Henry Yelverton as King's Attorney argued,

that at common law there be four manners of treasons, 1. Rebellion. 2. To deny the king's title and power, temporal or spiritual. 3. To advance and maintain superior power to the king. 4. In bearing his subjects in hand that the king's government is erroneous, heretical and unjust, whereby the manner of his government is impeached and called into question.[84]

There was less disagreement here, with Sir John Dodderidge (JKB) affirming that these four manners of treason were "undeniable maxims."[85] Denying the king's authority in both church and state, and maintaining a power greater than the king's, usurping his sovereign authority, were thus potentially treasonable either as compassing the king's death or as treason at common law.

An important issue relating to the first head of Bacon's definition of constructive compassing, controversial throughout the early modern period, was whether conspiring to levy war when no war had actually been levied constituted treason at common law. The authorities were somewhat divided on the question. While a statutory basis for this treason had briefly existed during the reign of Elizabeth I (13 Elizabeth I, c. 1), the provision declaring it treason was only in effect during the queen's lifetime.[86] Coke, who as Attorney-General had prosecuted the Oxfordshire rebels in 1597

[81] *State Trials* II: 873–874. [82] *State Trials* II: 874.

[83] Williams was a Catholic barrister who had written two "treasonable" books, *Balaam's Ass* and *Speculum Regali*.

[84] *State Trials* II: 1088. [85] *State Trials* II: 1088.

[86] Elton, *Tudor Constitution*, pp. 73–74.

under 13 Elizabeth I, c. 1 for conspiring to levy war, later averred that conspiracy to levy war did not fall under 25 Edward III.[87] However, there is good reason to believe that Coke's later opinions were far from ubiquitous in the years leading up to the Civil War. Sir James Dyer, a much-cited authority on the law of treason, stated that at the trial of Sir Nicholas Throckmorton in 1554, both during the arraignment and during the Star Chamber proceedings against the errant jurors afterwards, that it was the judges' expressed opinion "that if two or more conspire to commit treason, as in levying war, and if any of them afterwards put it in execution, that is treason in all, and this by the common law before the declaration made in 25. E. 3. stat. c. 2."[88] This text was cited with approval in Michael Dalton's widely disseminated treatise on the roles and functions of the justices of the peace, *The Country Iustice* (1618). Oliver St. John cited Dyer in 1641, arguing that not only was conspiracy to levy war treason by the common law but that it fell under 25 Edward III as constituting a compassing of the king's death.[89] This latter, particularly nasty construction would later form one of the more pernicious tenets of Restoration treason law.[90]

Printed reports and treatise literature suggest that treasonable words also continued to play a role in early Stuart treason law. This was in spite of the fact that no obvious statutory basis for them existed with the expiry of 13 Elizabeth I, c. 1 and the repeal of 26 Henry VIII, c. 13. Dalton stated that compassing the death of the king, queen, or eldest male heir was treasonable even when not brought to effect but merely declared "by any open act" or uttered "by words or letters."[91] Furthermore, while jurists may have generally accepted that words in and of themselves were not treasonable, treasonable words could still constitute evidence of treasonable intentions. In *Pine's Case* (1628), Hugh Pine, a Somerset barrister outspoken in his opposition to the Forced Loan, stood accused by two competent witnesses of having said of King Charles: "Before God, he is no more fit to be king than Hickwright" (Hickwright was described as "an old simple fellow who

[87] Coke, *The Third Part of The Institutes*, pp. 9–10. Coke, writing in the aftermath of the 1620s parliaments, has undoubtedly restricted his conception of the law of treason from his days as one of the king's servants: his discussion of the Oxfordshire rebels, Burton and Bradshaw, side-steps the question of whether conspiracy to levy war constitutes treason, instead referring to the case to distinguish the treason of levying war from mere riot; see also John Walter, "A 'Rising of the People'? The Oxfordshire Rising of 1596," *P&P* 107 (1986): 129–130.

[88] 1 Dyer 98b, 73 *Eng. Rep.* 215 (KB).

[89] Dalton, *The Countrey Iustice*, p. 198; St. John, *Argument*, pp. 7, 15–16.

[90] See the account of Algernon Sydney's trial in Jonathan Scott, *Algernon Sydney and the Restoration Crisis 1677–1683* (Cambridge, 1991), pp. 325, 328.

[91] Dalton, *The Countrey Iustice*, p. 198.

was then Mr. Pine's shepherd").[92] The judges agreed that Pine's words were insufficient evidence on which to base an indictment, and that words "of themselves" could not serve as the basis for an indictment of high treason. However, they also decreed that words could still "be . . . evidence to discover the corrupt heart of him that spake them." Although the judges also affirmed that there was no treason in England but what was laid out in 25 Edward III, they left the door wide open to the ideas of constructive compassing with treasonable words playing an evidentiary role.[93]

III

During the Tudor and early Stuart periods English jurists looked to the existing law of treason for the solution of novel problems. The break with Rome, the extension of English sovereignty over the whole of Ireland, and the growing forces of Counter-Reformation manifested in the rise in seminary priest and Jesuit activity in the last half of the sixteenth century presented hitherto unknown pressures on the law of treason. These pressures necessitated not only new statutes but the reinterpretation of the foundational statute of 25 Edward III in light of new circumstances. The law of treason defended and advanced the sovereignty of English monarchs over both the established church and the newly created neighboring kingdom of Ireland.

In spite of these developments and the availability of newer legislation, 25 Edward III remained the principal statutory foundation of English treason. The statute proved flexible and highly adaptable to new circumstances. However, as a result the definition of treason was far from clear at the outbreak of the English Civil War. While Bellamy has emphasized procedural reasons for the statute's retention there is every reason to believe that "constructive" and "common-law" treasons played a major role as well.[94] In addition, the attempts at repeal, originally intended to narrow the scope of English treason law, had had the unintended effect of throwing into question the status of Edward VI's legislation. As a result, procedural codicils set up during his reign such as the two-witness rule, were of uncertain force. By

[92] *State Trials* III: 359: T. G. Barnes, *Somerset 1625–40: A County's Government During the "Personal Rule"* (London, 1961), p. 34.

[93] *State Trials* III: 368; Sir George Croke, *The Reports of Sir George Croke*, ed. and trans. Harbottle Grimstone (London, 1657), sig. N4r, p. 89.

[94] Both Bellamy and Ward agree that 25 Edward III remained the principal English treason statute at the end of the Tudor dynasty. However, while Bellamy has suggested that the reason for this lay in the absence of any procedural codicils from 25 Edward III (two-witness rule etc.), Ward has suggested that more liberal constructions of the original statute ensured its survival. This author tends to concur with Ward.

the early seventeenth century English jurists had developed constructions of 25 Edward III that portrayed treason as a crime of usurpation or unlawful appropriation of the monarch's sovereignty tending to the compassing of their death. This was the case even if that had not been the original intention of the statute's framers. It is now necessary to address questions pertaining to the *nature* of that sovereign authority.

2

Sovereignty and state

I

In 1607 the civil lawyer John Cowell published *The Interpreter*, reputedly the first major attempt to compile a comprehensive legal dictionary in English. Cowell stated that "treason" came from the French "*trahison*" and that it "signifieth an offence committed against the amplitude and maiestie of the commonwealth." "High Treason," he continued, was "an offence done against the securitie of the commonwealth, or of the King's most excellent Maiestie."[1] The remainder of the entry went on, in rather uncontroversial fashion, to recapitulate the contents of 25 Edward III and outline the manner of punishments for convicted traitors.[2] Modern scholars usually read Cowell in order to evaluate his alleged "absolutism," paying particular attention to his controversial definition of the royal prerogative. However, his definition of treason as a crime against the commonwealth or common good – terms roughly analogous to the "state" in the English of the time – had far-reaching implications.[3] While initially suppressed, the book eventually became a best seller in the seventeenth century and was reprinted as late as 1701 in a supposedly expurgated edition.[4] Absolutist or not, the book was just too useful for practicing lawyers to discard, having no logical substitute in the professional literature of the day. Sir Edward Coke himself possessed a copy.[5]

[1] John Cowell, *The Interpreter: or Booke Containing the Signification of Words* (Cambridge, 1607), sig. Vvv 1v.
[2] Cowell, *The Interpreter*, sigs. Vvv 1v–2r.
[3] John Guy, "The King's Council and Political Participation," in Alistair Fox and John Guy, eds., *Reassessing the Henrician Age: Humanism, Politics and Reform 1500–1550* (Oxford, 1986), pp. 124–125.
[4] Johann P. Sommerville, *Politics and Ideology in England, 1603–1640* (London, 1986), pp. 122, 127; Sommerville notes that nothing was in fact changed in the 1701 edition.
[5] W. O. Hassall, ed., *A Catalogue of the Library of Sir Edward Coke, with a Preface by S. E. Thorne* (New Haven, 1950), p. 40; Richard Helgerson, *Forms of Nationhood: The Elizabethan Writing of England* (Chicago, 1992), p. 79.

W. R. Stacy, in discussing the trial of the Earl of Strafford before the House of Lords in 1641, has argued that the prosecution "bridged the gap between the legal definition of treason against the king's person and the unknown offense of treason against the state."[6] In this chapter I establish that this was clearly not the case: the idea of treason against the state was *not* unknown at the outbreak of the English Civil War but constituted part of a shared stock of commonplace political concepts available to early Stuart jurists and politicians. The argument here consists in four sections. The first section offers working definitions of "sovereignty" and "state" and locates them in the lexicon of late Tudor and early Stuart political life. While the term is usually associated with abstract, theoretical debates, the concept of "sovereignty" had a more commonplace meaning as simply the positive powers of the sovereign. Furthermore, the definition of these powers was heavily contested, particularly with regard to questions of church and state. The second section discusses the role of the king's two bodies as a hermeneutic in the interpretation of English treason law, the corporate nature of public authority, and the relationship between ruler, law, and polity in early modern Britain. It establishes that the corporate nature of the polity was deeply ingrained in English public law at the outbreak of Britain's civil wars in the late 1630s and provided means for redefining treason as more than a personal crime against the monarch. The third section considers the role of arguments based on what current scholarly fashion has termed "reason of state," the place of appeals to "necessity," and their relationship to established traditions of English law. The fourth section offers synthesis by way of a "general theory" of early modern treason.

II

In the 1970s Quentin Skinner argued that an important watershed in the evolution of the idea of the state occurred near the end of the sixteenth century when the peoples of western Europe began to conceive of political power in abstract, impersonal terms. Hitherto the idea of the "state" had referred to a ruler holding or maintaining their state. With the emergence of a more "modern" idea of the state, however, political power now stood free from the person or persons of any individuals, becoming the exclusive property of an abstract entity known as the "state."[7] Skinner has identified the key conceptual transition "from the idea of the ruler 'maintaining his

[6] W. R. Stacy, "Matter of Fact, Matter of Law, and the Attainder of the Earl of Strafford," *AJLH* 29 (1985): 343–344.

[7] Quentin Skinner, "The State," in Terence Ball et al., eds., *Political Innovation and Conceptual Change* (Cambridge, 1989), pp. 90–131.

state' – where it simply meant upholding his own position – to the idea that there is a separate legal and constitutional order, that of the State, which the ruler has a duty to maintain."[8] In the pre-modern formulation of the state, the legal and constitutional order depended on the king by virtue of the supra-personal powers of his office: the law was the king's law and the state was the king's state to acquire, to hold, and to maintain. As a result of this transition subjects no longer owed their allegiance to particular rulers, but to the abstract entity of the state, the host of sovereign power.[9]

Skinner has suggested that the key figure in this transition was the French jurist Jean Bodin, whose *Les Six livres de la république* first appeared in the original French in 1576. A Latin edition translated by Bodin himself appeared in 1586, thus enabling the author to reach an international audience. In 1606 an English edition entitled *Six Bookes of a Commonweale*, based on both prior editions, appeared in print.[10] It was perhaps the most important and influential treatise of comparative public law published in Europe during the early modern period. Skinner has argued that when Knolles translated Bodin into English this was one of the first instances in England where the term "state" was employed "with some consistency in a recognizably modern sense."[11]

Bodin characterized sovereignty as indivisible, perpetual, and absolute in the sense of being "not limited either in power, charge, or time certaine"[12] but bound only by the law of God and the law of nature.[13] Sovereign princes

[8] Quentin Skinner, *The Foundations of Modern Political Thought*, vol. I: *The Renaissance* (Cambridge, 1977), pp. ix–x.

[9] Skinner, "The State," p. 123.

[10] This edition was the translation of a possibly recusant schoolmaster named Richard Knolles. Jean Bodin, *Bodin, On Sovereignty*, ed. and trans. Julian H. Franklin (Cambridge, 1992), pp. xxxv–xxxviii; all quotations given here, however, will be from Kenneth D. McRae's 1962 facsimile edition of Knolles's 1606 English translation: Jean Bodin, *Six Bookes of a Commonweale*, trans. Richard Knolles and ed. Kenneth D. McRae (Cambridge, Mass., 1962).

[11] Quentin Skinner, *The Foundations of Modern Political Thought*, vol. II: *The Age of Reformation* (Cambridge, 1978), p. 355. More recently, however, he has suggested that Hobbes's *Leviathan* (1651) marked the true watershed in the emergence of a modern conception of statehood. Hobbes's mature thought marked not merely the transition from a supra-personal notion of kingship to an impersonal, corporate conception of the polity. It marked the emergence of a "purely artificial" or abstract conception of the "state" as "the name of an artificial person 'carried' or represented by those who wield sovereign power..." In *Leviathan* Hobbes used not only more conventional metaphors of the political body but also more explicitly mechanistic metaphors. The abstract conception of the state outlined in *Leviathan* was something altogether new and distinct from the public law category of corporation or *universitas*. This argument is derived from a close reading of both the Latin and English editions of *Leviathan*. Quentin Skinner, *Liberty Before Liberalism* (Cambridge, 1998), pp. 4–5; Quentin Skinner, *Reason and Rhetoric in the Philosophy of Thomas Hobbes* (Cambridge, 1996), pp. 386–390.

[12] Bodin, *Six Bookes*, book I, p. 85.

[13] Bodin, *Six Bookes*, book I, ch. 8 and for the limits on sovereignty p. 92: "But as for the lawes of God and nature, all princes and people of the world are unto them subject: neither is it

were bound neither by the laws of their predecessors nor by the laws of their own making.[14] Sovereignty in any commonwealth resided in either a prince, an aristocracy, or the people in the instance of a "popular state" such as republican Rome. Because sovereignty was indivisible, it could be held only by one of the three and a "mixed state" was impossible.[15] In states where princes exercised sovereignty, either inheritance or customary law (e.g. the Salic law) could govern succession. Bodin differentiated sovereignty from mere magistracy in that magistrates, whether appointed by a prince, elected by the people, or collectively chosen in an aristocratic state, were limited by their particular commissions both in the scope of their charge and in the time for which they were given it.[16]

It was Bodin's alleged "absolutism" that made him a controversial figure both in his day and in the century following. Even today seemingly endless academic debate revolves around the question of to what degree Bodin's scheme limited in practice the powers of the sovereign. Professor Julian Franklin has repeatedly argued that Bodin's supposed absolutism, especially with respect to issues of taxation and public finance, was much over-rated, as was his purported hostility to the Aristotelian idea of a mixed polity.[17] Such questions are of peripheral relevance to our purposes here as we are only indirectly considering the question of Bodin's influence in England and the myriad of textual ambiguities that subject would entail. Suffice to say that educated people in early Stuart England read Bodin. Some read him extensively and carefully. William Prynne, Archbishop William Laud, the young Thomas Wentworth, Sir Robert Filmer, and Thomas Hobbes all read Bodin – the last mentioning him "in tones of considerable respect."[18]

However, this did not stop Englishmen from envisioning their polity as "mixed monarchy" or embracing the idea that sovereign power operated

in their power to impugne them, if they will not be guiltie of high treason to the diuine maiestie, making warre against God: under the greatness of whome all monarchs of the world ought to beate the yoke, and bow to their heads in all feare and reuerence. Wherefore in that wee said the soueraigne power in a Commonweale to be free from all lawes, concerneth nothing the lawes of God and nature."

14 Bodin, *Six Bookes*, book I, pp. [90]–92 (pagination irregular).

15 This latter category was backed up in ch. 8 by a rather pained argument that the Roman constitution during the republican period was not mixed.

16 Bodin, *Six Bookes*, book I, ch. 8.

17 Julian H. Franklin, *Jean Bodin and the Rise of Absolutist Theory*, ch. 5 and Bodin, *Bodin, On Sovereignty*, Introduction.

18 For Wentworth see Anthony Milton, "Thomas Wentworth and the Political Thought of the Personal Rule," in J. F. Merritt, ed., *The Political World of Thomas Wentworth, Earl of Strafford, 1621–1641* (Cambridge, 1996), p. 154. At his trial Laud demonstrated his familiarity not only with the works of Bodin but with the writings of Hugo Grotius, with whom he had a correspondence: *Works* III, pp. 367–368. Prynne's engagement with Bodin is well known from his *Sovereign Power of Parliaments and Kingdomes: Divided into Four Parts Together with an Appendix* (London, 1643). For Hobbes see Skinner, *Reason and Rhetoric*, p. 236.

through customary forms of law.[19] It was possible to read and appropriate Bodin's writings as the work of either a "constitutionalist" who regarded the sovereign power as a set of legal capacities exercised by the monarch in concert with the governed, or an "absolutist" who regarded the sovereign as above the law and able to make laws according to his or her own will and pleasure.[20] What Bodin himself may have intended is less relevant than the uses to which political actors put his writings. For example, in his study of absolutist thought in the early Stuart period Glenn Burgess has rehabilitated the thesis of George L. Mosse that "as the seventeenth century progressed Bodin, perhaps contrary to the spirit of his own political beliefs, began to be pressed into service by the English as a symbol for absolutism."[21] Such "absolutist" readings, of course, were not necessary outcomes: the accretion of customary practices over a number of generations were subject to interpretation simply as the process through which natural law and the law of God became determined as positive law.[22] As a result, custom conceivably had the force of natural law and determined the mode through which the monarch exercised the marks and rights of sovereignty.[23] Thus, a Bodinian conception of sovereignty could be assimilated to a position in keeping with that of Sir Edward Coke that the English law was "immemorial" custom handed down from before the dawn of written records. The dichotomy between "constitutionalist" and "absolutist," and the accompanying debate on the "limits" of sovereign power, was a product of the seventeenth century's military, constitutional, and religious conflicts and not its long-term ideological cause.

Indeed, Johann Sommerville's contention that a fully mature understanding of royal absolutism was widespread among groups such as the clergy and

[19] Paul Christianson has argued that there were in fact competing conceptions of the ancient constitution in early Stuart England, some classically Cokean governed by the customary common law, others such as Selden interpreting the English constitution as "mixed monarchy." A third category, "constitutional monarchy created by kings," attributable to James I and VI held that the king as sovereign was bound both by his coronation oath and by the practices of his predecessors to govern by the law of the land: Paul Christianson, "Royal and Parliamentary Voices on the Ancient Constitution," in Linda Levy Peck, ed., *The Mental World of the Jacobean Court* (Cambridge, 1991), pp. 71–95.

[20] My thinking here has been influence by Roger Chartier's essay "Texts, Printing, Readings," in Lynn Hunt, ed., *The New Cultural History* (Berkeley, Calif., 1989), pp. 154–175.

[21] Glenn Burgess, *Absolute Monarchy and the Stuart Constitution* (New Haven, 1996), p. 64; George L. Mosse, "The Influence of Jean Bodin's *République* on English Political Thought," *Medievalia et Humanistica* 5 (1948): 73–83.

[22] Glenn Burgess, *The Politics of the Ancient Constitution: An Introduction to English Political Thought, 1603–1642* (London, 1992), ch. 2, esp. pp. 52–53.

[23] See, for example, Oliver St. John's argument in the *Ship Money Case*: J. P. Kenyon, *The Stuart Constitution, 1603–1688: Documents and Commentary*, 2nd edn. (Cambridge, 1986), p. 98; S. R. Gardiner, ed., *Constitutional Documents of the Puritan Revolution 1625–1660*, 3rd edn. (Oxford, 1906), pp. 110–111.

civilians before the Civil War has increasingly come under attack from both Burgess and Conrad Russell.[24] Sommerville, failing to engage with Franklin's arguments, has suggested that not only was Bodin's theory of sovereignty absolutist but that absolutist readings of his work predominated in the early Stuart period.[25] Whether one agrees with this bold contention or not, it is evident that both mature absolutist ideologies and absolutist readings of Bodin were available *before* the Civil War, however marginal to political life.[26] Their ubiquity among certain groups, however, is more difficult to establish. A more pertinent question is why the works of this handful of individuals either remained largely in manuscript during this period, as in the cases of John Cusacke and Sir Robert Filmer, or in other instances led to their authors' impeachment and public censure – the cases of Sibthorpe and Manwaring, impeached for preaching sermons in support of the forced loan, spring to mind in the latter regard.

A more commonplace aspect of Bodin's thought,[27] more central to our purposes here, was his demarcation of the marks of sovereignty.[28] This was one of the most rigorous attempts to define what in practice constituted the positive powers of the state available in early Stuart Britain. The most important of these was "power to give lawes to all... subiects in generall, and to euerie one of them in particular... without consent of any other greater, equall, or lesser than himselfe."[29] This basic mark of sovereignty was inalienable. While particular individuals were permitted to receive commissions to draft laws, these laws could not be brought into force without the consent of the sovereign, be they prince, people or aristocracy.[30] The other marks of sovereignty included (1) power of war and peace and the making of alliances; (2) the receiving of appeals from inferior magistrates; (3) the power to appoint and dismiss "great officers"; (4) the levying of taxes and subsidies on the subjects and the power to exempt subjects from them; (5) powers of pardon and dispensation "against the rigour of the law; (6) "power of life and death"; (7) coinage; and (8) "to cause all subiects and liegemen to sweare

24 Sommerville, *Politics and Ideology*, ch. 1; Burgess, *Absolute Monarchy*, *passim*; Glenn Burgess, "The Divine Right of Kings Reconsidered," *EHR* 107 (1992): 837–861; Conrad Russell, *The Causes of the English Civil War* (Oxford, 1990), ch. 6.

25 Johann P. Sommerville, "English and European Political Ideas in the Early Seventeenth Century: Revisionism and the Case of Absolutism," *JBS* 35 (1996): 168–194.

26 Burgess has easily conceded this point: *Absolute Monarchy*, p. 75; for a contrasting view see Linda Levy Peck, "Beyond the Pale: John Cusacke and the Language of Absolutism in Early Stuart Britain," *HJ* 41(1998): 121–149.

27 Julian Franklin in discussing Bodin's early theory of sovereignty has traced Bodin's first formulation of the rights of sovereignty in his *Methodus* of 1566 to a key passage from the *Histories* of Polybius: Franklin, *Jean Bodin*, pp. 32–33.

28 These are explained in great detail in book I, ch. 10.

29 Bodin, *Six Bookes*, book I, pp. 159, 162 [161] (irregular pagination).

30 Bodin, *Six Bookes*, book I, p. 162 [161].

for the keeping of their fidelitie without exception, unto him to whome such oath is due."[31] Bodin asserted that these "the true markes of soueraigntie, [were] comprised vnder the power of being able to giue a law to al in generall, and to euery one in particular, and not to receiue any law or commaund from any other, but from almightie God onely."[32] Power to give law was, therefore, not simply power to legislate and make commands that would be obeyed as positive law but pertained more generally to the administration of justice – power to judge causes and appoint magistrates to judge in the sovereign's place.

Bodin was, of course, not the only thinker to define practical sovereignty as a cluster of powers wielded by the sovereign. In early modern Europe the concept of sovereignty did not always allude to more abstract theorizing but was often merely a shorthand to denote the practical powers of the state. English civilians arrived at differing conceptions of the marks and rights of sovereignty independently of Bodin deriving them from such sources as the *Corpus Juris Civilis*. Thomas Hobbes would later offer a similar, more extensive scheme of twelve instead of nine "rights" of sovereignty in his *Leviathan* of 1651.[33] As English civilians and to some extent common lawyers were trapped in the same classical and Roman-law sources as Bodin, familial resemblances between their schema and his are not surprising. Bodin's demarcation of the true marks of sovereignty may have been the most rigorous and influential in the early Stuart period but it was not the only such catalogue of powers available. The marks and rights of sovereignty were not exclusive to Bodin's writings and were subject to a number of varying formulations in terms both of what constituted the marks and who lawfully held them among both civil and common lawyers alike.

For example, the Tudor statesman and civil lawyer Sir Thomas Smith, writing roughly contemporaneously with Bodin in the mid-1560s, stated that "all common wealthes and governmentes be most occupyed, and be most diverse in the fashion of five thinges." These were (1) the making of laws and ordinances for domestic governance; (2) power of war and peace and the making of alliances; (3) coinage; (4) the "choosing and election of the chiefe officers and magistrates"; and (5) the "administration of justice."[34] In 1612 Sir John Davies, a common lawyer who also enjoyed extensive knowledge of the civil law, cited Bodin on the true marks of sovereignty and argued that the English kings had not fully subdued Ireland until Elizabeth's time

31 Bodin, *Six Bookes*, book I, pp. 162 [161]–163 [162].
32 Bodin, *Six Bookes*, book I, pp. 162 [161]–163 [162].
33 Brian P. Levack has offered the example of Richard Zouch: Brian P. Levack, *The Civil Lawyers in England, 1603–1641: A Political Study* (Oxford, 1973), pp. 99–100; Thomas Hobbes, *Leviathan*, ed. Richard Tuck (Cambridge, 1990), pp. 121–129.
34 Sir Thomas Smith, *De Republica Anglorum*, ed. Mary Dewar (Cambridge, 1982), p. 88.

because they had failed to gather the marks of sovereignty into their sole possession within that realm.[35] Davies's argument in his *A Discovery of the True Causes Why Ireland Was Never Entirely Subdued [and] Brought Under Obedience of the Crown of England Until the Beginning of His Majesty's Happy Reign* was not simply that previous English monarchs had failed to achieve mere legal sovereignty over Ireland but that they had failed to extend the administration of English law, the common law, to the whole of Ireland.[36] Power to give law was, for Davies at least, power to judge as well as power to make and repeal law.

The Welsh royalist judge and common lawyer David Jenkins – himself a man under threat of trial and execution for treason in the late 1640s – defined "Soveraignty" as "the power of the Militia, of coyning of Money, of making leagues with forraigne Princes, the power of Pardoning, of making of Officers etc." As a royalist Jenkins went on to assert that these powers belonged to kings only and "had no beginning."[37] The similarities are, of course, superficial and no assertion is being made here about direct influence.[38] However, the examples of Davies and Jenkins illustrate that the marks and rights of sovereignty were a current commonplace with common lawyers as well as civilians. These commonplaces emerged both through the direct reception of Bodin's writings and indirectly through a more piecemeal process of the Roman law's "reception" in England over the course of the Middle Ages.

William R. Connolly, in his *Terms of Political Discourse*, once argued that political concepts such as sovereignty are essentially "cluster concepts": ideas defined by shared criteria, usually having some core of individual characteristics but seldom all features in common. Sovereignty was thus an imperfectly shared, *essentially contestable* concept.[39] A central division in the nature of sovereignty, for example, lay in the distinction between purely impersonal conceptions of sovereignty like that suggested in Bodin and supra-personal notions like that of the king's two bodies. These latter ideas envisioned the rights of sovereignty inseparably from the natural person of a single

[35] Sir John Davies, *A Discovery of the True Causes Why Ireland Was Never Entirely Subdued [and] Brought Under Obedience of the Crown of England Until the Beginning of His Majesty's Happy Reign*, ed. James P. Myers, Jr. (Washington, D.C., 1988), pp. 74–76.

[36] Davies, *A Discovery*, *passim*; Hans S. Pawlisch, *Sir John Davies and the Conquest of Ireland: A Study in Legal Imperialism* (Cambridge, 1985), ch. 4.

[37] David Jenkins, *Lex Terrae*, in *The Works of That Grave and Learned Lawyer Iudge Ienkins, Prisoner in Newgate upon Divers Statutes Concerning the Liberty and Freedome of the Subiect* (London, 1648), p. 8.

[38] Having said this a reader might consider the following: "The Regality of the Crowne of England; is immediately subiect to God and to none other. Plaine words shewing where the supreame power is." Jenkins, *Lex Terrae*, p. 13.

[39] William E. Connolly, *The Terms of Political Discourse*, 2nd edn. (Princeton, 1983), pp. 10–44.

individual or, alternately, a group of individuals. Key facets of sovereignty such as the power to make and repeal law, the power to make war or peace, coinage, and power to appoint magistrates may have gone undisputed, but other defining characteristics relating to the marks or rights of sovereignty remained subject to heated debate. Thus, the very definition of this key political concept stood at the heart of early modern political discourse. The struggle for sovereignty in early modern England was as much a struggle for precise definition of the positive powers of the state as it was for the control of those powers.

The perspective offered here might then be fairly characterized as "neo-Whig." Ideological conflict *did* occur in early Stuart England and it occurred over the practical definition of key political concepts. J. H. Hexter in his attack on the revisionism of the mid- to late 1970s argued that the events leading up to the Civil War saw conflict of constitutional principle over a cluster of issues. These were:

> (1a) What is the rightful source of political authority? What in effect legitimates the right of one man or group to command the obedience of others? (1b) Who – what person or persons – does or should possess the powers of command? (2a) What is the extent and what are the limits, if any, of the ruler's power of command over those subject to it? (2b) What are the limits on the subject's duty to obey?[40]

In this interpretation political power was the sovereign power to command obedience from the subjects of the realm. Debate over the precise locus and limits of this power drove constitutional conflicts from impositions, to Forced Loan, to ship money, to Militia Ordinance and, finally, armed conflict.

This framework, however, is far too inflexible. Conrad Russell has observed that the parliamentarians of early Stuart England had not had the opportunity to read Montesquieu.[41] Neither could they draw on the writings of John Austin or H. L. A. Hart. The problem with Hexter's criteria is that they are based on a narrow and anachronistic legal positivism. This does not, however, mean that the concept of "sovereignty" has no utility in the analysis of European political life in the late sixteenth and seventeenth centuries, merely that it needs a softer, more analytically flexible definition derived from the source materials of public law available at the time. After all, the concept of "sovereignty" was deeply embedded in the lexicon of the period. The people who conducted the war of words in the seventeenth century *did* have the opportunity to read Bodin and other similar authors and did have a loose understanding of sovereignty as a cluster of "state"

[40] J. H. Hexter, "The Early Stuarts and Parliament: Old Hat and the *Nouvelle Vague*," *Parliamentary History* 1 (1982): 207.

[41] Conrad Russell, *Parliaments and English Politics, 1621–1629* (Oxford, 1979), p. 3.

powers. Moreover, these powers were subject to heated debate over their precise definition.[42]

The Civil War was, as Hexter asserted, a struggle for sovereignty. However, in order to characterize that struggle historians should work from Bodin and similar authors forward, not from Austin and Hart backwards. *Bates' Case*, the forced loan, the *Ship Money Case*, and ultimately the Militia Ordinance stand among the most celebrated constitutional controversies of the early Stuart period and they all have one thing in common: all stood in direct relation to increasingly contested rights or marks of sovereignty. The rights of sovereignty were the loci of political, constitutional, and ultimately military conflict. This conflict occurred over the precise practical definition of these rights and marks and it occurred in spite of a prevailing consensus that the king was a lawful king, that this king was sovereign, and that he exercised control over the marks and rights of sovereignty. Legislature, judiciary, and crown were not separate and sovereignty was not a precisely delineated power of command. Parliament was both court and legislature and at the same time incorporated with the king as its head. The king summoned it by his writ and his premature death could end it, just as it did in 1625.[43]

In short, the marks of sovereignty were problematic because they were not always clear. They could vary from state to state in early modern Europe and increasingly did so with the progress of the Reformation and Counter-Reformation. For example, because of the particular course of the Reformation in England the royal supremacy over the Church of England constituted a mark of sovereignty. Brian P. Levack has identified this position among a number of English civilians concerned with rebutting Catholic polemicists in the late Tudor and early Stuart period.[44] The civil lawyer John Haywarde, writing in the wake of the Gunpowder Plot, went as far as to argue that this power constituted a mark of sovereignty in *all* states.[45] Haywarde also defended the royal supremacy in a language clearly evocative of Bodin, arguing that "it is necessarilie expedient, that they who beare the soueraigntie of [the] State, should alwaies manage the affaires of religion; either by themselves, or by some at their appointment within the same State; and neuer receiue direction and rule from a foraine power."[46] The foreign power immediately in question was, undoubtedly, the See of Rome.

In practice, as a result of the Reformation, power over the appointment of ecclesiastical offices, power to tax the clerical estate, right of final appeal

42 David Parker has questioned Bodin's affinity to legal positivism: David Parker, "Law, Society and the State in the Thought of Jean Bodin," *HPT* 2 (1981): 254.

43 Russell, *Parliaments*, ch. 1. 44 Levack, *Civil Lawyers*, p. 101.

45 [John Haywarde], *A Reporte of a Discourse Concerning Svpreme power in Affaires of Religion* (London, 1606), sig. B1r, p. 3.

46 [Haywarde], *A Reporte*, sig. C1r, p. 11.

in causes before ecclesiastical courts, and, most importantly, power to define the doctrine and enforce the discipline of the Church of England all fell exclusively to the crown. With regard to questions of doctrine, the act for the submission of the clergy of 1534 (25 Henry VIII, cap. 19) forbade the convocation of the Church of England from presuming "to attempt, alledge, claim or put in ure, or enact, promulge or execute any new Canons, Constitutions, Ordinance Provincial, or other . . . unless the King's most Royal Assent and License may to them be had."[47] Essentially the act surrendered the legislative powers of the church to the crown. Canons of the church would, like acts of parliament, require royal assent. One consequence of this, discussed in the previous chapter, was the growing tendency to conflate treason with the hitherto lesser cause of praemunire: accroaching the king's jurisdiction in spiritual as well as temporal affairs could be construed as treasonable – especially after Elizabeth's excommunication in 1570 and the subsequent growth in Jesuit and seminary priest activity.

The role of parliament in the governance of the church was less straightforward. Professor Elton has written of the Henrician reformation:

> In practice Henry claimed (and Parliament confirmed) all those powers over the Church in England which the pope had exercised: he controlled its laws, its courts, its appointments, its revenues, and also its doctrine. For it was an essential aspect of the Henrician supremacy that the determination of doctrinal and liturgical disputes should rest with the supreme head.[48]

Elton has characterized the Henrician supremacy as "personal" and argued that under Henry, "the carrying out of the supremacy was the personal duty and prerogative of the supreme head" with parliament playing a subordinate role.[49] Henry as "King-Bishop" exercised a sort of theocratic kingship over the church. Under Elizabeth, however, supremacy became "essentially parliamentary," with the queen taking the less clerical title of "supreme governor" and the final say in ecclesiastical matters lying with queen-in-parliament.[50]

Nevertheless, there was considerable dispute about the nature of the royal supremacy from the very beginning of the English Reformation. The common lawyer Christopher St. German had advanced a theory of parliamentary supremacy as early as 1535.[51] Indeed, a pivotal issue emerging from the Short Parliament was whether the formal declaration of the doctrine of the English

[47] *SL* II: 189; G. R. Elton, *The Tudor Constitution: Documents and Commentary*, 2nd edn. (Cambridge, 1982), p. 448.

[48] Elton, *Tudor Constitution*, pp. 341–342.

[49] Elton, *Tudor Constitution*, p. 343.

[50] Elton, *Tudor Constitution*, pp. 343–345; see also Claire Cross, *The Royal Supremacy in the Elizabethan Church* (London, 1969), pp. 23–24.

[51] Skinner, *Foundations* II, p. 104; John Guy, *Tudor England* (Oxford, 1988), pp. 374–375.

Church through the making of canons was within the powers of convocation alone acting with the king's consent or required the threefold consent of king, lords, and commons assembled in parliament.[52] That the king was supreme governor of the church was not in question. The mode of church government, the relationship of civil magistracy to the clerical estate, was an altogether different sack of incense. Debates on the nature of the royal supremacy were very much alive in the years leading up to the first Civil War in England.[53] For example, Esther S. Cope has reconstructed the parliamentary Erastianism of John Pym, who argued that an act of parliament was required if canons were to be binding on the laity,[54] and Conrad Russell has noted the growing popularity of a parliamentary supremacy among common lawyers in the 1630s.[55] Confronted with the episcopate's "Popish innovations" in the church during the personal rule of 1629–40, parliamentary Erastians in the years 1640–42 strove to return power over ecclesiastical affairs to the civil magistrate and end what they saw as a clerically inspired and led period of misgovernment. Legal-constitutional and religious perceptions of misgovernment were closely integrated for men such as John Pym, William Prynne, Oliver St. John, Sir John Maynard, John Hampden, and the future royalist Edward Bagshawe.[56]

The ideological positions on the supremacy fell roughly under four labels. The first and second, discussed above, were the personal and parliamentary conceptions of the supremacy. Both these positions were potentially Erastian: power to define the doctrine of the church lay with the civil magistrate,

[52] Sir Thomas Aston, *The Short Parliament (1640) Diary of Sir Thomas Aston,* ed. Judith Maltby, Camden 4th Ser., vol. 35 (1988), pp. 30–31, 50–52.

[53] Conrad Russell, "Whose Supremacy? King, Parliament and the Church, 1530–1640," *Lambeth Palace Library Annual Review* (1995): 53–64; Conrad Russell, "Parliament, the Royal Supremacy and the Church," *Parliamentary History* 19 (2000): 27–37; for example, see the debate in parliament on 15 December 1640 between the Erastians, Oliver St. John and John Pym, and Sir Robert Holborne, who defended the legislative autonomy of the clerical estate assembled in convocation: Wallace Notestein, ed., *The Journal of Sir Simonds D'Ewes from the beginning of the Long Parliament to the opening of the Trial of the Earl of Strafford* (New Haven, 1923), pp. 152–157.

[54] Esther S. Cope, "The Short Parliament of 1640 and Convocation," *JEH* 25 (1974): 175; Julian Davies has offered a contrasting view more sympathetic to a clerical supremacy in his study, *The Caroline Captivity of the Church: Charles I and the Remoulding of Anglicanism* (Oxford, 1992), ch. 7 and esp. pp. 273–274.

[55] Conrad Russell, *The Fall of The British Monarchies, 1637–42* (Oxford, 1991; reprinted Oxford, 1995), pp. 15–16.

[56] This study contests the argument of John Morrill, who has identified three separable and distinct perceptions of misgovernment: the legal-constitutional, the localist, and the religious; J. S. Morrill, "The Religious Context of the English Civil War," in Richard Cust and Ann Hughes, eds., *The English Civil War* (London, 1997), pp. 159–181; there have been numerous critiques of this framework, most notably that of Sommerville, *Politics and Ideology*, pp. 223–224; for a more recent critique of Morrill see Glenn Burgess, "Was the English Civil War a War of Religion?: the Evidence of Political Propaganda," *HLQ* 61 (2000): 173–201.

whether king alone as a "king-bishop" or the king-in-parliament. The third is that of popery: power to define religious doctrine lay with the See of Rome and not with any secular magistrate. In its strongest formulation in the decades from 1570 onwards this meant that, if the secular magistrate (i.e. the king) lapsed into heresy (or Protestantism), the Pope had a power to excommunicate and depose him and absolve his subjects from their bonds of allegiance. The fourth was, like the Catholic position, clerical, but acknowledged the necessity of godly reformation in the church. Power to define religious doctrine lay with an independent ecclesiastical body. This position could accommodate various conceptions of church government, most notably Presbyterianism and *iure divino* episcopacy. The first position corresponded roughly to the "Scottish" model of church government in which a largely autonomous ecclesiastical body, the assembly of the kirk, administered religious affairs, independently of the king and his parliament. In its episcopal variant this position, essentially that of Laud, acknowledged in accordance with the submission of the clergy of 1534 that the deliberations of convocation were subject to the king's ratification; however, it did not envision any active role for the civil magistrate in defining the doctrine of the Church of England.[57] The uncomfortable implication of this position for the parliamentarians of the early and mid-1640s was the implicit claim that the convocation or the episcopate had a "popish" power of excommunication over the king should he fall into heresy. This was an implication that "Laudian" writers such as Heylin were tactful in their refusal to explore, "his majesties pietie and zeale being too well knowne to give occasions to such queres."[58] A potential fifth position, that of separatism, attributable to Baptists and later Quakers, represented something of a non-position as it denied the necessity of a coercive and inclusive state church to godly reform.

A final side-issue relating to the royal supremacy was the question of the power to tax clerical estates. Prior to the Reformation the clergy assembled in convocation preferred to deal with the crown directly, voting their own subsidies without being subject to parliamentary approval. This was taxation by consent but it was the consent of the convocation, not that of parliament.[59] After Henry VIII clerical subsidies became subject to confirmation by act of parliament and statute forbade the payment of all clerical subsidies to the See of Rome.[60] Power of lay and clerical taxation thus became consolidated as

[57] *SL* II: 189–190; Elton, *Tudor Constitution*, p. 340; and for Laud see William Lamont, *Godly Rule: Politics and Religion 1603–1660* (London, 1969), pp. 56–77, and chapter 4, below.

[58] Heylin cited in Lamont, *Godly Rule*, p. 58.

[59] F. W. Maitland, *The Constitutional History of England*, ed. H. A. L. Fisher (Cambridge, 1908; reprinted Cambridge, 1965), p. 78; Elton, *Tudor Constitution*, p. 43.

[60] Maitland, *Constitutional History*, p. 311; Patrick Carter, "Parliament, Convocation, and the Granting of Clerical Supply in Early Modern England," *Parliamentary History* 19 (2000): 14–26.

a single mark of sovereignty, both, at least in theory, subject to the approval of king-in-parliament. Furthermore, convocation maintained the independent power to vote benevolences over and above the amount specified in the subsidy. Usually granted in time of war these benevolences were *not* subject to parliamentary approval. Convocation granted such a benevolence to the crown in 1545 and Patrick Carter has estimated that a similar grant in 1587 raised 15, 000*l.* in subsequent years – half the value of an actual clerical subsidy.[61] This latter precedent was crucial in justifying convocation's actions in the spring of 1640 when they continued to sit, make canons and vote supply after the dissolution of the Short Parliament.[62] The dispute over the autonomy of the clerical estate had important fiscal as well as legislative and doctrinal dimensions that demand consideration.

Another mark of sovereignty, pivotal at the start of the 1640s in England and subject to more detailed discussion below, relates to arguments from "necessity" or, in the lexicon of the period, "reason of state." Simply put, this argument held that in times of great extremity, when the very existence of the commonwealth, kingdom or state was jeopardized either by external threats or by internal dissension and revolt, the sovereign was empowered to command actions that in more settled times would be construed as unconstitutional, illegal, or against conventional standards of political morality. This mark could in some schemes be subsumed under power of war and peace, to which it was closely related. The question at the start of the Long Parliament was not whether this type of argument was a valid one but *how* the king exercised this power. Was the king alone or king-in-parliament the best judge of necessity and empowered to command accordingly?[63] Peter N. Miller has observed concerning the *Ship Money Case* "the real issue was not *whether* the *salus populi* could make licit the infringement of basic rights, but *who* was to determine when such a moment of crisis existed."[64] John Pym used arguments of this order to promote the Earl of Strafford's attainder as necessary to the preservation of the king and kingdom just as the Earl had appealed to necessity in defending himself against charges of counseling

61 Carter, "Parliament": 18.

62 Carter has questioned Julian Davies's contention that Charles I directed ecclesiastical policy himself during this period. Carter cites evidence that Peter Heylin the Westminster proctor discovered the precedent of 1587 and brought it to Archbishop Laud's attention. Laud subsequently informed the king: Carter, "Parliament": 22.

63 I disagree strongly with Michael Mendle, who has claimed that the claims of the Long Parliament to judge necessity and command accordingly amounted to a "parliamentary absolutism" – an already muddy term which confuses the issue rather than clarifies. I believe that he has simply confounded absolutism with reason of state: Michael Mendle, "Parliamentary Sovereignty: A Very English Absolutism," in Nicholas Phillipson and Quentin Skinner, eds., *Political Discourse in Early Modern Britain* (Cambridge, 1993), pp. 97–119.

64 Peter N. Miller, *Defining The Common Good, Empire, Religion and Philosophy in Eighteenth-Century Britain* (Cambridge, 1994), p. 13.

extra-parliamentary taxation.[65] Similarly, William Prynne argued for the necessity of Connor Maguire's trial in England because were he to have been tried in Ireland his confederates would have sought to rescue him.[66]

In Roman law, the relationship of the marks of sovereignty to the law of treason was one of infringement. According to J. A. C. Thomas, "the sovereignty of the state was infringed when anyone exercised powers other than those conferred on him, be it by unwritten law, statute, senatusconsult or any other entitlement."[67] For example, according to the *Digest* of Justinian, anyone who "being a private citizen, knowingly and with malicious intent acts as though holding office or magistracy" was guilty of treason.[68] This proviso and the crime of killing a magistrate were consistent with Roman law.[69] It was also potentially a usurpation of that mark of sovereignty by which the sovereign appoints and dismisses magistrates.[70] The inclusion of the latter offense in 25 Edward III, like that of levying war on the king, suggested a strong affinity with Roman law. The *Digest* made it clear that anyone waging war or raising forces to wage war without the command of the Emperor was subject to the penalties of treason, as was any provincial commander who refused to hand over his command when he had been superseded.[71] Furthermore, while it remained ambiguous whether 25 Edward III exerted a monopoly claim over power to make war, it was generally accepted in early Stuart England that, at least within the realm, power of war and peace lay solely with the king. As Sir Edward Coke clearly stated: "no subiect can levie warre within the Realme without authority from the king, for to him it only belongeth."[72] This was in spite of the fact that, as the

[65] The account of Pym's speech, ordered to be published after the attainder had passed the commons, is rich with the rhetoric of necessity as Pym rebuts Strafford's appeals to necessity and makes his own in turn: BL TT E.208(8), *The Speech or Declaration of John Pym, Esquire: After the Recapitulation or summing up of the Charge of High Treason against, Thomas Earle of Strafford, 12 April. 1641* (London, 1641), pp. 24–27.

[66] Bodl. Lib. Tanner MS 418, fol. 37; HLS MS 113, fols. 190–191.

[67] The habit of translators to interpret "contra" or "rem publicam" as "against the state" is something of an irritant as neither Justinian nor the authors he drew upon had any conception of the word "state" in the sense that Skinner attributes to Bodin and other early modern authors: J. A. C. Thomas, ed. and trans., *The Institutes of Justinian: Text, Translation and Commentary* (Cape Town, Wynberg and Johannesburg, 1975), p. 335.

[68] *Digest*, 48, 4, 3.

[69] *Digest*, 48, 4, 1; this included also the crime of conspiring to kill a magistrate.

[70] Bodin, *Six Bookes*, book I, pp. 166–168.

[71] These provisions seem to be clearly aimed at ambitious provincial governors who might consider the possibility of turning their armies on Rome and making themselves Emperor. However, the severity of these provisions were mitigated somewhat by the doctrine of dangerous neighbors whereby provincial governors could be excused from the law if they took pre-emptive actions against an enemy of Rome massing at their borders: Richard A. Bauman, *Crimen Maiestatis in the Roman Republic and Augustan Principate* (Johannesburg, 1967); *Digest*, 48, 4, 3.

[72] Sir Edward Coke, *The Third Part of The Institutes of the Laws of England concerning High Treason, and other Pleas of the Crown, and Criminall causes* (London, 1644), p. 9.

parliaments of the 1620s and the Anglo-Scottish conflagration of the late 1630s demonstrated, the crown's ability to pay for any sustained conflict depended largely on the beneficence of parliaments.

As noted in chapter 1, early modern legal writers appear to have been fully aware of the numerous points of convergence between the Roman law and the English law of treason. This awareness also spilled over into the realm of legal practice. In the trial of the Gunpowder Plotters in 1606 Coke as Attorney-General argued that, because parliament was a court, every member enjoyed a judicial place by virtue of the king's writ and their murders would have been "a several Treason and *crimen laesae majestatis*."[73] Considering Coke's well-documented engagement with Roman and civil law sources assertions about influence are more than credible. There can be no doubt that in practice the English conception of high treason bore strong familial resemblances to that of the Roman law and that the appropriation of Roman law concepts into the English law of treason was well advanced at the outbreak of the English Civil War. How this state of affairs came to pass is less important than the fact that English jurists of the early seventeenth century generally accepted these points of commonality as consistent with the traditions of the English law. Treason was far more than merely the homicide of the monarch's person.

The development of the idea of the state and the growth of the law of treason in England were coterminous and interdependent processes that cannot be considered in isolation from one another. The impact of Roman law ideas on the law of treason beginning at least from the end of the thirteenth century coupled with the emergence of impersonal conceptions of statehood and political authority constituted the broad ideological background of the English law of treason in 1641. A more specific idea that straddled the gap between treason as a personal crime against the monarch and the idea of an impersonal or abstract state was the theory of the king's two bodies. This concept and its role in the interpretation and expansion of the English law of treason is the subject of the next section.

III

The theory of the king's two bodies represented an important halfway house in the transition between personal monarchy and the emergence of the impersonal state. It was crucial because it provided a vocabulary for discussing the relationship of the king's supra-personal powers – his sovereignty – to his person.[74] While treason remained a crime against the king under 25

[73] *State Trials* II: 168.

[74] The classic discussion of the theory of the king's two bodies is Ernst L. Kantorowicz, *The King's Two Bodies: A Study in Medieval Political Theology* (Princeton, 1957); more pertinent

Edward III the advent of the mature theory of the king's two bodies in the late Tudor period rendered it not simply a crime against the king's person but a crime against his (or her) kingship in the abstract as a juristic fiction.[75] The theory of the king's two bodies, in short, provided jurists with an indispensable tool for redefining treason as a crime against the king by virtue of his sovereignty over the state of the commonwealth.

This theory held that the king had in him two capacities, one natural and the other corporate. The first capacity, wrote Coke in *Calvin's Case* (1608), was "a natural body, being descended of the blood royal of the realm". This natural body was "the creation of Almighty God, and... [was] subject to death, infirmity and such like." The second of these was the body politic, "or capacity, so called, because it is framed by the policy of man... and in this capacity the King is esteemed to be immortal, invisible, not subject to any death, infirmity, infancy, nonage, etc."[76] While the person of the king was mortal and inevitably perished the dignity of the kingly office was immortal and upon the death of one monarch the crown and kingdom of England would descend automatically without any necessary need for ceremony, "for coronation is but a royal ornament and solemnization of the royal descent, but no part of the title."[77] The realm was, in a sense, a perpetual corporate entity tied to the monarch and the heirs of his body in the same way that lands held in fee tail were to any private subject. Indeed, in English law there was often no clear distinction between public and private law – it was as though the crown and kingdom were a great entail.[78]

The role of law, and in particular the municipal law of England, was essential in constituting the king's political body. As early as the fifteenth century

to the events of 1641 and immediately afterwards is Michael J. Mendle, "Politics and Political Thought, 1640–1642," in Conrad Russell, ed., *The Origins of the English Civil War* (London, 1973), pp. 219–245.

75 By the "mature" theory of the king's two bodies it is meant the theory as expressed in the writings of Coke and Plowden with which Kantorowicz begins his analysis.

76 Coke, 7 *Reports*, fol. 10a; for a comprehensive discussion of the facts and issues surrounding *Calvin's Case* see Polly J. Price, "Natural Law and Birthright Citizenship in *Calvin's Case*," *Yale Journal of Law and the Humanities* 9 (1997): 73–145.

77 Coke, 7 *Reports*, fol. 10b; *The Third Part of the Institutes*, p. 7; Louis Knafla, ed., *Law and Politics in Jacobean England: The Tracts of Lord Chancellor Ellesmere* (Cambridge, 1977), p. 234. Kantorowicz has traced this aspect of the theory from the accession of Edward I to the throne in the thirteenth century; outside of the realm when his father died, Edward's coronation did not actually take place until two years after he became king: *King's Two Bodies*, pp. 328–329.

78 S. B. Chrimes and, more recently, J. H. Burns have remarked on the tendency, particularly in the writings of Sir John Fortescue, to borrow private law categories in discussion of the succession. Coke is clearly operating within these categories in his published report of *Calvin's Case*: S. B. Chrimes, *English Constitutional Ideas in the Fifteenth Century* (New York, 1966), p. 34; J. H. Burns, *Lordship, Kingship, and Empire: The Idea of Monarchy 1400–1525* (Oxford, 1992), pp. 60–61, 63.

Sir John Fortescue, another former Chief Justice of England, in a series of allusions to Aristotle, had likened the laws of the realm to the sinews of a physical body.[79] Among English jurists this image was a commonplace in the early seventeenth century. Sir John Davies referred to the law as the "soul" of the body politic and described magistrates as its "organs."[80] According to Coke, it was "by the policy of the law" that the king was rendered a political body[81] and this law, argued Coke, was the law of England of which the law of nature was a part.[82] In 1607 Nicholas Fuller argued that "the laws in a Commonwealth are like the sinews in a naturall body, by which hand, foot, and other parts of the body do readily move by the direction of the head" and warned that if any limb of the political body "bee forced above the strength of the sinew" it would be rendered weak or even useless.[83] John Pym referred to the law as that which unites king and people in a single political body and warned of the dire consequences to the whole political body should the law be subverted or destroyed.[84] The law, in this case the municipal law of England, was *fundamental* not in the sense that it limited the actions of the monarch but in that it gave form and composition to the corporate polity of king and kingdom. Although increasingly strained, this kind of language was still current at the outbreak of the first Civil War and parliamentary speeches and legal writings of the period are shot through with it.[85] Furthermore, it enjoyed a certain authority because of its authorship and its continued use among leading officers of state.

The theory was, of course, heavily indebted to Roman law not only in its borrowing of the doctrine of capacities but in its appropriation of the terms dignity (*dignitas*) and majesty (*maiestas*).[86] While the body natural was mortal the kingly dignity was immortal and lent continuity to the English constitution that the common lawyers of the late Tudor and the early Stuart period valued.[87] While the king's person could be in only a single place at any given time, the king's majesty and thus his power, his authority, and his law extended to all corners of his realms.[88] This latter aspect of the theory

79 Sir John Fortescue, *On the Laws and Governance of England*, ed. and trans. Shelley Lockwood (Cambridge, 1997), p. 21.

80 Sir John Davies, *Le Primer Report des Cases & Matters in Ley resolues & adiudges en les Courts del Roy en Ireland. Collect et digest per Sr. John Dauys Chiualer Atturney Generall del Roy in cest Realme* (Dublin, 1615), fol. 8b.

81 Coke, 7 *Reports*, fols. 10a, 12a.

82 Coke, 7 *Reports*, fol. 12b.

83 Nicholas Fuller, *The Argument of Nicholas Fuller of Grayes Inne Esquire, in the Case of Thomas Lad, and Richard Mansell his Clients* (London, 1607; reprinted London, 1641), sig. B3r, p. 14.

84 *The Speech ... of John Pym*, pp. 3, 16.

85 Mendle, "Politics and Political Thought, 1640–1642," p. 221.

86 Kantorowicz, *King's Two Bodies*, *passim*.

87 Kantorowicz, *King's Two Bodies*, pp. 383–401.

88 Kantorowicz, *King's Two Bodies*, pp. 382–385.

was crucial to the law of treason in that it meant treason against the king could be committed at great distances from the king's natural person in the furthest corner of his realms and dominions.

This was essential to maintaining the king's authority in Ireland, where no English monarch actually set foot from the time of Richard II until 1689. For example, the attainder of Shane O'Neil passed by the Irish parliament at Dublin in 1569 asserted that the accused had,

> ... to the perpetuall damage of his name and lineage, refusing the name of a subject, and taking upon him as it were the office of a prince, hath proudly, arrogantly, and by high and perilous practices enterprised great sturres, insurrections rebellions and horrible treasons against your royall Majestie, your crown and dignitie imagining and compassing thereby to deprive your Highnesse, your heires and successors, from the reall and actuall possession of this your Majesties kingdom of Ireland ...[89]

There are two points of interest in this passage. The first, in keeping with our earlier discussion of Tudor treason statutes, was the description of treason as a crime of usurpation or deprivation. The second was the use of the terms "majesty," "dignity," and "crown." In the Irish context it was necessary for English monarchs to project their power through supra-personal legal and constitutional fictions such as the king's two bodies in order to maintain their authority.[90] Ireland may have been a separate and distinct kingdom but it was (unlike Scotland) rendered a body politic by the same policy of law as England, that of the English common law.

The final aspect of the theory of the king's two bodies to be addressed here is the idea of *inseparability*. While the king's political body was distinct from his (or her) natural body it was also inseparable from it.[91] This led to a blurring of the relationship between the two capacities that had grave ramifications for the law of treason. Because the king's two bodies were distinguishable in politic and natural capacities yet indivisible, crimes against the body politic were necessarily also crimes against the body natural. The clearest implication here was that attempting to destroy a king's political body was necessarily an attempt to destroy the king's person. This was the foundation of constructive treason under English law: a crime against the king's realm such as subverting or interfering with the operation of his laws, the soul or sinews of his body politic, could be adjudged treasonable as a compassing of the death of his *natural* body. The blurring of the distinction between the king's two capacities, the lack of a clear distinction between public and private roles, enabled early modern jurists to effect a continued

89 *Irish Statutes* I: 323.

90 For the crown as fiction see Kantorowicz, *King's Two Bodies*, pp. 335–383 and F. W. Maitland, "The Crown as Corporation," *LQR* 17 (1901): 131–146.

91 John B. Sanderson, *"But the People's Creatures": The Philosophical Basis of the English Civil War* (Manchester, 1989), p. 51.

expansion of the law of treason to include such seemingly innocent actions as the encroachment of forensic jurisdiction.

Furthermore, the powers that the king enjoyed by virtue of his role as the lawful sovereign could not be separated from his person. The indivisibility of the king's two bodies was a common assumption among early Stuart jurists like Bacon and Coke,[92] but perhaps the clearest expression of this idea came from the Welsh royalist judge David Jenkins writing in the mid-1640s. Jenkins stated categorically that,

> the king hath the governmeht [sic] of his Subiects, the body politick and the naturall body of the King make one body, and not divers, and are inseperable and indivisable.
>
> The body naturall and politique make one body, and are not to be severed: Ligeance is due by nature, Gods Law, and Man's Law cannot be forfeited nor renounced by any meanes, it is inseparable from the person.[93]

Jenkins was, of course, responding to parliamentary theorists such as Henry Parker who had as early as 1642 asserted the rather strained claim that the king, while *personally* absent from parliament, remained *legally* present at Westminster assembled in parliament.[94] By contrast, William Prynne appropriated the idea of inseparability to the parliamentarian cause by arguing that it was the "Cavaliers about him" who had procured the king's absence from Westminster, thus unkinging him.[95] Jenkins was, no doubt, also concerned to rebut parliamentary theorists like Henry Parker who had argued that to levy war against the king's *personal* commands was not treasonable.[96]

Calvin's Case had repudiated both the idea of a fully abstract state and the impersonal conception of allegiance that it entailed. The key issue of this case was whether or not Robert Calvin, a Scot born at Edinburgh after the accession of James I to the English throne, was entitled to inherit land in England and enjoy the benefit of English law. In Coke's report of the decision the judges insisted that allegiance was owed not only to the monarch's crown, that is the corporate body or state, but also to his or her natural person as well. Conversely, the losing side, seeking to disinherit Calvin from his

92 *Kantorowicz, King's Two Bodies*, p. 382; Coke argued that allegiance was due not only to the king's office but to his person as well: *Coke*, 7 *Reports*, fol. 11a–b.

93 Jenkins, *Lex Terrae*, pp. 21–22.

94 C. C. Weston and Janelle Greenberg, *Subjects and Sovereigns: The Grand Controversy over Legal Sovereignty in Stuart England* (Cambridge, 1981), pp. 56–57.

95 Prynne, *Sovereign Power*, pt. I, sig. L3r, p. 105.

96 Henry Parker, *Observations upon some of his Majesties late Answers and Expresses*, in William Haller, ed., *Tracts on Liberty in the Puritan Revolution* (New York, 1933), vol. II, p. 45 [211]. Philip Hunton also made the distinction between the king's commands given as a public magistrate and as a private person: Philip Hunton, *A Treatise of Monarchie, Containing two Parts: 1. Concerning Monarchy in generall 2. Concerning this particular Monarchy* (London, 1643), sig. H4v, p. 56. See also Sanderson, "*People's Creatures*," p. 36.

English possessions, argued an impersonal conception of political authority: because Calvin was a Scot his allegiance was to the crown of that country and not to the natural person of the king who was king of both England and Scotland. Therefore he was an alien in England and to be denied the benefit of law.[97]

Conrad Russell has characterized the losing position in *Calvin's Case* as impersonal allegiance.[98] This constitutional stance, usually attributed to the traitorous Despensers of the fourteenth century, had a dubious heritage. Lord Ellesmere in his speech touching the *post-nati* vigorously denounced it as making the king "a king divided in himselfe" and as creating "a dangereous distinction betweene the King and the Crowne, and betweene the King and the kingdome."[99] The position of Judge Jenkins was thus the customary stance of early Stuart jurists who sought place and preferment from the crown: allegiance was owed to the king's body natural as well as the body politic and the two were not to be severed.[100] In practical terms what this meant was that treason of levying war could happen in any corner of the realm and still be adjudged a crime against the king's person. This could be the case even if he were five hundred miles away and asleep in bed or if the treason had been committed in the king's realm of Ireland against his political body there. Most importantly, however, it meant that any attempt to destroy the king's kingdom, his "state," or his political body was a constructive compassing of his death.

The criterion of inseparability sets the notion of the king's two bodies well outside of Skinner's conditions for the emergence of the modern concept of the state. While it provided a supra-personal conception of kingship and the king's powers, it continued to identify the object of allegiance as the natural person of the king *as well* as his crown. The lawful subject owed allegiance not merely to the corporate entity of the state, commonwealth, or crown but to the hereditary occupant of the kingly office. While more abstract, impersonal, or "modern" conceptions of statehood were undoubtedly very much available to English jurists at the outbreak of the first Civil War, they lacked the validity that the king's two bodies enjoyed in English public law. The writings of former Chief Justices, Attorneys General and Lord Chancellors such as Fortescue, Coke, Ellesmere, and Davies were a considerable source

97 Coke, 7 *Reports*, fols. 2b–3a.

98 Russell, *Causes*, pp. 157–158.

99 Ellesmere, unlike Coke, exhibited a marked hostility and distrust of the king's two bodies and any legal distinction between king and crown in his consideration of *Calvin's Case*. More in keeping with Fortescue, he expressed a marked hostility to the doctrine of separate capacities: Knafla, *Law and Politics*, pp. 244–245; Chrimes, *Constitutional Ideas*, p. 35; Lockwood, Introduction to Fortescue, *Laws and Governance*, p. xxxix.

100 This aspect of the inseparability of the king's two bodies was brought to my attention by Conal Condren in a paper I delivered to the Cambridge University Tudor–Stuart seminar on 7 February 1996.

of authority. The emergence of newly modeled conceptions of public authority did not necessarily supplant the notion of the king's two bodies as an accepted component of the English law. The two conceptions of statehood – both of which could be characterized as fictional juristic entities – continued to coexist in the political discourse of England in the early 1640s. Necessity now demands that the question of what current fashions call "reason of state" be integrated into our argument, with respect to both the idea of the state and the theory of the king's two bodies.

IV

Kevin Sharpe, in his compendious study of the personal rule of Charles I (1629–40) has noted that "during the period 1626 to 1629 we hear increasingly a new language: the language of necessity, and of public safety contrasted with private interests."[101] Richard Tuck has identified arguments from "necessity" with the emergence of "New Humanism" in western Europe at the end of the sixteenth century. In public life "New Humanism" manifested itself as an "anti-constitutional" and occasionally "anti-ethical" language of *interest* and *necessity* envisioning an instrumental and calculated view of political life that owed more to the renaissance of Tacitus than to that of Cicero.[102] The relevance of such appeals to our discussion here is indisputable. However, the following section will demonstrate that the language of "necessity" was not necessarily "anti-constitutional" or "anti-ethical" but rather formed an integral part of the English law at the beginning of the Civil Wars in Britain.[103]

Broadly speaking, actions flowing from appeals to "necessity" operated in two senses in the early modern period. The first considered those actions a ruler must take for the necessary maintenance of their "state." In this scheme the legal and constitutional order was inextricably bound up with both the authority and the person of the king: the "state" as a constitutional order

101 Kevin Sharpe, *The Personal Rule of Charles I* (New Haven, 1992), p. 59.

102 Richard Tuck, *Philosophy and Government, 1572–1651* (Cambridge, 1993).

103 This point has been strongly asserted in Nicola P. Perkins, "The Judiciary and the Defence of Property in the Law Courts during the Personal Rule of Charles I," unpublished Ph.D. dissertation (Cambridge, 1999); see also Paul Christianson, "John Selden, the Five Knights Case and Discretionary Imprisonment in Early Stuart England," *Criminal Justice History* 4 (1985): 65–87; and David S. Berkowitz, "Reason of State in England and the Petition of Right, 1603–1629," in Roman Schnurr, ed., *Staatsrason: Studien zur Geschichte eines politischen Begriffs* (Berlin, 1975), pp. 164–212. Christianson argues that the debates over the crown's power of discretionary imprisonment centered on conflicting interpretations of the "ancient constitution" with the crown lawyers making few appeals to "reason of state" and debate being conducted within the conventions of the common law. Berkowitz suggests in contrast a confrontation between "reason of state," absolutism, and prerogative on the one side and the "sovereignty of law" on the other.

depended on the king's and the laws of the realm were the king's laws to enforce, promote and maintain.[104] The second pertained to those deemed necessary for the maintenance of the "state" as an abstract entity – a free-standing legal and constitutional order. The state became a moral end in and of itself. It is tempting to characterize the former as a "medieval" understanding of the term and the latter as a characteristically "modern" understanding. However, it must be remembered that in 1641 both sets of meanings were available to English parliamentarians and jurists of all political stripes. They constituted parallel threads with the former, more "medieval" understanding prevailing in English public law: the law was unquestionably the king's law and the kingdom or "state" was the king's to hold and maintain. Early modern jurists allotted those actions necessary for the preservation of the king and kingdom the highest moral priority. This was relatively unproblematic. Actions that might normally be considered unconstitutional, illegal, or, in the short view, even immoral were justifiable if taken towards the preservation of king and state. Extraordinary courses of action were justified by virtue of their "necessity" for the preservation of king and kingdom, king and state, or, potentially, in a more explicitly "modern" sense the abstract "state" as a moral end in and of itself. Appeals to "necessity," therefore, related to the law of treason on two levels: (1) as a mark of sovereignty (an issue previously discussed); and (2) as a substantive argument deployed in English state treason trials.

By the reign of James I English prosecutors could argue that treason was not only an attempt to destroy or subvert the king but also the kingdom, the state, or the commonwealth. Indeed, there is every reason to believe that John Cowell's understanding of treason as a crime against the majesty of the commonwealth was not merely the opinion of an eccentric and ultimately condemned academic. The killing of a kingdom was the killing of a king. Coke as Attorney-General at the trial of the Gunpowder Plotters remarked that, "this treason doth want an apt name, as tending not only to the hurt, but to the death of the king, and not the death of the king only, but of his whole kingdom, *Non Regis sed Regni*, that is to the destruction and dissolution of the frame and fabrick of this antient, famous, and ever flourishing monarchy..."[105] Elsewhere in the trial he remarked that the traitors "might as it were with one blow, not wound, but kill

[104] This, I believe, is the sense in which Gaines Post employs the term: Gaines Post, *Studies in Medieval Legal Thought: Public Law and the State* (Princeton, 1964), pp. 241–309; see also Peter Burke, "Tacitism, Sceptisism, and Reason of State," in J. H. Burns and M. Goldie, eds., *The Cambridge History of Political Thought, 1450–1700* (Cambridge, 1991), pp. 484–490.

[105] *State Trials* II: 167.

and destroy the whole state."[106] Similarly the Jesuit Henry Garnett stood accused of conspiring and compassing "To dispose the king, and to deprive him of his Government" as well as overthrowing "the whole state of the commonwealth."[107] The integral relationship of king and state was a given.

The relationship of reason of state in its continental form with common-law jurisprudence was more problematic. The first and most obvious problem, one of origins, cannot be resolved here (or possibly anywhere) – in particular the question of whether the common lawyer's appeal to necessity in key state trials was evidence of the influence of continental "statist" thinking or "New Humanism." For example, Levack has suggested that the opinion of Chief Baron Sir Thomas Fleming in *Bates' Case* reflected some "untraditional views" borrowed from civil law which distinguished between the king's ordinary and his absolute power.[108] This resulted in "a new definition of royal power and a concept analogous to the Continental theory of 'reason of state.'"[109] Levack has argued: "Instead of describing the royal prerogative as a constellation of specific rights, he [Fleming] was conceiving of it in much more general, abstract terms that it could be exercised whenever 'matters of state' needed to be resolved."[110]

106 *State Trials* II: 177.

107 *State Trials* II: 218; see also 225: "sithence the Jesuits set foot in this land, there never passed four years without a most pestilent and pernicious treason, tending to the subversion of the whole state." Garnett's indictment was framed under 25 Edward III ostensibly because of a general pardon of 1603 for offenses under 27 Elizabeth I, c. 2 for priests who had "treasonably" entered the kingdom (Garnett had arrived in 1586): *State Trials* I: 222–225, 228–229.

108 The full quotation that Levack draws on is: "The King's power is double, ordinary and absolute, and they have several laws and ends. That of the ordinary is for the profit of particular subjects, for the execution of civil justice, the determining of *meum*; and this is exercised by equity and justice in ordinary courts and by the civilians is nominated *jus privatum*, and with us common law; and these laws cannot be changed without Parliament; and although their form and course may be changed in substance. The absolute power of the King is not that which is converted or executed to private use, to the benefit of any particular person, but is only that which is applied to the general benefit of the people, and is *salus populi*... and this power is guided by the rules which direct only at the common law and is most properly named policy and government; and as the constitution of this body varieth with the time, so varieth this absolute law, according to the wisdom of the King for the common good; and these being general rules, and true as they are, all things done within these rules are lawful." Brian P. Levack, "Law and Ideology: The Civil Law and Theories of Absolutism in Elizabethan and Jacobean England," in Heather Dubrow and Richard Strier, eds., *The Historical Renaissance: New Essays on Tudor and Stuart Literature and Culture* (Chicago, 1988), p. 232; for the original see *Lane's Exchequer Reports being a reprint of Reports of Cases in the Court of Exchequer from 1605 to 1612 by the Hon. Richard Lane with Notes and a Life of the Reporter by Charles Francis Morrell* (London, 1884), pp. 44–45 [27].

109 Levack, "Law and Ideology," p. 233.

110 Levack, "Law and Ideology," pp. 232–233.

The second problem, that of compatibility with common-law thought, is more tractable because it involves questions of validity and usage. Glenn Burgess has argued that, "The idea that necessity could justify the abandonment of law, even the destruction of property rights, was a central principle of English common law."[111] What should be clear from our earlier discussion of reason of state as a mark of sovereignty is that the rhetoric of necessity was a commonplace, a shared resource available to both sides in state treason trials. The notion that there was an extraordinary power in the state that could be exercised in time of great extremity was not particularly contentious, and before the 1640s it was even generally accepted that this power lay in the king. As Oliver St. John remarked in questioning the validity of the ship money writ, the issue was not "*de persona*, in whom the *suprema potestas* of giving the authorities the powers to the Sheriff... for that is in the King; but the question is only *de modo*, by what medium or method this supreme power, which is in His Majesty, doth infuse and let out itself into this particular."[112] The validity of appeals to necessity as consonant with the traditional forms of lawful governance was not at issue. The larger issue was whether the king should act without parliament in taking such measures. Whether the traditions of the English common law can be reconciled with continental reason of state theories or not, the fact remains that the appeal to necessity was an established and valid part of the common lawyers' arsenal in the waging of state trials. As Burgess has concluded, in the final analysis, "it matters less where the ideas came from (and their exact pedigree in this instance is probably irrecoverable, in any case) than the uses for which they were employed."[113]

Appeals to necessity were, therefore, not the exclusive property of apologists for the personal rule of Charles I. For example, the parliamentarian lawyer John Marsh argued in his defense of the Militia Ordinance that, although the king's power to proclaim war and peace ordinarily gave him control over the militia, the two houses of parliament could, in times of "imminent danger" to the kingdom and "extream necessity" place the militia in a defensive posture without the king's consent.[114] What is remarkable here, however, is the nature of the proofs that Marsh produced in defending the Long Parliament's actions. He buttressed the appeal to necessity not with allusions to the sources of "New Humanism" but with citations from Bracton's *On the Laws and Customs of England* and Coke's report of the

[111] Burgess, *Absolute Monarchy*, p. 50.
[112] Gardiner, *Constitutional Documents*, pp. 110–111.
[113] Burgess, *Absolute Monarchy*, p. 81.
[114] John Marsh, *An Argument or, Debate in Law: of the Great Question concerning the Militia; As it is now settled by Ordinance of both the Houses of Parliament* (London, 1642), sig. B3r, p. 5, and sig. B4r, p. 7.

Bishop of Salisbury's Case to the effect that, "In time of necessitie, illegal acts, are made legall: and things utterly against law justifiable."[115] He continued to cite Plowden's *Commentaries*, arguing the example of the prisoner who, finding himself in a burning prison, must commit the felony of breaking jail in order to save himself from certain death.[116] Marsh, an educated man, may indeed have been familiar with the materials of "New Humanism." What is noteworthy, however, is that he couched the appeal to necessity in terms consistent with the central authorities of the English law. Just as the *Ship Money* judge, Sir Richard Weston, later an ardent royalist, had justified the extra-parliamentary levy in terms consistent with previous custom, usage, and history, Marsh justified his position and openly derived his key arguments from the sources of the common law.[117] While Michael Mendle's assertion that the early 1640s saw the emergence of a "parliamentary absolutism" may be somewhat overstated, parliamentary lawyers certainly employed the language of "necessity" in the defense of the Long Parliament's actions.[118]

Our conclusions here are twofold. Firstly, despite the appearance of more fully abstract conceptions of political authority, prosecutors on the eve of the Civil War continued to rest their arguments largely on their claims to be acting in the king's name for the preservation of the kingdom, state, and commonwealth. This was not a fully impersonal conception of the "state" but depended on supra-personal conceptions of the king's authority such as that of king's two bodies. This was definitely true of Coke and, according to Kantorowicz, Bacon. The inseparability of the king's natural person from his public authority as manifested through his political body meant that depriving the king of his state, or destroying "the whole state," meant killing the king. Crimes against the state were de facto crimes against the king and the treason of destroying the state or kingdom necessarily constituted constructive compassing. Secondly, prior to the outbreak of hostilities "reason of state" or, more generically, the appeal to "necessity," was part and parcel of a shared and increasingly contested vocabulary on which both sides would draw in the coming conflict. The appeal to "necessity" was by no means exclusively reserved to the king and the defenders of his prerogative. This was the case well before the shooting started in 1642.

[115] Marsh, *An Argument*, sig. B4r, p. 7; Coke, 10 *Reports*, fol. 61a; the maxim in Latin as quoted in Coke and Marsh is "*illud quod alias licitum, & necessitas inducit privilegum, quod jure privatur.*" Thorne's edition of Bracton differs slightly: Henry de Bracton, *On the Laws and Customs of England*, ed. and trans. S. E. Thorne (Cambridge Mass., 1968), vol. III, p. 231. Alan Cromartie has recently emphasized Marsh's use of Plowden and Coke but his direct citation of Bracton 247a–b was of equal if not greater importance: Alan Cromartie, "The Constitutionalist Revolution: The Tranformation of Political Culture in Early Stuart England," *P & P* 163 (1999): 115.

[116] Marsh, *An Argument*, sig. B4r, p. 7; 1 Plowden 13, 75 *Eng. Rep.* 21 (KB).

[117] *State Trials*, III: 1078.

[118] See Mendle, "Parliamentary Sovereignty," *passim*.

V

These two opening chapters have presented not simply a discussion of the statutory basis of English treason law but a general theory of treason. Simply stated: high treason occurs whenever any words, counsels, or actions tend towards depriving the lawful sovereign of his or her sovereignty. Thomas Hobbes, whose perspicacity remains the envy of modern commentators, put it succinctly when he stated in the English-language edition of his *De Cive* that the traitor was he who averred that the sovereign "had no Right to wage warre at this own will, to make Peace, list soldiers, levie monies, electing Magistrates, and publique Ministers, enacting Lawes, deciding controversies, setting penalties, or doing ought else, without which the State cannot stand."[119] This was treason not only by the law of the land but, according to Hobbes, the law of nature in all states.[120] To be sure, Hobbes revolutionized our understanding of sovereignty and political obligation. His conception of treason, however, was in many respects a garden-variety Roman law concoction. Hobbes was in this aspect very much a product of his time. Treason was not simply the homicide of the monarch's person but the denial or unlawful seizure of sovereign power. This was so whether sovereignty was purely impersonal or found expression through supra-personal constitutional fictions such as the king's two bodies. In the particular context of early modern England the lawful sovereign was the king. However, while the king enjoyed certain prerogative powers such as coinage, the appointing of magistrates, and the declaring of war and peace, he could neither exercise legal sovereignty nor levy subsidies without parliament.

It is crucial to observe that, although the English law of treason evolved in a monarchical setting, the general theory of treason as an unlawful appropriation of sovereignty remained relevant when removed from this context. Usurpation of sovereign power remained treasonable in both a republic and in a frankly absolutist state in which all the rights of sovereignty were held exclusively by the prince. This should be unsurprising. Whatever the precise nature of a regime – aristocratic, monarchic, or democratic – the claimants of sovereign power needed the law of treason in order to advance their claims to govern. For example, the first treason "act" of the Commonwealth, passed on 14 May 1649, used similar language to the Elizabethan statutes discussed above:

> Be it Enacted by this present Parliament, and by the authority of the same, That if any person shall maliciously or advisedly publish by Writing, Printing, or openly Declaring, That the said Government is Tyrannical, Usurped or Unlawful; or that

119 Thomas Hobbes, *De Cive: The English version entitled in the first edition Philosophicall Rudiments concerning Government and Society*, ed. Howard Warrender (Oxford, 1983), pp. 180–181; also cited in Sanderson, "*People's Creatures*," p. 101.

120 Hobbes, *De Cive*, p. 181.

the Commons in Parliament assembled are not the Supreme authority of this Nation; or shall, Plot, Contrive or Endeavor to stir up or raise Force against the present government, or for the subversion or alteration of the same, and shall declare the same by open deed, That then every such Offence shall be Taken, Deemed and Adjudged, by the authority of this Parliament, to be High Treason.[121]

In 1649 the English constitution was fundamentally redefined as a republic. However, in drafting their treason legislation the Commonwealths-men struck a chord of continuity with England's monarchical past: actions declared treasonable were those tending towards the diminishing of the claims of the Commons assembled in parliament to exercise the rights of sovereignty as the "supreme authority." On 4 January 1649 the Rump Parliament had declared itself the "the supreme power in this nation" and claimed the exclusive right to give law.[122] Henceforth, the term "ordinance" that the Long Parliament had used to characterize its orders was abandoned as the Rumpers claimed power to make "acts" of parliament without the threefold consent of king, lords, and commons. Such claims to sovereign power needed defending and in order to secure them the Commonwealths-men turned to the law of treason.

While the events of 1649 represented, however briefly, a fundamental break with England's monarchical past it remains somewhat questionable whether this reflected any far-reaching redefinition of political power in and of itself. Through the use of political theories like the king's two bodies kingship had by 1641 undergone a transformation. In keeping with the growth of the idea of the state, the role of the king had been redefined as the lawful wielder of the sovereign power. This power was, at least before 1642, customarily defined in supra-personal rather than strictly impersonal terms: the authority of the kingly office could not be separated from the king's natural person and that of the heirs of his body. In early Stuart England the king wielded this sovereign power both by virtue of his prerogative and in concert with parliaments when new law was made, old law repealed, or subsidies levied. To usurp his power, whether it was wielded by his prerogative or through parliament, was treason.

VI

The body of this study consists of four case studies of major English state treason trials beginning with the trial of Thomas Wentworth, First Earl of Strafford, in March 1641 and ending with the trial of Charles Stuart, King of England, Ireland, and Scotland, in January 1649. While this may seem

121 C. H. Firth and R. S. Rait, eds., *Acts and Ordinances of the Interregnum* (London, 1911), vol. II, pp. 120–121, 193.
122 Kenyon, *Stuart Constitution*, p. 292.

extremely focused, it must be borne in mind that, of these four trials, two have already formed the basis for scholarly monographs and a full consideration of all aspects relating to any one of them could easily form the basis of a full-length book.[123] The four trials are analyzed in relation to themes delineated in part I; that is, treason is addressed as a political and juristic concept with respect to contemporary notions of "sovereignty" and "state." The result should add considerably to our understanding of the nature of political authority and the relationship of political thought to political action in early modern England.

Use is made of both manuscript and printed sources. While the project of revisionist political history has emphasized the importance of manuscript sources as the best means of accurately reconstructing early Stuart political life, the use of manuscript sources here emphasizes their ideological content. Printed material, while of questionable value in reconstructing an "accurate" picture of historical events, has been used by Quentin Skinner and others in order to reconstruct the myriad of shifting ideological positions, or "moves," of participants in the pamphlet debates of the Civil War and interregnum.[124] The following study will accordingly attempt a reading of manuscript sources as ideological statements taking into account as far as possible, when they can be accurately identified, the prejudices of the authors.

[123] J. H. Timmis III, *Thine is the Kingdom: The Trial for Treason of Thomas Lord Wentworth, Earl of Strafford, First Minister to King Charles I and Last Hope of the English Crown* (Tuscaloosa, Ala., 1974) and C. V. Wedgwood, *The Trial of Charles I* (Glasgow, 1964; reprinted Harmondsworth, 1983).

[124] Quentin Skinner, "History and Ideology in the English Revolution," *HJ* 8 (1965): 151–178; Quentin Skinner, "Conquest and Consent: Thomas Hobbes and the Engagement Controversy," in G. E. Aylmer, ed., *The Interregnum* (London, 1972), pp. 79–98.

Part II

PRACTICE

3

Thomas Wentworth, First Earl of Strafford

He hath encroached jurisdiction, where none was, taking upon him a power to repell the lawes, and to make new lawes, *and in domineering over the lives and goods, and what ever else was the subjects.*[1]

I

The trial of Thomas Wentworth, First Earl of Strafford before the House of Lords in the spring of 1641 remains one of the most controversial state treason trials in English history. Essentially, Strafford stood trial for his role in Charles I's personal rule of 1629–40 and his impeachment represented more than simply a political vendetta of a leading faction within the early Long Parliament. The proceedings against Strafford were an indictment of the methods, practices, and policies of Charles I's government during the personal rule in both England and Ireland.

Scholarly debate has focused heavily on the question of the legality of Strafford's impeachment and attainder. Historians have been divided over whether or not the charges against the earl fell within commonly accepted definitions of treason or represented an unprecedented innovation in the law. Conrad Russell has been the leading proponent of the former view, arguing in an important 1965 article that the theory of treason in Strafford's trial fell within "accepted doctrines of law and political theory."[2] Russell asserted that, aside from the literal sense of 25 Edward III, there was another tradition of treason law "possibly owing something to Roman law . . . of treason against the state, or against the stability of the kingdom." Essential to this conception of treason was "the idea of making a division between the king and the people."[3]

1 BL TT E.196(45), *Mr. Maynards Speech Before Both Houses in Parliament, upon Wednesday the xxiiiij. of March, in reply upon the Earle of Straffords Answer to his Articles at the Barre* (London, 1641), p. 4.

2 Conrad Russell, "The Theory of Treason in the Trial of Strafford," *EHR* 80 (1965): 30.

3 Russell, "Theory of Treason": 31.

Also falling within this category has been the position of J. H. Timmis III. Timmis has argued that the fifteenth and twenty-third articles against Strafford – the two which would later form the basis of the bill of attainder – fell within the accepted statutory definition of treason as a levying of war against the king. The managers of the evidence against Strafford resorted to bill of attainder not because of any legal weakness in their position but because they had failed to prove the case in fact.[4] This argument was not unlike that of George, Lord Digby during the debates on the bill of attainder. Digby advocated "laying aside this Bill of Attainder" not over questions of law but questions of fact: he was simply not satisfied that the proofs to the key twenty-third article were sufficient.[5]

The competing interpretation holds that the proceedings against Strafford were unprecedented in law and unsupported in fact. C. V. Wedgwood initially stated this position in her 1961 biography of Wentworth[6] and W. R. Stacy has since forcefully restated this view in a 1985 article.[7] This view holds that the case against the Earl of Strafford derived from an unprecedented theory of accumulative treason and that the prosecution's abandonment of the impeachment proceedings in favor of a bill of attainder occurred because of the weakness of their case both in law and in fact. Stacy has argued,

> Throughout the trial and attainder the key charge against Strafford was that through an accumulation of lesser offenses, he had endeavored to subvert law and government and thereby divide the king and his people. This amounted to an unprecedented theory of accumulative treason, and the arguments of the prosecution advanced to support and supplement this charge were indeed novel and severely strained the law.[8]

Stacy's argument was essentially a "retrying" of the case according to a literalist interpretation of the statutes without any proper consideration of the range of ideological positions available to the participants in the trial. The argument did not address the broader issues that the trial brought into focus. These include, most notably, relationship between monarch and polity, king and state.

A literalist position was certainly available in the early modern period; however, its use was usually confined to individuals standing accused of

[4] J. H. Timmis III, "Evidence and 1 *Eliz. I, Cap.* 6: The Basis of The Lords' Decision in the Trial of Strafford," *HJ* 21 (1978): 680; and his book, *Thine is the Kingdom: The Trial for Treason of Thomas Lord Wentworth, Earl of Strafford, First Minister to King Charles I and Last Hope of the English Crown* (Tuscaloosa, Ala., 1974).

[5] John Rushworth, *The Tryal of Thomas Earle of Strafford upon an impeachment of high treason* (London, 1680; 2nd edn. 1700), pp. 50–53.

[6] C. V. Wedgwood, *Thomas Wentworth First Earl of Strafford, 1593–1641: A Revaluation* (London, 1961), pp. 310–379.

[7] W. R. Stacy, "Matter of Fact, Matter of Law, and the Attainder of the Earl of Strafford," *AJLH* 29 (1985): 323–347.

[8] Stacy, "Matter of Fact, Matter of Law": 324.

treason and their counsels. It was not a generally accepted body of law. For example, at his trial in 1554 Sir Nicholas Throckmorton stated, "There is a Maxim or principle in the law, which ought not to be violated, That no penal Statute may, ought, or should be construed, expounded, extended, or wrested otherwise than the simple words and nude letter of the same statute doth warrant and signify."[9] This account of Throckmorton's trial appeared in Holinshed's *Chronicle* and was certainly available during the Civil War and interregnum.[10] Although this position was not unheard of in early modern England, to identify it as an accepted body of law, as Stacy has, is completely unfounded. It was simply one of a range of legal/ideological positions that were available to the participants in a state treason trial and, for an accused traitor such as Throckmorton or Strafford, it was undoubtedly the most attractive.

The arguments of Stacy and Timmis, while reaching different conclusions, share the same flaw: they seek to establish the "legality" of Strafford's trial and attainder simply on the basis of its statutory definition without reference to broader ideological issues. This approach is erroneous because, as should be clear from chapter 1, the statutes themselves are subject to interpretation as expressions of ideological positions concerning the nature of political authority. Furthermore, these analyses concentrated almost exclusively on the fifteenth and twenty-third articles that eventually formed the bill of attainder. They virtually ignored the general charges and in particular the pivotal notion of the subversion of the fundamental law of the land. If only two of the twenty-eight specific articles in Strafford's impeachment were good in law, then why did the managers of his prosecution bother with the rest? Furthermore, why did they spend valuable time reiterating the charges contained in the seven general articles drawn up in November 1640? This was especially true when considering that the anti-Strafford camp perceived themselves to be grievously short of time.[11] The answer to this question is that the definition of treason in the trial of Strafford necessarily comprehended the relationship of treason to sovereignty as political practice.

[9] *State Trials* I: 889–890. The account contained in this volume is drawn from Raphael Holinshed, *The Chronicles of Ireland* in *Holinshed's Chronicles: England, Scotland and Ireland with a New Introduction by Vernon F. Snow*, 6 vols. (New York, 1965; reprinted New York, 1976).

[10] Annabel Patterson has argued that John Lilburne modeled his successful 1649 defense on that of Throckmorton from a reading of Holinshed: Annabel Patterson, "For Words Only: From Treason Trial to Liberal Legend in Early Modern England," *Yale Journal of Law and the Humanities* 5 (1993): 389–416. This account differs significantly from that of Dyer I: 98b in that it clearly asserts that conspiracy to levy war was *not* treason.

[11] Sir Simonds D'Ewes, a decidedly hostile observer to Strafford, claims to have remarked in the House of Commons on March 25 that he "...could not without great astonishment behold the delaies of this day of the triall of the Earle of Strafford..." Whether or not D'Ewes actually did make these remarks is less material than the sense of haste and urgency that compelled him to record them: BL Harl. MS 162, fol. 359r.

The argument is structured as follows. The first section contains an analysis of the general articles and their relationship to the ideas of sovereignty, state, and the king's two bodies as discussed in the previous chapter. The second section consists of (1) an analysis of the twenty-eight particular articles; and (2) a consideration of the arguments of the managers of Strafford's trial in pursuing these articles during the impeachment proceedings. This section demonstrates that the substance of the particular articles against the earl constituted specific cases where Strafford had overstepped the boundaries of his lawful jurisdictions and infringed on numerous marks of sovereignty. As a result his actions had subverted the fundamental law of the land, denying the king's law and justice to his subjects in both England and Ireland and creating a division between the king and his subjects, the king and his kingdoms. Like the Despensers of the fourteenth century, he sought to separate king from kingdom and from crown. The third section is a consideration of the attainder proceedings and the ideological implications of the subversion of the law.

The argument here is a refinement of Conrad Russell's. It will examine how the prosecution made use of pre-existing political vocabularies, that is, commonplaces of political language, in order to redescribe and legitimate an extreme course of action – the execution of leading minister of state. The case against the earl demands assessment not simply according to anachronistic standards of legality but according to a set of criteria that consider the range of ideological positions available relating to the nature of sovereignty, the state, and public authority in early modern England. Seen in this light, the theory of treason in the trial of Strafford *did* fall within the accepted conceptions of English treason law. Extra-statutory treasons *did* exist and were known in 1641. The Roman law conception of treason was not only a commonplace but stood largely in conformity with accepted English law. The idea of treason against the realm or state was not an unprecedented innovation.

The substance of the articles against the Earl of Strafford was that he had unlawfully appropriated to his person the sovereign power in derogation of the king's authority in both England and Ireland. This occurred first during his presidency of the Council of the North, then during his tenure as lord deputy in Ireland, and, finally, during the Scottish conflagration of 1638–40 and the hectic events leading up to the calling of the Long Parliament. The natural consequence of the earl's usurpations was the subversion of the law and consequently the emergence of a division between ruler and ruled, between the king, his parliament, and his people. This division, the prosecution would argue, tended toward the destruction of both the king and his state, who were inseparable. In other words, Strafford had endeavored to sever the king's bodies politic, both English and Irish, from his body natural.

II

The articles of impeachment against the Earl of Strafford consisted of seven general articles and twenty-eight specific articles. The general articles were read to the prisoner at the bar of the House of Lords on 25 November 1640, two weeks after the House of Commons made their accusations against Strafford to the Lords.[12] The twenty-eight specific articles were prepared over the following two months, being first produced on 30 January 1641 when they were read to the Earl of Strafford at the bar of the Lords.[13] The accused requested a copy of the charges in writing in order to prepare his answers and they were provided.[14] After much stonewalling Strafford made his answers to the articles verbally in the king's presence before the bar of the Lords on 24 February 1641[15] – two days before Archbishop Laud was to appear to hear the articles of high treason being pressed against him.[16]

Much procedural wrangling then ensued, after which the Lords resolved that Strafford would have access to counsel in questions of law, but not in questions of fact, and that his counsel would be allowed only to speak to matters of law and not to the evidence, thus leaving the embattled earl to his own devices for the majority of the proceedings.[17] The Lords reserved judgment to themselves when question arose as to what constituted matter of law and what constituted matter of fact.[18] Strafford also petitioned on 18 March that he be allowed to call his own witnesses and examine them under oath.[19] The Lords resolved further on 18 March that this request would be only partially granted: Strafford would be allowed to examine whatever witnesses he chose but not under oath.[20] This represented a hollow victory for Strafford as many of his key witnesses – Archbishop Laud and Sir George Radcliffe most prominently – also stood accused of high treason. This was in accord with common-law rules of procedure that did not permit witnesses to give testimony under oath if there was a possibility of them giving self-incriminating evidence. It also provided the prosecution with a handy and legitimate pretext for denying Strafford access to the

[12] *CJ* II: 26; *LJ* IV: 88, 97. [13] *LJ* IV: 148; MM, 30 January 1641. [14] *LJ* IV: 148.

[15] Strafford was originally supposed to make his replies on 17 February but he and his counsel, Richard Lane, after petitioning unsuccessfully for extra time to answer the charges on the 13th and 16th finally succeeded in securing an extra week to prepare on the 17th: *LJ* IV: 162 164. His answers were delivered and read to the commons the following day: Maija Jansson, ed., *Two Diaries of the Long Parliament* (Gloucester, 1984), pp. 9, 90.

[16] *LJ* IV: 172–173.

[17] *LJ* IV: 178–179; MM, 9 and 13 March 1641. The managers of the evidence against Strafford in the House of Commons appear to have attempted to limit the role of Strafford's counsel as much as possible. Lane did speak on question of law to the bill of attainder on 17 April: BL Harl. MS 163, fol. 452r; Sir Ralph Verney, *Verney's Notes of the Long Parliament*, ed. J. Bruce (Camden Series 31, 1845), pp. 50–52; and Rushworth, *Tryal*, p. 671.

[18] MM, 9 March 1641. [19] *LJ* IV: 177–178. [20] *LJ* IV: 189.

testimony of his friends and allies just as it had provided Attorney-General Coke and Chief Justice Popham with a handy pretext for denying Sir Walter Ralegh the right to question his single accuser Lord Cobham at his trial over three decades before.[21] In spite of Strafford's continued pleas for more time the trial opened on 22 March 1641. On 10 April, frustrated at the success of Strafford's delaying tactics, the commons resolved to proceed by bill of attainder.[22]

Any credible attempt to reconstruct the legal case against the Earl of Strafford must begin with a consideration of the seven general articles sent up to the Lords on 25 November 1640. The first of these was arguably the most significant, charging

> That . . . *Thomas*, Earl of Strafford hath traiterously endeavoured to subvert the Fundamental Laws and Government of the Realms of *England* and *Ireland*, and, instead thereof to introduce an arbitrary and tyrannical Government, against Law, which he hath declared by traiterous Words, Counsels, and Actions, and by giving His Majesty Advice by Force of Arms, to compel His loyal Subjects to subvert thereunto.[23]

The second article charged Strafford with treacherously assuming "Regal Power over the Lives, Liberties of Persons, Lands and Goods of His Majesty's Subjects, in *England* and *Ireland*" to effect of their "Subversion and Undoing." The third article accused him of appropriating the king's revenues to his own use during his tenure as Lord Deputy in Ireland in the 1630s. The fourth purported that he had abused his offices as President of the Council of the North and Lord Deputy of Ireland, "to the increasing, countenancing, and encouraging of Papists" so that they might assist him in his "malicious and tyrannical Designs." The fifth charged him with endeavoring to create "Enmity and Hostility" between the Scottish and English subjects of Charles I. The sixth blamed Strafford for the defeat of the English army by the Scots at Newburn the previous summer and the subsequent fall of Newcastle. The seventh and final general, undoubtedly related to the dissolution of the Short Parliament earlier that year, charged that he had "laboured to subvert the Right of Parliaments, and the ancient Course of Parliamentary Proceedings, and, by false and malicious Slanders, to incense

[21] Both Ralegh and Cobham had been implicated in the Main Plot, an alleged conspiracy to replace James I on the throne with Arabella Stuart. Cobham appears to have made a deal to save his own skin: *State Trials* II: 19.

[22] BL Harl. MS 164, fol. 965v. There is evidence that this course of action had been contemplated even before the general articles were read on 25 November 1640: on 19 November St. John, Glynne, Palmer, Grimstone, Maynard, D'Ewes, Whistler, Selden, and Widdrington had been appointed to a select committee, any two of whom "were to search the Records of Attainder in the King's bench, in such Manner and at such Time, as they shall think fit, for the Furtherance of the Charge in Hand against the Earl of *Straford*": *CJ* II: 31.

[23] *LJ* IV: 97.

His Majesty against Parliaments." In summing up the general articles the charge concluded that Strafford had "laboured to alienate the Hearts of the King's liege People from His Majesty, to set a Division between them, and to ruin and destroy His Majesty's Kingdoms."[24]

Conrad Russell has suggested that the idea of creating a division between king and people may have been appropriated from Scots law, and in particular from the treasonable offense of "leasing making" which consisted "of making division by giving ill counsel." As Russell has noted, this, of course, had no status in English law but was a useful source of ideas.[25] Lord Chancellor Ellesmere had also expressed the idea of creating a division between ruler and ruled or king and kingdom and identified it with the doctrine of impersonal allegiance.[26] Furthermore, there was the case of Roger Manwaring, who was impeached in the parliament of 1628 for preaching sermons in support of the forced loan. Manwaring stood charged (among other things) with plotting and practising "to alter and subvert the frame and fabric of this estate and commonwealth" and by his "most scandalous speech" endeavoring "to set a division between the head and the members, and between the members themselves."[27] He essentially stood accused of sowing discord in the body politic between the king as head and his subjects as members. Manwaring was, of course, not charged with high treason but the similarity in political vocabulary with the charges against Strafford remains striking.

Another key source that has been largely ignored is the law of praemunire. In part I we noted that the advent of the royal supremacy resulted in an increasing tendency to conflate treason with this lesser, largely jurisdictional, crime. Indeed, much of the substance of the charges against both Strafford and Laud consisted of the disruption of the ordinary course of justice in the common-law courts to the advantage of both the equitable jurisdiction of the Lord Deputy in council in Ireland and the ecclesiastical courts in England. While English common lawyers generally accepted praemunire as an offense pertaining only to the jurisdiction of the ecclesiastical courts, Coke had as early as 1615 expressed the view that equitable jurisdictions, such as Chancery in England and Council Board in Ireland, were subject to the same sanctions as the ecclesiastical courts should they infringe on the jurisdiction of the common-law courts.[28] In the third volume of his *Institutes*, first published in 1644, Coke argued that praemunire extended

[24] *LJ* IV: 97.
[25] Conrad Russell, *The Fall of the British Monarchies, 1637–1642* (Oxford, 1991; reprinted Oxford, 1995), p. 286.
[26] Louis Knafla, ed., *Law and Politics in Jacobean England: The Tracts of Lord Chancellor Ellesmere* (Cambridge, 1977), pp. 244–245.
[27] *State Trials* II: 336–337.
[28] S. E. Thorne, "Praemunire and Sir Edward Coke," *HLQ* 2 (1938–9): 85–88; Charles M. Gray, "The Boundaries of the Equitable Function," *AJLH* 20 (1976): 193–194.

to all courts within the realm that were governed by laws other than the common law. This included all courts of equity and those such as Admiralty which functioned according to civil law.[29] More importantly Coke cited the statute of 27 Edward III, c. 1 and described praemunire as tending to "the prejudice and dishersion of the king and his Crowne . . . the dishersion of all his subiects . . . the undoing and destruction of the common law of this Realme."[30] Elsewhere in this work he referred to praemunire as "the subversion of the common law."[31] While Coke's views on the applicability of the statutes of praemunire to equitable jurisdictions may have been at variance with the other authorities of the day, Holdsworth has noted that the controversy of 1615 "lingered on during the rest of the seventeenth century."[32]

The questions of the availability of Coke's views to the managers in Strafford's trial, and of their exclusivity to Coke are problematic. While the third volume of his *Institutes* did not reach print until 1644, the House of Commons had appointed a committee on 5 December 1640 to inquire after Coke's books, papers, and manuscript writings seized at his death in 1634 and to inquire by whose authority they were seized.[33] Whether the managers of the evidence against Strafford had access to Coke's manuscripts of the second, third, and fourth parts of the *Institutes* before this date when they were drawing up the general charges remains a matter of speculation. However, the idea of praemunire as a destruction of the law was common currency before the calling of the Long Parliament if only because the statute of 27 Edward III described it as such. For example, Sir John Davies in his report of the praemunire trial of the priest Robert Lalor in Ireland early in the reign of James I argued that the statute of 16 Richard II, c. 5 and the statutes against provisors "were made to vphold and maintaine the Soueraigntie of the King, the liberty of the people, the common lawe, and the common-weale, which otherwise had beene undermined and vtterly ruined by the vsurpation of the *Bishop of Rome*."[34] While Coke's views on the applicability of praemunire

[29] Sir Edward Coke, *The Third Part of the Institutes of the Laws of England concerning High Treason, and other Pleas of the Crown, and Criminall causes* (London 1644), pp. 121–122.

[30] Coke, *The Third Part of the Institutes*, p. 120.

[31] Coke, *The Third Part of the Institutes*, p. 123.

[32] The other authorities of the day, Selden, Ellesmere, and Hale all held contrary views about the applicability of the statutes of praemunire to equitable jurisdictions: Sir William Holdsworth, *A History of the English Law*, 6th edn. (London, 1903; reprinted London, 1938), vol. I, pp. 462–463.

[33] The members named to this committee were "Mr. Henry Cooke, Sir Thomas Coke, Mr. Hide [presumably Edward Hyde, later Lord Clarendon], Mr. Hatcher, Lord Falkland, Sir Simonds D'Ewes, Mr. Maynard [presumably Sir John Maynard, who prosecuted both Strafford and Laud]": *CJ* II: 45–46.

[34] Sir John Davies, *Le Primer Report des Cases & Matters in Ley resolues & adiudges en les Courts del Roy en Ireland. Collect et digest per Sr. John Dauys Chiualer Atturney Generall del Roy in cest Realme* (Dublin, 1615), fol. 85b.

to those of the king's courts not governed by the common law may have been controversial, the description of praemunire as tending toward the destruction of the common law was not. Considering the willingness of common lawyers to identify the common law as fundamental to the constitution of England as a body politic, the implications of the general charges against Strafford were far-reaching.

Aside from the idea of the subversion or destruction of the law the prosecution also enjoyed access to the notion of the destruction of the king's kingdom as treason. This was nothing new, having been raised, for example, during the prosecution of the Gunpowder Plotters.[35] Furthermore, while the development of this argument proved unnecessary to the success of the prosecution's case, it was potentially consistent with purely impersonal conceptions of the state as an abstract juristic entity defined by law.[36] If it was through the policy of law that the king was rendered a body politic and the law constituted the sinews of the body politic, giving it form and definition, then to subvert the law was to destroy the political body of the whole state.[37] This law, of course, was the common law of England that, at least in theory, also governed the king's realm of Ireland. Because the king's natural body was inseparable from his political body, it was impossible to intend the destruction of the king's state or kingdom without also compassing the death of the king's natural body. Thus, the treason of destroying the kingdom could be brought under the first head of 25 Edward III as a compassing or imagining of the king's death.

This idea of destroying the king's kingdoms as expressed in the conclusion to the general articles also left the door open to arguments deriving from necessity: if the actions of the accused intended the destruction of the state, then the accused's execution was justifiable as necessary to the preservation of the king and kingdom, commonwealth or state – or at least as justifiable as the collection of ship money. The use of the words "assuming regal power" argues strongly that the means of affecting this destruction was the accused's usurpation of the lawful sovereign's powers and his unlawful, tyrannous and arbitrary exercise without the customary restraint of law. Thus, the idea of subverting the fundamental law, when placed in the broader marketplace

[35] *State Trials* II: 167.

[36] The managers do not seem to have appealed to an impersonal notion of state but there is no reason to deny Skinner's argument that the concept was available to them at this time. Russell has noted its use by the Scots as early as 1638: Russell, *Fall*, p. 55.

[37] For use of the term "whole state" or "state" in this sense see *R. v. Garnett*. Henry Garnett, head of the Jesuit order in England stood accused of, among other things, attempting to "overthrow the whole state of the commonwealth" and of endeavoring the "subversion of the whole state": *State Trials* II: 218, 225. Another example of the use of the term "whole state" is *R. v. Peacham*: *State Trials* II: 870.

of political ideas, was pregnant with onerous connotations for the Earl of Strafford.[38]

III

The twenty-eight specific articles of impeachment brought against the Earl of Strafford were an indictment not only of his role in the personal rule of Charles I but of the methods and practices of government in England and Ireland during the 1630s. These practices included the frequent resort to legislation by conciliar orders, either proclamations or "acts of state," and their enforcement through the prerogative courts, the raising of extra-parliamentary subsidies such as ship money, the perceived expansion of equitable and ecclesiastical jurisdictions at the expense of the common-law courts, and, the king's disastrous Scottish policies of 1637–40. Seen in this light the process of impeachment dovetailed with the normal process of redress of grievance before the voting of supply in early Stuart parliaments. Strafford was one of Charles I's most prominent ministers during the personal rule, serving both as President of the Council of the North and later as Lord Deputy of Ireland. Accordingly, his prosecutors laid at his door a myriad of accumulated grievances pertaining to the administration of justice, foreign policy, and public finance stemming from the perceived misrule of the 1630s. More generally the articles of impeachment charged that while serving in these public capacities Strafford had endeavored to subvert the fundamental law in both England and Ireland and erect an arbitrary government above law. The method of misrule was the usurpation of powers that were reserved to the exercise of the lawful sovereign – these sovereign powers were inalienable. The term "lawful sovereign," of course, refers here to the king both by virtue of his prerogative powers and his powers exercised in concert with parliament.

The first two articles of the impeachment dealt with Strafford's tenure as President of the Council of the North and pertained to the administration

[38] Although his correspondence does not suggest it, it is likely that Wentworth had some idea of the gravity of the charges against him. Shortly after first seeing the twenty-eight specific articles, Wentworth made these remarks in a letter to Sir Adam Loftus, the Vice Treasurer in Ireland: "The Charge is now at last come in, and a long one it is; but I thank God I see no Capital Matter in it, nor any Misdemeanour, which I am not I trust able to clear, if I might but answer, as they have had to gather the Accusation." However, even if Strafford had seen treason in the charges it is unlikely that he would have said so in a letter intended to reassure his supporters in Ireland that could have easily been intercepted and used as evidence against him: Wentworth to Loftus, 4 February 1641, in William Knowler, ed., *The Earl of Strafforde's Letters and Dispatches with an Essay towards his Life by Sir George Radcliffe* (London, 1739), vol. II, p. 415.

of justice. The first concerned the jurisdiction of the Council as a court of equity[39] and Strafford's purported enlargement of that jurisdiction to stay common-law actions concerning the possession and title of lands.[40] The article charged further that he had, according to Robert Baillie, later taken steps to procure further instructions to "hinder prohibitions or appeals from his Court to any other, and had committed sundrie for bringing of prohibitions, even before these instructions were obtained."[41] The charge was essentially that Wentworth had enlarged the legal jurisdiction of the council at the expense of the common-law courts – a charge Strafford was willing to admit readily in fact, arguing that it did not constitute treason.[42]

The charge was consistent with Coke's peculiar conception of praemunire and concerned that general mark of sovereignty, "power to give lawes to all . . . subiects in generall, and to euerie one of them in particular." This power, when seen in the context of English constitutional history, was not simply legislative sovereignty in the positivist sense in which a sovereign body makes commands that are obeyed as positive law.[43] The power to judge and the power to legislate were not clearly distinguished in the articles of impeachment. The power to give law was not simply legislative sovereignty but referred more generally to the administration of justice in the king's courts: the subversion of the law was simply the disruption of the ordinary course of justice in the king's courts at common law. When considered in relation to the general theory of treason outlined above and the Roman law of *maiestas*, Strafford's response to the charge can only seem naive.[44] If treason was a crime of infringed or abrogated sovereignty then a magistrate's enlargement of his jurisdiction was necessarily treasonable if it were to the deprivation of the lawful sovereign. The encroachment of sovereign jurisdiction was the essential element of the fundamental law, the common law of

[39] I.e. it followed proceedings patterned after Chancery and not the common-law courts.

[40] The expansion of the jurisdiction of the equity and prerogative courts as a more efficient means both of administering the personal rule and of raising revenue was commonplace in the 1630s: W. J. Jones, *Politics and the Bench* (London, 1971). I use the term "title" here because the charge includes the term "freehold": Rushworth, *Tryal*, pp. 61–62.

[41] Robert Baillie, *Letters and Journals of Robert Baillie*, ed. D. Laing (Edinburgh, 1841–42), vol. I, p. 320; Rushworth, *Tryal*, p. 62; for writs of prohibition see chapter 4, below, and R. Helmholz, *Roman Canon Law in Reformation England* (Cambridge, 1990), pp. 169–170.

[42] Baillie recalls: "He alleadged, that what was charged in the first article, was bot ane enlargement of his own jurisdiction: and this in a judge was a very chaste ambition." *Letters and Journals* I, p. 321.

[43] C. H. McIlwain, *The High Court of Parliament and its Supremacy: An Historical Essay on the Boundaries Between Legislation and Adjudication in England* (New Haven, 1910), p. viii.

[44] J. A. C. Thomas, ed. and trans., *The Institutes of Justinian: Text, Translation and Commentary* (Cape Town, Wynberg and Johannesburg, 1975), p. 335.

England's subversion. As Sir John Maynard remarked at Archbishop Laud's trial three years later, "Nothing can bee more fundamentall then that w[hi]ch bennds Jurisdiction."[45]

The second article asserted that Wentworth upon the occasion of an assize at the city of York, "to bring His Majesties Leige-people into a dislike of His Majesty, and of his Government," had said publicly "that some of the Justices were all for Law, and nothing would please them but Law; but they should find that the king's little finger should be heavier than the Loines of the Law."[46] This article appeared to be well witnessed[47] although Strafford argued, and Sir William Pennyman confirmed, that he had in fact asserted the opposite: that the little finger of the law was heavier than the loins of the king.[48] The inclusion of this incident in the articles was more than a belated attempt by the managers of the trial to inject an element of comic relief into the proceedings. While it was generally established in the leading cases of the early modern period that words in themselves could not constitute treason, evidence of treasonable words could still serve to establish the treasonable *intent* of the accused. Words, in accordance with *Pine's Case*, could constitute evidence of a compassing or imagining of the death of the king but could not form the basis for an indictment.[49] Although Croke's report of the case did not see print until 1657, it is almost certain that the managers had access to the opinion. One of the managers of the evidence, Harbottle Grimstone, was Croke's son-in-law and at Croke's death in 1642 became the late judge's executor, subsequently translating and editing an English language edition of his *Reports*.[50]

Articles 3–19 concerned Strafford's tenure as Lord Deputy of Ireland and represented, along with article 23, the guts of the prosecution's case. Although many of the articles were factually based in the grievances of private individuals against Strafford, there is a unifying theme running through them. Simply, put the managers of the evidence argued that Thomas

[45] Worcester College, Clarke MS LXXI, 28 March 1644 (the section of the manuscript relating to Laud's trial is not foliated).

[46] Rushworth, *Tryal*, p. 62.

[47] Wentworth's remarks appear to have been witnessed by no fewer than four people, including a sheriff, Sir Thomas Layton: MM, 24 March 1641; Rushworth, *Tryal*, p. 155.

[48] Baillie, *Letters and Journals* I, p. 321; Rushworth, *Tryal*, pp. 151–152.

[49] Although the judges in *Pine's Case* were divided over the question of treasonable words, those judges who held that words could be taken as evidence of treasonable intent still affirmed that the indictment must be framed under a head of 25 Edward III: *State Trials* III: 368; Sir George Croke, *The Reports of Sir George Croke*, ed. and trans. Harbottle Grimstone (London, 1657), sig. N4r, p. 89; and chapter 1, above.

[50] Lois Spencer, "The Printing of Sir George Croke's Reports," *Studies in Bibliography* 11 (1958): 236; Adrian Johns, *The Nature of the Book: Print and Knowledge in the Making* (Chicago, 1998), p. 301; the report now forms the basis of the account in Cobbett and Howell's *State Trials*.

Wentworth did not have the legal authority in Ireland to conduct himself as Lord Deputy in the manner that he had. Through his actions he had conducted himself in a more than quasi-regal manner, abrogated the authority of the lawful sovereign, accrued to himself in practice many of the marks of sovereignty, and sought to dissolve the very fabric of the king's political body of Ireland – the common law.

In order to make their argument stick the anti-Straffordians[51] had to make a certain set of assumptions about the constitutional relationship of England and Ireland. Although Ireland maintained its own separate parliament, had its own church, privy council, and law courts similar to those of England, the managers needed to assume that Ireland was akin to England by virtue of a shared heritage of the common law and that the common law was not simply the birthright and inheritance of all Englishmen but of all Irishmen, whether Anglo or Gaelic, as well. As will be clear from chapter 1, the constitutional relationship of England and Ireland was ambiguous to say the least. Poynings' Law had stipulated that acts of the Irish parliament were first to be submitted to the king and his English council for approval. Another statute of Poynings' Parliament, sometimes also confusingly referred to as Poynings' Law, had brought all English statutes made to that point in time into effect in Ireland (including 25 Edward III); however, it remained doubtful whether an English parliament could legislate for Ireland.[52] Also, there were important questions raised by the revival of parliamentary judicature in the 1620s: while it had been tenuously established by the outbreak of the Civil War that a writ of error in the King's Bench in Ireland was maintainable in King's Bench in England, the reemergence of the English and Irish Houses of Lords as courts of record created a whole new set of jurisdictional conundrums.[53] As Michael Perceval Maxwell has asserted, "Strafford's invulnerability in Ireland depended on his separation of Ireland from England in all respects save the crown."[54] The managers and those who supported them, by contrast, needed to presume a commonalty of legal heritage albeit not a unity of legal institutions. While the king's political body of Ireland may have been separate and distinct from his political body of England, it was rendered a political body by virtue of the same fundamental rule of law,

[51] By this group I mean the managers and the principal parliamentary opponents of the earl: Oliver St. John, John Pym, Sir John Maynard, Sir John Glynne, Bulstrode Whitelocke, Geoffrey Palmer.

[52] I have developed this line of argument more thoroughly in chapter 5, below, and in D. Alan Orr, "England, Ireland, Magna Carta and the Common Law: The Case of Connor Lord Maguire, Second Baron of Enniskillen," *JBS* 39 (2000): 389–421.

[53] A very useful and informative discussion of the constitutional issues raised during the tumultuous year of 1641 is Michael Perceval-Maxwell, *The Outbreak of the Irish Rebellion of 1641* (Montreal and Kingston, 1994), ch. 7; see also chapter 1, above.

[54] Perceval-Maxwell, *Outbreak*, p. 163.

the English common law. Accordingly, the subversion of the fundamental law of Ireland was as great an evil as the subversion of the fundamental law of England. While Strafford claimed legal exception in defending his actions in Ireland, the managers adopted a constitutional position emphasizing a shared heritage of legal values.

This, of course, required some rather pained historical mythologizing about the shared history of the two realms. The notion of an ancient constitution, customary in nature, handed down from time immemorial was, according to J. G. A. Pocock, one of the hallmarks of English common-law thought in the early Stuart period.[55] The "common-law mind" was, in the words of Conrad Russell, "deeply allergic" to the idea that England had at some point been conquered and its ancient laws superseded by those of the conqueror's making.[56] The extension of this kind of thinking to Ireland required some degree of historical imagination. For example, one of the titles set out in the attainder of Shane O'Neil at Dublin in 1569 was that the Irish came originally from Biscay and that they were granted "some land in the West" by the British king Gurmonde and thus they had from their first coming into the western archipelago been under the allegiance of the English king and subject to English law. Another less fanciful title suggested in the attainder was that, although Ireland had been conquered by Henry II of England, he had not given the Irish laws as a conqueror but had bestowed upon them English laws and customs and was bound to rule Ireland under the same restraints of law that he ruled England.[57] Conquest did not abrogate the rule of law in Ireland because the binding force of the common law derived from its rationality and from its immemoriality in England.

The third article against the Earl of Strafford asserted the more familiar claim that the realm of Ireland had "been time out of mind annexed to the Imperial Crown of this His Majesties Realm of England, and Governed by the same Laws."[58] It charged that, shortly after taking up his office as Lord Deputy in 1634, the earl had made a public speech in Dublin before the citizens, mayor, recorder, and "Divers Nobility and Gentry of that kingdom" in which he asserted: "That Ireland was a Conquered Nation, and that the king might do with them what he pleased: And speaking of the Charters of former kings of England made to that City, he further said, That their Charters were nothing worth, and did binde the king no further than he pleased."[59] Essentially the article charged that Strafford had asserted publicly

[55] J. G. A. Pocock, *The Ancient Constitution and the Feudal Law: A Study of English Historical Thought in the Seventeenth Century*, 2nd edn. (Cambridge, 1987), ch. 2; and for a more recent critique see Glenn Burgess, *The Politics of the Ancient Constitution, An Introduction to English Political Thought, 1603–1642* (London, 1992), ch. 2.

[56] Russell, *Fall*, p. 282. [57] *Irish Statutes* I: 329. [58] Rushworth, *Tryal*, p. 62.

[59] Rushworth, *Tryal*, pp. 62–63.

that the ancient constitution in Ireland was either abrogated or never relevant and that the realm might be ruled without the customary restraint of law.

In his defense Strafford acknowledged that he had spoken the words in question but denied that by them he had meant "that [the] k[ing] might deale with them as a Conquered Nation."[60] Henry II *did* conquer Ireland, asserted Strafford. However, although he was in a position to do so, he did not give them whatever laws he wished but the laws of England.[61] Thus, argued Strafford, there was a sense in which these words could be "understood w[it]hout any falte of Treason."[62] While acknowledging the article proven, he denied that the words spoken constituted treason and cited in his defense the thirty-day time limit for the reporting of treasonable words established by the statute of Edward VI.[63] Strafford also acknowledged that he had remarked at the opening of the Irish parliament seven years earlier "that the Chartours of Dublin were Truelie faultie in manie things... yet that he had never questioned them."[64]

The idea of conquest was undoubtedly acceptable before the Civil War among certain groups of learned antiquaries and jurists – men such as Sir John Davies or Samuel Daniel.[65] Nor was the idea necessarily inconsistent with the proposition that the common law was in force in Ireland. Stating that Ireland had been conquered and English law imposed there was far less controversial than the suggestion that William I had conquered England in 1066 and imposed Norman laws and customs in the place of English ones. The idea of the ancient constitution depended on the historical continuity of the common law in England and the subsequent imposition of English

60 MM, 25 March 1641; see also BL Harl. MS 162, fol. 358r.

61 Rushworth, *Tryal*, p. 162. Strafford's referral to *Calvin's Case* here is very confusing because it is unclear if he is citing it to emphasize the similarities or the differences between England and Ireland in terms of their laws and institutions. Rushworth refers to fol. 23a to the effect that "where the words are, *So as now the Laws of* England, *became the proper laws of Ireland*," while the manuscript minutes of the house for 25 March suggest that Strafford was using Coke to emphasize the *differences* in laws and institutions between England and Ireland: "In Calvins case S[i]r Edward Cookes Reports that Ireland is governed by different lawes and Institutions... from England." Robert Baillie's narrative of the trial reveals that Strafford's response to this was somewhat disorganized as he first petitioned for more time and then sat down with his secretaries for half an hour to pen a response: Baillie, *Letters and Journals* I, p. 322.

62 MM, 25 March 1641.

63 MM, 25 March 1641; BL Harl. MS 162, fol. 358r; Baillie, *Letters and Journals* I, pp. 322–323; Rushworth, *Tryal*, p. 161.

64 Baillie, *Letters and Journals* I, p. 323.

65 For Davies see chapter 2, above, and for Daniel see D. R. Woolf, *The Idea of History in Early Stuart England* (Toronto, 1990), p. 99. Woolf has noted a discrepancy between Daniel's views on the pre-conquest origins of parliament as expressed in his *The First Part of the Historie of England* (1612, 1613) and his *The Collection of the Historie of England* (1618): in the former the parliament of 1116 on Salisbury plain was referred to as the "first parliament" and in the latter as the "first parliament *after* the conquest."

law on Ireland by conquest was no threat to this. There was indeed a set of meanings available by which the idea of an Irish conquest could be expressed without controversy. In the *Case of Tanistry* Davies distinguished between conquest by a tyrannical or despotic monarchy on the one hand and by a "royal" monarchy on the other:

> ...under a royal monarchy the subjects are freemen, and have a property in their goods, and a freehold and inheritance in their lands; but under a despotick monarchy or tyranny, they are all as villains or slaves, and proprietors of nothing but at the will of their *Grand Seignor* or tyrant, as in *Turkey* and *Muscovy*.[66]

The conquest of Ireland fell under the rubric of conquest by a royal monarchy and the subjects there were to be afforded the full benefit of English law and their property rights respected. It was more likely Strafford's alleged remark that the king could give law in Ireland arbitrarily according to his will and pleasure that landed him in hot water than the bare suggestion of conquest. The notion of conquest in general was not so damning as the suggestion of a tyrannical conquest.

Strafford's response to the article was suggestive of a developing pattern in his defense: he would concede the case in fact unless the article fell clearly within the terms of 25 Edward III and argue against the prosecution's case in law. The managers, for their part, seem to have been all too happy to engage the embattled earl on questions of law. For example, Strafford's appeals to the time limits for the reporting of treasonable words were, according to Rushworth, neatly riposted by the managers: the words themselves were not treasonable but merely evidence of the earl's endeavors to subvert the law.[67] The rule established in *Pine's Case* took precedence.

The fourth article derived from the grievances of Richard Boyle, Earl of Cork, a prominent "New English" landowner whom Strafford had put out of possession of certain ecclesiastical properties and the tithes attached to them in a decision of Council Board in Ireland.[68] When the Earl of Cork approached the Lord Deputy and asked that his case might be considered in King's Bench rather than at Council Board, he was threatened with

[66] *A Report of Cases and Matters in Law, Resolved and Adjudged in the King's Courts in Ireland. Collected and Digested by Sir John Davies, Knight, The King's Attorney-General in that Kingdom. Now first translated in to English* (Dublin, 1762), p. 111; it is possible that the dichotomy derived from Bodin.

[67] Rushworth, *Tryal*, p. 169: "It is said here is no Treason in this Article, no Argument of Treason: but the Commons never pressed these words single and dividedly, to be Treason; but take all together, they discover that Disposition, that Counsel, that Resolution that my Lord of *Strafford* had taken on him, the ruine and subversion of the Common Law, in both kingdoms."

[68] Rushworth notes that Cork had been "in Possession as Tenant of the Crown thirty-five years, or a Rectory and certain Tythes in the County of *Tipperary*, for which he paid a yearly Rent." Rushworth, *Tryal*, p. 175.

imprisonment.[69] More importantly, in speaking of a similar such order from the Council Board Strafford allegedly said that he "would make the said Earl, and all Ireland know, that so long as he had the Government there, any Act of State there made, or to be made, should be as binding to the Subjects of that kingdom, as an Act of Parliament."[70] Sir Pierce Crosby and Lord Kilmallock witnessed the words.[71] The charge was consistent with Sir Edward Coke's unusual views on the law of praemunire being based on a supposed miscarriage in the administration of justice flowing from the conflict between the common-law courts in Ireland and the equitable jurisdiction of Council Board. The first part of the charge was not in itself serious. Strafford was able to establish that Council Board in Ireland had traditionally functioned as a court of equity.[72] Furthermore, Cork's cause involved only a lease on church lands and not a question of title – an issue that even the prosecution's witnesses admitted was within Council Board's equitable jurisdiction.[73]

Strafford's unwillingness to acknowledge the case in fact concerning his views on the relationship of acts of state to acts of parliament suggested the importance of the issue at stake.[74] He had excepted against Sir Pierce Crosby from the beginning as a hostile witness from the outset "as one who pretended to be wronged and grieved" by the accused.[75] He also, once again, invoked the thirty-day time limit for the reporting of treasonable words as specified by 1 Edward VI, c. 12. As for the actual contention that an act of state was equal to an act of parliament, Strafford asserted that, provided an act of the Council Board did not conflict with any act of parliament or be contrary to the fundamental law, it should have the force of an act of parliament.[76]

Strafford's response to this charge, reported by Baillie, D'Ewes and Rushworth,[77] was extremely ill judged. He had successfully established that

69 MM, 26 March 1641: "... E[arl] [of] Strafford told him call it in [the action at common-law presumably] or that hee would laye[?] him in the Castle."

70 Rushworth, *Tryal*, p. 63.

71 MM, 26 March 1641.

72 Sir Adam Loftus, Robert Lord Dillon, and later even Cork himself confirmed this contention: MM, 26, 29 March 1641; Rushworth, *Tryal*, p. 178; BL Harl. MS 162, fol. 362r; Jansson, *Two Diaries*, p. 30.

73 Patrick Little has suggested that Cork may have been a reluctant recruit to the anti-Straffordian camp in any event, fearing that Strafford would expose Cork's irregular dealings during the 1630s over the college of Youghal and his attempts in the late 1630s to gain the favor of the Catholic queen Henrietta Maria: Patrick Little, "The Earl of Cork and the Fall of the Earl of Strafford, 1638–1641," *HJ* 39 (1996): 630.

74 Jansson, *Two Diaries*, p. 91; Verney, *Notes*, p. 18. In both accounts Strafford asserted that he did not remember the comparing of acts of Council Board to Acts of Parliament.

75 Crosbie had during Strafford's Irish administration been ejected from council and then sentenced in Castle Chamber (the Irish Star Chamber) for accusing Strafford of having killed a man. The Earl of Arundel, the Lord Steward, had disallowed this exemption and allowed Crosby to be sworn: Verney, *Notes*, pp. 30, 33; Baillie, *Letters and Journals* I, p. 318.

76 Rushworth, *Tryal*, p. 182; Baillie, *Letters and Journals* I, p. 325; BL Harl. MS 162, fol. 363r.

77 These were three decidedly hostile observers to the Earl of Strafford's cause.

the Council Board in Ireland was a court of record and that Cork's cause, because it involved only a lease on church lands and not title, was actionable within it. Also, while his attempt to except against Crosby had failed, it was bound to damage his credibility as a witness. However, to assert that an act of the Council Board could have the same force of law as statute was clearly an abrogation of the power of king-in-parliament to give law. Statute law may have been seen by common lawyers as simply declaratory of custom but that power was the preserve of the king-in-parliament or, in the case of seventeenth-century Ireland, the king's legally appointed deputy in parliament. The method of the personal rule, governance by executive order, stood trial as well as its advocate and practitioner.

Sir John Glynne adroitly turned aside Strafford's contention that under the provisions of 1 Edward VI, c. 12 any report of treasonable words must be made to the proper authorities within thirty days. D'Ewes reported:

> Mr. Glynne answered that the statute of E[dward] 6 did not all take away or prevent us the use of the wordes which wee intended to make of them for wee did not charge them as a direct Treason but onlie to evidence those Treasons wee charge from withall. That the former proceedings of the Councell of Ireland being against the rules of the common law and against Acts of Parliament cannot iustifie him.[78]

Assuming that subversion of the fundamental laws was treason, either as a constructive compassing of the king's death or as a common-law treason, the ill-considered outbursts of a long public life offered a veritable treasure trove of evidence against the accused. In accordance with *Pine's Case* words had evidentiary value without any regard for the procedural codicils of 1 Edward VI, c. 12. The floodgates were open.

The fifth article was related to a series of incidents in which Strafford stood accused of exceeding his jurisdiction by exercising martial law during time of peace. The first of these related to proceedings in 1635 against Lord Mountnorris, a privy counselor, condemned to death by a Council of War for treason,[79] without benefit of common law.[80] The second related to the execution of a common soldier, Thomas Denwitt, executed under martial law for "flying from his colours, and for stealing some Beef."[81] The potential seriousness of the charge lay in the implication that, by exercising martial law in time of peace against individuals who were not in open rebellion, Strafford had taken upon him the king's powers to decide war and

[78] BL Harl. MS 162, fol. 363r.

[79] Mountnorris was condemned for a bizarre incident when he had trodden on the Lord Deputy's gouty toes and purportedly remarked: "that man had a brother in England, who would not be content with such a revenge for such ane affront": Baillie, *Letters and Journals* I, p. 326.

[80] Rushworth, *Tryal*, p. 63.

[81] Rushworth, *Tryal*, p. 195.

peace. In his defense Strafford took an exceptionalist line concerning the constitutional relationship of the two realms.[82] Producing the king's letters to him as evidence, he argued that the exercise of martial law was within his commission as Lord Deputy and that the customs regarding the use of martial law were different in Ireland than in England. He added further that he had simply been following the practice of previous deputies, and that Mountnorris being an officer in the Irish army was under the jurisdiction of martial law.[83] Finally, he noted that he had very quickly taken steps to secure Mountnorris's pardon from the king.[84]

Mountnorris, understandably, was not in a forgiving mood and testified against Strafford. More damning, however, was probably the testimony of Lord Loftus, Viscount Ely, who had forty years earlier served as Provost Marshal in Ireland. Loftus testified that "he had never used martiall law, bot upon manifest rebells; and that my Lord Falkland's instructions carried expresslie the cases of warre and rebellions."[85] The *Book of Instructions* given to Lord Falkland was produced and read to the effect that martial law should only be exercised in time of war[86] and the prosecution denounced Strafford's actions against Mountnorris as not only contrary to the Petition of Right but also to 25 Edward III.[87] While it may have been true that previous lord deputies had de facto been able to exercise considerable discretion in the exercise of martial law, the prosecution's contention was that the common law was in force equally in Ireland. Strafford's resort to martial law in time of peace, when ordinary proceedings at common law should have taken precedence, was therefore against law.

82 The term "exceptionalist" is borrowed from Louis Hartz's *The Liberal Tradition in America* (New York, 1955; reprinted New York, 1991) and is discussed in greater detail in chapter 5, below. Hartz was concerned with the divergent course that American liberalism took from its European counterpart: lacking the opposition of a feudal past, liberalism in America developed unhindered and became the shared ideology of *all* sectors of society. As a result the class struggles that wracked Europe in the nineteenth and twentieth centuries failed to develop and as a result no credible socialist movement emerged. The constitutional relationship between England and Ireland can be cast in a similar light: the two kingdoms lacking a shared feudal past, representatives of the crown such as Strafford felt free to interpret their powers more expansively than even the king would in his own realm of England.

83 BL Harl. MS 162, fol. 368r; BL Harl. MS 164, fol. 946r; Baillie, *Letters and Journals* I, p. 327; Rushworth,*Tryal*, pp. 197–198. In fairness to Strafford he appears to have been correct about the practice of previous Irish administrations: Steven G. Ellis, *Tudor Ireland: Crown Community and the Conflict of Cultures, 1470–1603* (London, 1985), pp. 178–179.

84 MM, 27 March 1641.

85 Baillie, *Letters and Journals* I, p. 328; compare with BL Harl. MS 164, fol. 946r: "The Lord Viscount Ely late Lord Chancellor of Ireland witnesses in Marshall's court alwaies proceed by Articles: and never any condemned by Marshall law but in time of open warre or open rebellion."

86 Rushworth, *Tryal*, p. 203; MM, 27 March 1641; BL Harl. MS 162, fol. 368r.

87 BL Harl. MS 162, fol. 369r.

The managers then proceeded to article 6 and the third part of article 8 with the seventh and the first two parts of the eighth being passed over. These were similar to the first part of article 4 in that they involved decisions at Council Board over the possession of lands but differed in that they included equitable causes not involving church lands.[88] Again, the general theme was the subversion of the law through the disruption of the ordinary course of justice at common law. Article 6 involved the perennially persecuted Mountnorris being put out of possession of the manor of Tynmour and article 8 concerned the cause of the Lady Mary Hibbots, the widow of the former Chancellor of the Irish Exchequer. Strafford, for his part, maintained that these causes had been equitable, that by his commission the Council Board in Ireland enjoyed powers analogous to the courts of Requests and Chancery in England, and that he had acted within the law.[89]

Ranelagh, Sir Adam Loftus, the Earl of Bath, the Earl of Cork and Lord Dillon, "Strafford's own witness," all testified that they had not heard of a Lord Deputy determining causes concerning title to land except in issues involving plantation and church lands.[90] The enlargement of the Lord Deputy's equitable jurisdiction to hear private causes not involving church and plantation lands was, according to Strafford, not treason and he produced the king's letters authorizing him to hear such equitable causes.[91] The managers – Glynne and Maynard at this point – responded that the king's letters were just in their intention, but that they empowered the Lord Deputy to hear only those equitable causes that had traditionally been within his provenance and that they provided no commission for expanding the equitable jurisdiction of Council Board.[92] Strafford, in enlarging his forensic jurisdiction beyond that traditionally wielded by previous lord deputies, had taken upon him a sovereign power to give law, to judge, that derogated from that emanating from the crown.

The ninth article involved a warrant that Strafford had allegedly issued to the Bishop of Down and Connor, to imprison "the Bodies of the meaner sort" who either refused to appear in his ecclesiastical courts or who had appeared

[88] Interestingly, article 7 and the second part of article 8 dealt with Strafford allegedly deciding questions of title in the causes of Thomas, Lord Dillon and George, Earl of Kildare. As Strafford was able to establish only that Council Board functioned as a court of equity, and was thus incompetent to determine titles, these charges were potentially more damaging. This suggested a certain lack of confidence on the part of the managers.

[89] Hibbots' case involved a 99-year lease on lands bequeathed to her by her husband and not a title: Baillie, *Letters and Journals* I, pp. 328, 331; BL Harl. MS 162, fol. 372r; Rushworth, *Tryal*, pp. 207, 213.

[90] MM, 29 March 1641; Rushworth, *Tryal*, p. 216.

[91] Rushworth, *Tryal*, pp. 213, 230; BL Harl. MS 162, fol. 372r; BL Harl. MS 164, fol. 946v; Baillie, *Letters and Journals* I, pp. 328–329.

[92] BL Harl. MS 162, fol. 372r.

and subsequently refused to obey the orders of the court.[93] An attested copy of the warrant was then produced in evidence.[94] The article seems to have been only half-heartedly pursued. Although too sick to attend in person, Archbishop Usher's deposition was read to the effect that such warrants had been commonplace in Falkland's time. More pertinently, Robert Little, Strafford's secretary, then testified that he had seen a similar letter of assistance to the bishops from Falkland's administration upon which he had modeled the warrant.[95] Perhaps sensing that there were weightier matters at hand, the managers offered to proceed to the next article.

The tenth article concerned Strafford's alleged appropriation of the revenues of the Irish customs farm to his own use.[96] It charged that Strafford had altered the Book of Rates, inflating the values of customable goods resulting in a dramatic increase in customs revenues.[97] Strafford protested that the raising of the Book of Rates was not his doing, that it was done before his going into Ireland and that it had been done against his advice.[98] He argued further that his only treason had been the making of a profit and this profit was to the king and not himself.[99] While there may have been more damaging articles among the twenty-eight, this article revealed more clearly than most the prosecution's strategy of portraying Strafford as an unlawful usurper not only of the authority of king-in-parliament but of those rights the king enjoyed by virtue of his prerogative.[100] Whether the ancient constitution was balanced toward a generous conception of the king's prerogative or emphasized the king's parliamentary role as legal sovereign in a mixed monarchy, the Earl of Strafford had acted treasonably. The embattled earl's problem was that he was neither a king nor a parliament yet his accusers contended that he had unlawfully acted as both during his tenure as Lord Deputy in Ireland.

They passed on the eleventh article involving a scheme whereby Strafford had required licenses for the export of "pipe staves and other commodities."[101]

93 Rushworth, *Tryal*, p. 65; Baillie, *Letters and Journals* I, p. 332.

94 Baillie, *Letters and Journals* I, P. 332.

95 MM, 30 March 1641; Baillie, *Letters and Journals* I, p. 332.

96 Strafford had originally purchased the farm from the widow of George Villiers, Duke of Buckingham: MM, 31 March 1641.

97 Rushworth, *Tryal*, pp. 65–66; BL Harl. MS 162, fol. 381r; Michael Perceval-Maxwell has argued that the dramatic increase in Irish customs revenue in the 1630s was due as much to a real growth in trade and a burgeoning Irish economy as to increased efficiency in collection: *Outbreak*, pp. 32–34; and for the latter interpretation see Hugh Kearney, *Strafford in Ireland, 1633–1641* (Manchester, 1959), pp. 159–168.

98 Baillie, *Letters and Journals* I, p. 333; BL Harl. MS 162, fol. 382r.

99 BL Harl. MS 164, fol. 949r.

100 BL Harl. MS 162, fol. 383r. Sir John Maynard to the tenth article argued, "... Poundage that is the Kings inheritance in Ireland noe man questioned it; but wee question the customes exacted in Ireland by the Earle of Strafford against law."

101 Rushworth, *Tryal*, p. 66.

The twelfth article concerned Strafford's erection, to his personal profit, in 1638 of an Irish tobacco monopoly by means of a series of proclamations.[102] Strafford argued in his defense that while monopolists had been censured by parliament in the past it had not been adjudged treason and that a similar situation existed in England, where the landing of tobacco had been restricted to London by a series of royal proclamations.[103] Finally, he produced the king's letter authorizing his actions.[104] Glynne for the prosecution responded that the king's letters had been *procured* by the earl under false pretenses and that their *procurement* by his own agency aggravated rather than mitigated the seriousness of Strafford's crime. Glynne argued further that "Proclamacons cannot raise monopollies ag[ains]t lawe"[105] and that the proclamations issued by Strafford in Ireland restricting the unlicensed importation of tobacco had been issued before similar proclamations in England.[106] The article was similar in structure to the tenth: Strafford had unlawfully sought to deprive the king of valuable revenue needed for the maintenance of his state and thus constituted a constructive compassing of the king's death.[107]

The thirteenth article dealt with Strafford's ill-fated project to encourage the manufacture of linen in Ireland.[108] Strafford had sought to force the development of an indigenous linen industry by restricting the export of linen yarn through the imposition of strict quality controls on exports. The project, while visionary and far-sighted considering the subsequent success of the Irish linen industry, was an abysmal failure with many poor people left holding valueless yarn upon whose profits their livelihoods had depended.[109] The key issue to emerge in the trial was not, however, the economic rationality of the

[102] Rushworth, *Tryal*, pp. 66–67.

[103] Baillie, *Letters and Journals* I, p. 333; Rushworth, *Tryal*, p. 412.

[104] Baillie, *Letters and Journals* I, p. 333.

[105] MM, 31 March 1641; BL Harl. MS 162, fols. 385–386r; BL Harl. MS 164, fol. 949v. The use of the word "procure" is significant in that it implies at the very least agency; for example, in BL Harl. MS 162, fol. 386r Sir John Glynne is recorded to have argued that the king's letter, "being procured by him [Strafford] did rather aggravate then lessen his crime."

[106] BL Harl. MS 162, fol. 386r: "... the proclamation inhibiting the importation of tobacco without licence into Ireland was sett foorth in Januarie @. 13. Caroli; and the proclamation published in England to the same effect came not out till the March next ensuing."

[107] The full implications are clearly drawn out by Glynne in Rushworth, *Tryal*, p. 414: "His depriving the King of His Estate, under Colour of Advancing His Revenue, which is to deprive the King of His Government: For, if one takes away my meanes of Livlihood, and defence against an Enemy, it is a killing of me round about, though it were a more immediate killing of me to run me through.

"If he take away the King's Livlihood and Just Revenue, whereby He is enabled to Govern and Protect His People, Is it not to take away the Government out of his Hand?"

[108] Rushworth, *Tryal*, p. 67.

[109] Linen yarn and linen from Ireland was at this time, according to C. V. Wedgwood, of poor quality and the majority of the yarn was exported to Lancashire "for its growing textile industry": Wedgwood, *Thomas Wentworth*, pp. 194–195.

project but the means of its implementation: the proclamations of the Lord Deputy. In his response to the article Strafford argued that proclamations were temporary laws that were "revocable when inconvenience appeared." The managers of the evidence must have smelled blood.[110] D'Ewes recounted in his diary that they were quick to pounce, with Maynard arguing,

> for his saying that a proclamation was a temporarie law; that was a dangereous speech to call a proclamation a law and to establish a law by it against law to take away the goods of the subiect by violence and oppression. Nor did it mitigate the phraise to call it a temporarie law w[hi]ch is noe lesse then to say it is a law that shall end or continue according as the will of him that makes it.[111]

The implication was very clear: Strafford's rule by proclamation in Ireland was a usurpation of the law-giving role of parliament and king. This was the practical substance of his subversion of the fundamental law.

The rule by proclamation was a standard method of the personal rule. In the Tudor period proclamations were, in the words of Elton, "legislative orders issued by the king, with or without the advice of his Council."[112] Star Chamber enforced them and they were subject to the limitation that they could neither disseize subjects of their freeholds nor take life or limb. The role of proclamations as instruments of law-making, according to Elton, became a bone of contention with the accession of James I and the issue of their status as positive law remained unresolved by 1641.[113] The events of the 1640s reflected a struggle for sovereign power – a struggle for the positive powers of the state. This struggle was also for definition: at stake was not only who in practice controlled state powers but the extent and nature of those powers. The problematic relationship between statute, proclamation, and common law reflected a prevailing uncertainty over the exact nature of the law-giving powers of the state.

The managers of Strafford's trial were at pains to secure parliament's future role in the law-making process. Sir Edward Coke had argued in his famous opinion of 1610 that the king could not by his prerogative "change any part of the common law, nor create any offence by his proclamation, which was not an offence before, without parliament."[114] In this scheme proclamations

110 BL Harl. MS 162, fol. 388r; BL Harl. MS 164, fol. 950r.

111 While there may be some question as to the precise accuracy of D'Ewes account of the trial, on this issue his report of Maynard's speech dovetails neatly with the constitutional issues raised during the attainder debate later in the month of April (see below): BL Harl. MS 162, fol. 388r.

112 G. R. Elton, *The Tudor Constitution: Documents and Commentary*, 2nd edn. (Cambridge, 1982), p. 21.

113 Elton, *Tudor Constitution*, pp. 20–23.

114 *State Trials* II: 725; F. W. Maitland, *The Constitutional History of England*, ed. H. A. L. Fisher (Cambridge, 1908; reprinted Cambridge, 1965), p. 257.

were simply a means of admonishing subjects to keep the laws established by custom and declared by statute and not to offend against them. Although this opinion did not see print until its publication in *The twelfth Part of the Reports* in 1656, it was certainly available in manuscript.[115] The professional culture of early modern barristers was not exclusively a print culture and it was not unusual for manuscript reports to circulate for years prior to publication. Furthermore, although manuscript copies of Coke's works were suppressed even before his death in 1634, it is highly conceivable that manuscript copies of his opinions were available to the prosecution by the time of the trial.[116] Indeed, the Long Parliament made the recovery of Coke's library an early priority.[117]

Both Strafford and Laud appear to have entertained the idea that both the king-in-council and the Lord-Deputy-in-council wielded an *inferior* legislative power and that their orders and proclamations would have the full force of positive law, provided, of course, that they did not conflict with statute or common law. In practice this meant that if a parliament was not called for an extended period of time (as in France, for example) ordinary legislative power would fall completely to the king-in-council. Furthermore, Esther S. Cope has argued that the delivery of Coke's famous opinion in 1610 did not actually alter royal practice in the three decades leading up to the Civil War.[118] As Maitland remarked over a century ago: "The proclamations of Charles I were far more numerous than those of his father. Prices were fixed by proclamation; houses were demolished, shops were shut in order that the Cathedral of St. Paul might appear to better advantage; all persons who had houses in the country were directed to leave London."[119] Thus the question of sovereignty stood at the center of a seemingly innocuous charge. The question was not necessarily what Strafford actually did but whether he had the lawful power to do it. The methods of the personal rule, the issuing of proclamations, and their enforcement through the prerogative courts, were on trial as well as their advocates and practitioners.

The fourteenth article involving a new oath that was imposed on the owners, masters, boatswains, and pursers of all vessels arriving in Ireland was laid aside. The fifteenth article deriving from the forcible billeting of troops was undoubtedly the weightiest. It accused Strafford of laying troops "by force of Arms and in a Warlike manner" first in order to levy "great Sums of Money upon the Towns of Baltemore, Bandenbridge, Talowe, and divers other Towns and Places in the said Realm of Ireland" and secondly in order to enforce orders of the Lord Deputy and Council Board.[120] This,

115 Esther S. Cope, "Sir Edward Coke and Proclamations, 1610," *AJLH* 15 (1971): 215–221.
116 Kevin Sharpe, *The Personal Rule of Charles I* (New Haven, 1992), pp. 656–657.
117 *CJ* II: 45. 118 *CJ* II: 219–221. 119 Maitland, *Constitutional History*, p. 302.
120 Rushworth, *Tryal*, pp. 67–68.

the prosecution argued, was a levying of war against the king under 25 Edward III and treason under the Irish statute of 18 Henry VI, c. 3.[121] This latter statute held that the billeting of troops on the king's subjects without their consent was treasonable and was probably aimed at the extirpation of the practice of "coign and livery" in which troops, rather than receiving regular pay, would be quartered on the country collecting the means of their support directly.[122] Although originally a Gaelic practice, various cash-starved lord deputies throughout the early modern period adopted and periodically revived this custom.[123]

The article was one of the most complex to argue because it raised not only the obvious question of what constituted "levying war" under 25 Edward III but also the thorny question of how the legislative power in Ireland related to that in England. By framing their argument under both an Irish and an English treason statute the managers adopted a conscious strategy of undermining the Earl of Strafford's obvious constitutional defense: the assertion that, because the laws, customs, and legal institutions of Ireland differed in their particulars from those of England, his actions did not amount to a subversion of the fundamental laws of that realm. The experience of earlier articles had taught the prosecution that this was a very likely strategy for Strafford to follow and their use of the Irish statute reflected an adjustment in their own constitutional position. The defense of Irish constitutional exceptionalism thus became problematic for Strafford.

The task of managing this key article fell to Geoffrey Palmer, a man whom Robert Baillie described as "a materiall man, bot not eloquent, nor quick, nor vehement," who would later serve as Charles II's Attorney-General at the Restoration.[124] The managers received a minor set-back when a copy of a warrant to Serjeant Savill for the levying of troops was disallowed for not being properly attested; however, the managers were able to establish the existence of such a warrant issued under Strafford's hand through the testimony of witnesses and the damage to their case was minimized.[125] The prosecution also produced numerous witnesses detailing the effects of the forcible billeting.[126] Ranelagh testified further that in previous times soldiers

121 Rushworth, *Tryal*, p. 441; BL Harl. MS 164, fol. 950r; MM, 1 April 1641.

122 The exact words of the statute are: "It is agreed and established, that no Lord, nor any other of what condition soever he be, shall bring or lead hooded men, neither English rebels, nor Irish enemies, nor any other people, nor horses, to ly on horseback or on foot upon the good wills and consents, but on hurt doing to the Commons of the county. And if any so do, he shall be adjudged a traitor." *Irish Statutes* I: 4; the text of this statute in Rushworth, *Tryal*, p. 441, is highly corrupt.

123 Ellis, *Tudor Ireland*, p. 321.

124 Baillie, *Letters and Journals* I, p. 334.

125 Rushworth recounted that Richard Welsh and Patrick Gough both testified to seeing the warrant issued under Strafford's hand: *Tryal*, pp. 433–434; see also MM, 1 April 1641.

126 This included one Edmond Berne who was forced to enter military service abroad by the earl's actions: Rushworth, *Tryal*, pp. 433–437; Baillie, *Letters and Journals* I, p. 335.

were laid upon the populace in only three instances: (1) in cases where the king's rents were due; (2) to levy a contribution for the direct maintenance of the army; and (3) in order to seize the lands and horses of manifest rebels. Troops were not used to enforce judicial decisions in private causes.[127]

Strafford's legal response included some tortuous reasoning concerning what statutes remained in force in Ireland. He cited the Irish statute of 10 Henry VII, c. 22, which had brought all previous English statutes into force in England. Among these statutes was 1 Henry IV, c. 10, made for the repealing of the augmentative treason statutes of Richard II, ordaining "That in no Time to come any Treason be judged otherwise than it was ordained by the Statute in the Time of his Noble Grandfather King Edward the Third, whom God assoil."[128] Strafford argued that 1 Henry IV, c. 10, when brought into effect by the Irish Statute of 10 Henry VII had repealed the Irish statute of 18 Henry VI, c. 3. In this he made argument that a statute made before another statute could have the effect of repealing one made after it – a convoluted, subtle line of argument of which St. John was later highly dismissive.[129] The repeal statute of 1 Mary was not in force in Ireland, having been made after the Irish statute of 10 Henry 7, c. 22, and, unless he was willing to concede that the legislative power in Ireland was not separate and distinct from that of England, Strafford could not invoke it. Thus the constitutional exceptionalism upon which so much of his defense rested was turned against him.

Strafford found himself reduced to arguing that 18 Henry VI, c. 3, being an Irish statute, was not enforceable in an English court and that, in any event, the statute did not apply to the Lord Deputy.[130] He held that because the Irish statute did not explicitly mention the king then neither the king nor his deputy were bound by it.[131] Here Strafford appeared to have come dangerously close to asserting that the Lord Deputy enjoyed power to command war and

[127] BL Harl. MS 164, fol. 950r; Rushworth, *Tryal*, p. 445.

[128] *SL* I: 428; *Irish Statutes* I: 56. He also cited the Irish statute 8 Edward IV, c. 1 which had brought the rape statute of 6 Richard II, c. 6 into force in Ireland: *Irish Statutes* I: 34.

[129] Strafford did not appeal to the repeal statute of 1 Mary, suggesting that he continued to see the legislative power in Ireland as separate and distinct from that of England: BL Harl. MS 164, fol. 950r; Rushworth, *Tryal*, p. 452; BL TT E.208(7), Oliver St. John, *An Argument of Law concerning the Bill of Attainder of High Treason of Thomas Earle of Strafford: At a Conference in a Committee of both Houses of Parliament* (London, 1641), pp. 39–40: "The rule of Law is that *Leges posteriores priores abrogat*, that latter lawes repeale former, but by this construction a former Lawe should repeale and make voide a *Non ens*, a Statute that then was not."

[130] BL Harl. MS 164, fol. 950v.

[131] Compare the following: Baillie, *Letters and Journals* I, p. 335: "He alleadged, that the acts alleadged were old and antiquat; but I understood not his probation. He said, that in these statutes the King was not included, because not expresslie mentioned, and so the King's Deputie was in the same case . . . "; and BL Harl. MS 164, fol. 950v: "For the Irish statute de @ 18. H. VI it did not concerne the Deputie of Ireland but others."

peace. He claimed that he had power to dispose soldiers as he saw fit and cited another Irish statute of 10 Henry VII, c. 17 that decreed no war or peace be made in Ireland except by the Lord Deputy's license.[132] He protested further "that it was a poor and unheard of warre which three or five or ten souldiers could make."[133]

Palmer's reply was devastating, arguing that Strafford had overstepped the jurisdiction of the Lord Deputy and usurped power of war and peace. Robert Baillie reported:

> Palmer replyed to all prettie well, that Ireland was a portion of the English Crowne; that he did answer there according to the Irish law; that his taking of regall and soveraigne power and priviledge was the charge; that the Deputie hath power to levie warre bot upon rebells, not in tyme of peace on the King's peacable subjects, answerable to legall Courts ...[134]

Aside from a usurpation of the sovereign power to levy war, Strafford's actions were a levying of war against the supra-personal properties of the kingly office: his majesty, dignity, and crown or, in language more reminiscent of Sir John Davies, his crown dignity and protection. The king's natural person remained in England but the protection of the king's laws extended to all of his Irish subjects and to levy war on them, in time of peace, when

132 Rushworth, *Tryal*, p. 450.

133 Quoted from Baillie, Letters *and Journals* I, p. 335; see also Rushworth, *Tryal*, p. 453; and BL Harl. MS 164, fol. 950v.

134 Baillie, *Letters and Journals* I, p. 336; Rushworth's account is fuller and includes a lengthy discourse on the subordinate and derivative relationship of Irish law to English law:

> The Laws of *Ireland* are devised from the Crown of *England*, the King being seized of it in the right of his Crown of *England*, and as a parcel of this Crown; The power they have to make Laws there is derivative from the Crown of *England*, and they did thankfully accept from the first Conqueror [Henry II presumably]: Since that, they had power to make Acts of Parliament, but that is subordinate, the Laws there are the Laws of *England* applyed to that place: As any particular custom of a place, not the general Law of the Land, is the Law of that place by a general custom, and yet may be judged out of the precincts of that custom; so the Laws of *Ireland* are the Laws of that Kingdom; yet may be judged by this Supream Court, out of the limits of Ireland. Though in an inferior Court, when a thing questioned in *Ireland*, is brought by Writ of Error, they judge according to the Laws of *Ireland*, not of *England*.
>
> And my Lord hath prayed, and we require, that he may be judged according to the Laws of *Ireland*. So this Law of 18. H. 6 may be judged by their Lordships, though it be a Law in *Ireland*. But my Lord urges that this Law is repealed, and for that he gave reasons of many Acts of Parliament; First, a *Statute* made 8 Edw. 4. That is made to a particular purpose, reciting one particular Statute, and repealing that, and then a general clause ratifying and introducing all the *Statutes* of *England* into *Ireland*. This being but a particular occasion, with such a general Clause, will not be applyable, however, it will be the Answer to that that follows. It is a general Clause to introduce the Laws of *England* and shall not have that reflexion to repeal any Law of force in *Ireland*. This introducing of our Laws thither, shall not work to repeal their Laws, but make a consistance of both Laws, so far as they may stand together. (Rushworth, *Tryal*, pp. 457–458)

they were not in rebellion, was a levying of war on the political body of the king[135] and subsequently on his natural person.[136]

The sixteenth article charged that Wentworth had procured permission from the king to issue a proclamation restricting travel between England and Ireland with the intent, "that no complaint of Injustice or Oppression done in Ireland should be received in England against any, unless . . . the party made first his address to him the said Earl."[137] As Michael Perceval-Maxwell has recently observed, the result of this was that the Lord Deputy "effectively cut Ireland off from the English judicial system, which in theory widened the gap between the Irish state and the English one, though not from the crown."[138] Strafford defended his actions, producing the king's letter of authorization.[139] He also argued that travel restrictions on leaving Ireland were necessary to prevent young Irishmen from attending seminaries abroad and conspiring with O'Neil and Tyrconnell.[140] He also cited the Irish statute 25 Henry VI, c. 2, which decreed "that none of the Kings Liege men . . . or Officers of the Land go out of the Land, but by Commission from the King or his Heirs, Lieutenant-Justices etc."[141]

Viewed from the perspective of the general theory of treason this article was very serious. Right of final appeal was, of course, a mark of sovereignty. Strafford, in appropriating the right to judge final appeals, had unlawfully

135 A key example of this particular conception of the king's two bodies came from Pym: "The *King* and his *people* are *obliged* to one another in *nearest relations*; He is a *Father*, and a *childe* is called in *Law, Pars Patris*: Hee is the *Husband* of the *Commonwealth*, they have the *same interests*, they are inseparable in their *condition*, be it *good* or *evill*; He is the *Head*, they are the *Body*, there is such an *incorporation* as cannot be dissolved without the destruction of both." BL TT E.208(8), *The Speech or Declaration of John Pym, Esquire: After the Recapitulation or summing up of the Charge of High Treason against Thomas, Earle of Strafford, 12 April 1641* (London, 1641), pp. 16–17.

136 There are textual ambiguities in the assertion being made here, especially in the use of the term "protection" in preference to "majesty," but I believe that it is borne out by the evidence. For example, Robert Baillie recalled that Palmer construed Strafford's actions, "to be treason, violating the King's protection, and so his crown and person," while D'Ewes recorded the words "crown and dignitie . . . and protection" and Rushworth more fully recounted: " . . . this levying of War, it was on the King's people; perhaps there was no intent upon the King's Sacred Person; yet if it be against the King's People, such a levying of War is Treason; ordinary Cases of Felony are to be against the King's Crown and Dignity, though it be the Homicide of a mean Subject, it is against the King's Crown and Dignity because it is against the protection and safety of that man that is the king's Subject; and so the levying of War on the King's People, by laying Soldiers in this hostile manner, being against the protection, by which the king is to defend them: It is a War against the King, his Crown, and Dignity." Baillie, *Letters and Journals* I, p. 334; BL Harl. MS 164, fol. 950v; Rushworth, *Tryal*, p. 458.

137 Rushworth, *Tryal*, pp. 67, 460.

138 Perceval-Maxwell, *Outbreak*, pp. 162–163.

139 Rushworth, *Tryal*, p. 473; BL Harl. MS 163, fol. 396r.

140 Baillie, *Letters and Journals* I, p. 336; BL Harl. MS 163, fol. 396r; BL Harl. MS 164, fol. 953v.

141 Rushworth, *Tryal*, p. 472; BL Harl. MS 163, fol. 396r.

erected a sovereign jurisdiction separate from that of the king, his parliament, and his judges in England. Indeed, there is much evidence for Perceval-Maxwell's suggestion that Strafford saw himself as governing a completely separate kingdom in all respects but the crown.[142] Rushworth recorded soberly that, "this thing is not so petty as my Lord makes it, to deny access of the Subject to their Sovereign."[143] Palmer in response denied that the Irish Statute of 25 Henry VI had abrogated the subject's right to petition the king and his judges in England, wryly noting the absence of a Jesuit college in England and accusing Strafford of obtaining the king's letter by misinformation.[144] The king could, theoretically at least, still do no wrong.

The seventeenth and eighteenth articles were passed over and, Whitelocke taking over from Palmer, the managers proceeded to the nineteenth article.[145] This article related to the Lord Deputy's imposition of a new oath on the Scottish population in Ireland during the Bishops' Wars. The oath was to the effect that the subject "should not protest against any his Majesties Royal Commands, but submit himself thereunto."[146] It appeared to be the second part of the oath, however, that created difficulty for the non-conforming Scots because it bound the subject "in point of ecclesiastical duties."[147] One Henry Stuart and his wife were fined 5,000*l.* each while their two daughters and one James Gray were fined 3,000*l.* each. All were imprisoned for not paying the fine.[148]

Whitelocke's contention was that no new oath could be introduced without an act of parliament and that Strafford did not have authority to create a new oath by executive order. Furthermore, Strafford's letter from the king asking that steps be taken to impose an oath on the Scots was insufficient because the king alone did not have the authority to frame a new oath.[149]

142 Perceval-Maxwell, *Outbreak*, p. 163. 143 Rushworth, *Tryal*, p. 486.

144 Rushworth, *Tryal*, p. 486; MM, 3 April 1641; Baillie, *Letters and Journals* I, pp. 336–337; BL Harl. MS 164, fol. 953v: D'Ewes reported "A specious shew to gett this granted was needfull."

145 The seventeenth article concerned the earl's purported declaration in the sixteenth year of Charles I's reign "That his Majesty was so well pleased with the Army of Ireland, and the consequences thereof, that his Majesty would certainly make the same a Pattern for all his Three kingdoms." The eighteenth accused Strafford of leaguing with papists in Ireland in that he (1) "restored divers Fryeries and Mass-Houses"; (2) raised a new Irish army of 8,000, "all of which, except one, or thereabouts, were Papists"; (3) that this new army was permitted the practice of the Catholic religion; and (4) that he allowed recusants in the north of England during his presidency of the Council of the North to compound at lower rates than decreed by statute: Rushworth, *Tryal*, pp. 69–70.

146 Rushworth, *Tryal*, p.70.

147 Rushworth, *Tryal*, pp. 496–497; a full text of the oath is reprinted on p. 494.

148 Rushworth, *Tryal*, p. 70.

149 Rushworth, *Tryal*, pp. 504, 509; BL Harl. MS 164, fol. 952v; Baillie, *Letters and Journals* I, p. 339; Baillie reported "he usurps a power more than royall; for non est penes principem

Whitelocke pressed the point further, arguing that the existing oath of allegiance should have been adequate to the task of fulfilling the king's request to secure the allegiance of his Scottish subjects in Ireland.[150] This seemingly insignificant article summed up the case against the earl most concisely: that he had, in Bodinian terms, unlawfully assumed the sovereign right "to cause all subiects and liegemen to sweare for the keeping of their fidelitie without exception, unto him to whome such oath is due" independently of the king and his parliament.[151]

The prosecution then proposed to handle the next five articles, the twentieth to the twenty-fourth, jointly on the grounds that they were interdependent. In spite of vigorous objections from Strafford, the Earl of Arundel, presiding as Lord High Steward, approved this course and Whitelocke proceeded.[152] These articles dealt with Strafford's conduct during the Bishops' Wars and the Short Parliament and more specifically with alleged treasonous counsels he had given the king during 1639–40. The twentieth article accused Strafford of provoking the king into pursuing an offensive war against the Scots and, "by his Counsels, Actions and Endeavours" creating war and discord between the king, his Scottish and his English subjects. The twenty-first accused Strafford first of procuring the king to break the pacification with the Scots and to renew hostilities; secondly, it accused him of counseling the king to call the Short Parliament and then procuring its dissolution when it would not supply the king; the article further accused Strafford of declaring in council "that he would serve his Majesty in any other way, in case the Parliament should not supply him."[153] The first part of the twenty-second article purported that Strafford had conspired with Sir George Radcliffe in the raising of the new Irish army of 8,000 foot and 1,000 horse to employ it "for the ruine and destruction of the kingdom of England, and of his Majesties Subjects, and of altering and subverting of the fundamental Laws and established Government of this kingdom." The second part of the article accused Strafford of declaring.

> to sundry persons . . . his Opinion to be, that his Majesty should first try the Parliament here, and if that did not supply him . . . he might use his Prerogative as he pleased, to levy what he needed, and that he should be acquitted both of God and man; if he

solum to frame a new oath, in all acts of parliament, you my Lords, and the Commons, have [an] interest."

150 Rushworth, *Tryal*, p. 509.

151 Jean Bodin, *The Six Bookes of a Commonweale*, trans. Richard Knolles and ed. Kenneth D. McRae (Cambridge, Mass., 1962), book I, pp. 162 [161]–163 [162].

152 BL Harl. MS 164, fols. 954r–v; Baillie, *Letters and Journals* I, p. 340; Strafford pushed to have the articles considered individually and in order – a process which would have been undoubtedly more time consuming.

153 Rushworth, *Tryal*, p. 71.

took some other Courses to supply himself, though it were against the wills of his Subjects.[154]

The key twenty-third article held that Strafford had firstly, together with Archbishop Laud, counseled the dissolution of the Short Parliament and, secondly, counseled the employment of the new Irish army in England with words to the effect that

having tried the affections of his People, he was loose and absolved from all rules of Government, and that he was to do every thing that Power would admit, and that his Majesty had tried all ways, and was refused, and should be acquitted towards God and man; and that he had an Army in Ireland... which he might imploy to reduce this kingdom.[155]

The twenty-fourth article, which was not significantly pressed, involved Strafford's role in causing the publication of "a false and scandalous Book, Entituled, *His Majesties Declaration of the Causes that moved him to Dissolve the last Parliament*" after the dissolution of the Short Parliament.[156] In brief, the five articles charged that Strafford had (1) procured a Scottish war; (2) raised an army of papists in Ireland with an intent to using it to invade and conquer England; (3) counseled the king to the same effect; (4) procured in conspiracy with Laud the dissolution of the Short Parliament; and (5) counseled the king to seek extra-parliamentary taxation.

The key witness to these articles was the Secretary of State, the older Henry Vane. Vane testified to the twentieth article that, on 5 May 1640, shortly after the breach of the Short Parliament, he had moved in council for a defensive war against the Scots while Strafford had advocated an offensive war.[157] This testimony was corroborated by the deposition of the Earl of Northumberland, the Lord Admiral, who was too ill to attend proceedings that day.[158] In maintenance of the charges of counseling extra-parliamentary taxation the deposition of Archbishop Usher was read: it recalled that Strafford had asserted in a discourse with the Lord Primate in April 1640 "that in case of eminent necessity he [the king] might make use of his prerogative, but in his opinion he was to try parliament first."[159] Vane and Lord Conway offered similar testimony.[160]

154 Rushworth, *Tryal*, p. 72. 155 Rushworth, *Tryal*, pp. 72–73.
156 Rushworth, *Tryal*, p. 73.
157 Conrad Russell has argued that Charles I had already decided on the necessity of an offensive war and was simply asking his counselors what was the best course for pursuing an offensive war against the Scots: Russell, *Fall*, p. 125.
158 BL Harl. MS 164, fol. 954v; Jansson, *Two Diaries*, p. 35.
159 Quotation is from William Drake's parliamentary note-book: Jansson, *Two Diaries*, p. 35.
160 Jansson, *Two Diaries*, p. 35; Baillie, *Letters and Journals* I, p. 341; BL Harl. MS 164, fol. 956r. Baillie reported: "My Lord Conway deponed, he said if the Parliament gave not these twelve subsidies, the king was justifiable before God and man to take some other course to

The most significant of this cluster of articles, however, was the twenty-third, charging that Strafford had counseled the employment of the new Irish army in England. While supported by the thinnest of evidence – the sole, highly questionable testimony of old Harry Vane – it was the article that, taken jointly with the fifteenth, probably struck the most fear into the hearts of the English. Read together, they accused Strafford of conspiring to invade England with an army of papists from Ireland and then to billet them forcibly in the homes of ordinary people. The case was undoubtedly weak: The Earl of Clare challenged Vane concerning the meaning of the words "this kingdom" – did he mean Scotland or England?[161] Conrad Russell has argued that, although he believes Strafford probably *did* speak these words in council, because he did so at a meeting for the discussion of Scottish affairs, it seems almost certain that "this kingdom" meant Scotland.[162]

Strafford for his part insisted that the Irish army had been intended for Scotland and was to have landed at Ayr in the south-west of that kingdom. From there it was to have marched north to attack the Earl of Argyle.[163] He also denied having spoken the words in question, noting that neither the Marquess of Hamilton, the Earl of Northumberland, the Bishop of London, nor Lord Cottington, who were all present at the time, could recall his speaking of the words in question.[164] With regard to the case in law, he cited once again the evidentiary proviso of 1 Edward VI, c. 12 questioning the validity of only a single testimony and argued that mere words could not constitute treason.[165] He also asserted that his words were spoken in council under oath where he was obliged to voice his opinion and that if mere words spoken at the council table were to be construed as treason the king would soon have none to advise him.[166] He responded to the charge of counseling the king to seek extra-parliamentary supply, arguing that this was justified by the necessity of preserving the commonwealth against the depredations of a foreign invader – an appeal to necessity reminiscent of the *Ship Money Case*.[167]

supplie himself, though against their will; – Sir Harie Vane, that if the Parliament did not succeed, he would be readie to serve the King any other way ..."

[161] Jansson, *Two Diaries*, p. 36; Rushworth, *Tryal*, p. 545; Baillie, *Letters and Journals* I, p. 342.

[162] Russell, *Fall*, pp. 126–127.

[163] BL Harl. MS 164, fol. 956r–v. the minutes of the House of Lords for 5 April 1641 indicate that Strafford was supported in this contention not only by his stalwart supporters Slingsby and Pennyman but by the Lord Admiral, Northumberland: MM, 5 April 1641 and Rushworth, *Tryal*, p. 554.

[164] BL Harl. MS 164, fol. 956v.

[165] BL Harl. MS 164, fol. 956r–v; Rushworth, *Tryal*, pp. 561–562, 565.

[166] BL Harl. MS 164, fol. 956r; Baillie, *Letters and Journals* I, p. 342.

[167] BL Harl. MS 164, fol. 956v: "He confest hee onlie saied That In cases of absolute necesssitie upon an invasion of a foraigne enemie when all ordinarie meanes shall faile that then to

Whitelocke responded that the port of Ayr was one hundred miles from Argyle's lands and that impassable mountains blocked the way. Consistent with the precedent of *Pine's Case* he also argued that while the earl's words may not have been themselves treasonable they were admissible as evidence of his treasonable intent.[168] Whitelocke and Maynard sought to overcome the demand for two witnesses by linking the five articles: while Vane's testimony to the twenty-third article may indeed have been a single testimony, the Earl of Northumberland's testimony had confirmed "divers of other word" that other witnesses had been unable to recall.[169] Maynard added the argument that Strafford had not simply spoken treasonable words but made treasonable counsels to the king and brought them into effect in the dissolution of the Short Parliament.[170] While mere words could not constitute treason, counsels were not simply words.

Of the remaining four articles only the next three were pursued. All concerned either the counseling, intending, or the actual levying of extra-parliamentary subsidies. Article 25 concerned Strafford's counseling of ship money in the aftermath of the Short Parliament and his role in the crown's attempts to secure a loan from the city of London. He purportedly remarked of the recalcitrant lord mayor and aldermen "That they deserved to be put to fine and Ransom, and that no good would be done with them, till an example were made of them, and that they were laid by the heels, and some of the Aldermen hanged up."[171]

Strafford denied the speaking of the words against the mayor and aldermen but asserted that, even if he had spoken them, they could not constitute treason as they were words spoken "in heate and passion."[172] He responded to the charges of counseling ship money, arguing that he had

preserve the Commonwealth ther is a supreame power . . . in his Ma[ies]tie that he may provide for the present danger. And at that time when hee gave this advice tidings weere brought to the King that the Scottish armie had marched into England." See also Rushworth, *Tryal*, p. 560.

168 BL Harl. MS 164, fol. 956r: "Mr. Whitelock saied that heere his words shewed his heart." Rushworth, *Tryal*, p. 574.

169 BL Harl. MS 164, fols. 956v–957r: D'Ewes reported Maynard's speech as follows: "Hee answered severallie to all the severall testimonies but to take them all together they are unanswearable . . . And wheereas hee alledgeth that the testimonie of Mr. Treasurour Fane should not because it is single touching the bringing of the Irish armie into England because others then present remember it not; that is of noe validitie. For the maine matter is proved by the Earle of Northumberland alsoe of w[hic]h this was but a consequent; and others not that neither."

170 BL Harl. MS 164, fol. 957r; Maynard argued that the "Sta[tute] 1 E[dward] 6, c. 12 . . . concernes words etc. But that wee accuse the E[arl] of Straff[ord] of are wicked counsels brought into action."

171 Rushworth, *Tryal*, p. 73.

172 BL Harl. MS 163, fol. 408r; BL Harl. MS 164, fol. 959r.

been persuaded of the legality of the levy by the favorable decision of the judges in the *Ship Money Case*.[173] Maynard responded that Strafford's words had not been spoken in passion but were evidence of his treasonable designs. He argued further that the illegality of ship money had been exposed in the Short Parliament and that the false judgments of Justice Berkeley and his colleagues provided no defense.[174] Glynne added the observation that Strafford in pronouncing a judgment of death against Mountnorris had not scrupled in construing rash words as treason.[175]

Article 26 alleged that Strafford had counseled the king to seize the bullion in the mint and urged the imbasement of the coin with brass. The article further alleged that, when the officers of the mint protested against the imbasing of the coin, he responded by quoting a letter from the Earl of Leicester in France to the effect "That the French king did use to send Commissaries of Horse with Commission to search into men's estates, and to peruse their Accounts, that so they may know what to levy by force which they did accordingly levy ..."[176] While the prosecution was able to prove that Strafford had spoken the words in question they were less successful in proving his role in the schemes to seize the mint and imbase the coin.[177] Strafford also denied that the king would ever be so impious as to follow the course of action suggested by "that foolish letter."[178]

The twenty-seventh article was the last prosecuted and it resembled the fifteenth very closely. It concerned the collection of an extra-parliamentary levy in York during September 1640 for the direct maintenance of the county's trained bands. Strafford was alleged to have said "that he would commit them that refused the payment thereof, and the Souldiers should be satisfied out of their Estates; and they that refused it, were in very little better condition than of High Treason."[179] Maynard argued that initially "about 100 of the nobilitie and gentrie of yorkshire" had presented a petition for delivery to the king to Strafford who was commanding the King's forces in the north. The petition had offered to support the trained bands for the period of a month conditional upon the summoning of a parliament. Strafford, the prosecution

[173] BL Harl. MS 164, fol. 959r; MM, 7 April 1641; Baillie, *Letters and Journals* I, p. 342; Rushworth, *Tryal*, p. 586.

[174] BL Harl. MS 163, fol. 408r; BL Harl. MS 164, fol. 959r; Rushworth, *Tryal*, pp. 587–588. The act declaring ship money illegal would not be passed until 7 August 1641, but already the Long Parliament had moved to impeach the *Ship Money* judges on 22 December 1640: Gardiner, *Constitutional Documents*, pp. 189–192; *LJ* IV: 114–116.

[175] BL Harl. MS 163, fol. 408r; BL Harl. MS 164, fol. 959r; Baillie, *Letters and Journals* I, p. 343; Rushworth, *Tryal*, p. 588.

[176] Rushworth, *Tryal*, pp. 73–74, 591; Baillie, *Letters and Journals* I, p. 343; Baillie cites the letter as coming from Leicester's secretary.

[177] Rushworth, *Tryal*, pp. 594–595.

[178] Baillie, *Letters and Journals* I, p. 343.

[179] Rushworth, *Tryal*, p. 74.

alleged, offered in turn to join the petitioners but only if the clause calling for a parliament was left out.[180] It was further charged that many who joined in this second petition were papists – not particularly unlikely considering that the Catholic population of Yorkshire probably had even less reason to love the Scots army than the rest of the county's inhabitants.[181] The subsidy was accordingly levied, door-to-door, at musket-point.[182]

Strafford conceded the case in fact. He acknowledged that he had advised the exclusion of the clause calling for a parliament, though not with the intent of hindering the calling of a parliament, "but that it might bee his Ma[ies]ties sole act" and that "hee might have the glorie of it."[183] The principal aspect of the earl's defense, however, was that he had both the king's consent and that of the people of York. He argued further that it was within his commission as Lord General to maintain the trained bands as he thought necessary and that the contribution of two pence per diem was voluntarily paid.[184] Maynard responded that Strafford's commission extended only to the employment of the trained bands and not to the exaction of taxes for their support.[185]

The final three articles were united by their equation of illegal taxation with treason. The power to levy subsidies was, of course, a mark of sovereignty in the Bodinian scheme.[186] Furthermore, the idea that the king could do no wrong and that his evil counselors were to blame for the ills of the Bishops' Wars and the personal rule was still very strong in 1641. Considering this, it was not surprising that the managers sought to portray Strafford as a usurper of the marks of sovereignty regardless of whether they were exercised by the king alone as in the case of power of war and peace, by the king-in-parliament as in the case of the law-making power, or by the consent of parliaments as in the instance of subsidies. The idea of treason as a usurpation of sovereign power thus had relevance both with regard to the king's powers by virtue of his prerogative (war and peace, coinage, etc.) and those exercised in concert with parliament (subsidies, statute-making, judiciature). This unlawful appropriation of sovereign power was essential

180 BL Harl. MS 164, fols. 959v–960r. 181 BL Harl. MS 164, fol. 960r.

182 BL Harl. MS 164, fol. 960r: D'Ewes recounted testimony that "Mr serjeant maior ... did levie the saied monies by the trained bands ... Hee did levie divers small summs on severall persons w[i]th the helpe of four musketiers who came with him and a constable or two to an house."

183 BL Harl. MS 164, fol. 960v. Baillie's account differs from that of D'Ewes here: "... he made them delete that clause of a Parliament, knowing the King's resolution to call it of his own goodness, without petition from any"; Baillie, *Letters and Journals* I, p. 344.

184 BL Harl. MS 164, fol. 960v; Baillie, *Letters and Journals* I, p. 344.

185 BL Harl. MS 164, fol. 961r; Baillie, *Letters and Journals* I, p. 344.

186 Bodin, *Six Bookes*, book I, ch. 10, pp. 154–155: Bodin referred to the example of "Galeace the first, viscount of Milan, [who] was accused, attainted, conuinced, and condemned of treason by the emperour, for hauing without leaue raysed taxes vpon his subiects, and that hee therefore died in prison."

to the idea of the subversion of the fundamental law. The implications of this subversion became fully evident after 10 April when the impeachment was abandoned in favor of proceeding by bill of attainder.

IV

The interpretations of Stacy and Timmis have emphasized the question of the legality of Strafford's attainder. This narrow conception of "legality" defined treason strictly in terms of whether or not Strafford's alleged actions in the fifteenth and twentieth articles fell within the terms of 25 Edward III. As a result the idea of the subversion of the law has been inexcusably neglected. Accepting the defense's contention that the subversion of the law was no treason within 25 Edward III, these historians have failed to explore its relationship to conceptions of kingship, sovereignty, and state.

Much of the attainder speeches and debates after April 10 were simply a rehashing of the issues raised during the impeachment. In the interest of brevity, therefore, this section does provide a narrative of the proceedings like that given above for the impeachment (an inevitably repetitive exercise) but reconstructs the foundations on which the prosecution's case proceeded. The result is a more substantive and satisfying account of the cumulative theory of treason than has hitherto been provided.

We have established that central to the idea of the subversion of the law was the unlawful appropriation of sovereign jurisdiction, in particular the power to give law. This power to give law, as the substance of the impeachment will have made clear, encompassed not only the power of king-in-parliament to declare law in statute but also the ordinary administration of justice in the king's courts. The unlawful assumption of these powers, whether legislative or judicial (the distinction not always being clear), was a subversion of the law. Pym made this explicit in debate on 15 April charging: "He hath taken a legislative power from the parliament, and assumed it to himselfe, and put it in execuition, and this is subvertion."[187] The response of Orlando Bridgeman was a familiar one, taking the exceptionalist position on the constitutional relationship between England and Ireland. The subversion of the law in Ireland was different from the subversion of the law in England because the legislative power in Ireland differed from that of England, upon which it depended.[188] Indeed, since the end of the fifteenth century and the introduction of Poynings' Law, under which legislation in

[187] Verney, *Notes*, p. 48; for similar remarks see also Jansson, *Two Diaries*, pp. 37, 39; and *Mr. Maynard's Speech ...*, p. 4.
[188] Jansson, *Two Diaries*, p. 39; Verney, *Notes*, p. 48.

Ireland had been made subject to the approval of the king and his English council, the situation had become even murkier.[189]

The effect of the subversion of the law was, according to the prosecution's most prominent spokesmen, understood in terms of the king's two bodies and their inseparability. Glynne accused Strafford of intending the destruction of the law itself.[190] Making explicit reference to *Calvin's Case*, the barrister Robert Nicholas argued that the law was the "soul" of the political body by which the king held his crown and to destroy it was to destroy also the king and his kingdom along with it.[191] What was the subversion of the law, argued Glynne, but "the subversion of the king and state"?[192] Pym argued that the subversion of the law "dissolved the ligaments of protection between Prince and people." He responded to Strafford's defense of necessity by accusing him of bringing the king into necessity by his ill counsels.[193] Strafford made the rather feeble argument that he had not so much subverted the law but merely diverted it into a different channel – a different issue entirely![194] His counsel, Richard Lane, made the rather more technical argument against common-law treasons and the process of attainder itself. According to Lane the statute of 1 Henry IV, c. 10 had in fact repealed not only all treasons at common law but also the salvo clause of 25 Edward III.[195] Lane's argument threw into question the very mode of procedure.

Lane's arguments, however, were not able to alter the course of events as the attainder gathered momentum. Despite the learned and eloquent arguments of such men as Orlando Bridgeman, George Lord Digby, and Robert Holborne, the attainder passed the Commons on 20 April with votes to both the question in law and in fact.[196] St. John and Glynne presented the

189 Perceval-Maxwell, *Outbreak*, p. 8.

190 BL Harl. MS 164, fol. 971r; Rushworth, *Tryal*, pp. 708, 714.

191 I have little doubt that the Mr. Nicholas in question was Robert Nicholas, a barrister of the Middle Temple, who sat for Wiltshire in the Long Parliament, subsequently played a key role in prosecuting Laud, and later became a Baron of the Exchequer under Cromwell: Mary Frear Keeler, *The Long Parliament, 1640–41: A Biographical Study of its Members* (Philadelphia, 1954), p. 285; BL Harl. MS 164, fol. 981r: "Mr. Nicholas[:] to destroy the law is to destroy kingdome and the king in it. the Law soule of political bodie. *Calvins* c[ase] 7r king inherits his crowne by the common law, take away that and this is to deprive the king of his crowne."

192 BL Harl. MS 164, fol. 971v.

193 BL Harl. MS 164, fol. 972v; *The Speech ... of John Pym*, pp. 16, 24.

194 BL Harl. MS 164, fol. 970v; Rushworth, *Tryal*, p. 650.

195 BL Harl. MS 163, fol. 452r; BL Harl. MS 164, fol. 979r; Verney, *Notes*, p. 52; Rushworth, *Tryal*, p. 671; Stacy has questioned the validity of this argument citing the role that the salvo played in the fifteenth-century evolution of attainder: Stacy, "Matter of Fact, Matter of Law": 336.

196 There were fifty-nine "noes" to the vote in the commons according to Verney but accounts vary from fifty-four to fifty-nine: Verney, *Notes*, p. 57.

prosecution's final arguments to the Lords on 29 April 1641 arguing the case under six heads: (1) that the fifteenth article constituted a treason of levying war under 25 Edward III; (2) that the twenty-third article, intending the levying of war, was a constructive compassing of the king's death and treason under 25 Edward III; (3) that the fifteenth and twenty-third articles taken cumulatively were a constructive compassing of the king's death; (4) that the fifteenth article was treason under the Irish statute of 18 Henry VI; (5) that, in refutation of Lane's argument, the subverting of the law and introducing of an arbitrary government remained treason at common law; and finally (6) an appeal to necessity in the use of the supreme legislative power.[197]

The upper house passed the bill of attainder on 8 May. On 10 May the king gave his assent and on 12 May Thomas Wentworth, First Earl of Strafford, was executed on Tower Hill. "This day my Lord Strafford lost his head," an anonymous diarist wrote.[198]

V

W. R. Stacy has argued that the case in law against the Earl of Strafford was bad both in law and in fact and that the decision to proceed by bill of attainder was a result of the managers' failure "to convince the House of Lords of the soundness of its case in law or fact."[199] Attainder provided a more "flexible" means of securing the hated earl's execution than continuing the impeachment. This explanation is flawed in that it considers political action divorced from political thought. The argument is erected on a narrow and possibly anachronistic understanding of the law of treason which, even if conceded, does precious little to illuminate the integral relationships of political thought to political action, law to polity, king to kingdom in early modern England.

Strafford, in endeavoring to subvert the law, stood accused of attempting to destroy the king and his kingdom by dividing ruler from ruled, dissolving the reciprocal bonds of allegiance, and ultimately destroying the fundamental law of the land without which England was not England and Ireland not Ireland. Concomitantly, an adequate historical inquiry of the charges against him is impossible without considering the range of conceptual tools available for the redefinition of treason, not simply as a crime against the king's person, but against the state. The justification for his execution was the preservation

197 Verney, *Notes*, pp. 60–61; St. John, *Argument of Law*, pp. 7–8; the account of D'Ewes, interestingly enough, appears to have left out the sixth head appealing to necessity and instead emphasized the declaratory nature of the legislative power and its relationship to the idea of common-law treasons: BL Harl. MS 164, fol. 993r.

198 Jansson, *Two Diaries*, p. 118.

199 Stacy, "Matter of Fact, Matter of Law": 324.

of the king and state, king and kingdom. This use of the term "state" was, however, not the fully impersonal and abstract entity divorced from the person or persons of any individual but an incorporation of ruler and ruled in a single political body or state. It was not the "state" that Quentin Skinner has identified as recognizably modern. This argument, or something similar, was certainly available to the managers of the evidence in Strafford's trial. To deny this is an assertion that cannot be intelligently made on the basis of the evidence here presented. However, it remains highly significant that the managers of the evidence against Strafford – the men acting in the name of the legitimate sovereign authority – claimed to be acting in the king's name for the preservation of the king's kingdom, his law, and his person and not in the interest of an impersonal state.

The idea of the "state" figured in prosecution's arguments only insofar as it was the king's state to hold and maintain and it was the theory of the king's two bodies upon which the prosecution's case hinged. St. John made this clear in his *Argument in Law*: "Machination of warre against the Lawes or kingdome is against the king[,] they cannot be severed."[200] As Glynne argued before the Lords on 29 April 1641, a levying of war to subvert the laws was necessarily a war against the king as the king was the fountain of the law and bound to maintain it.[201] The endeavoring of the subversion of the law was the endeavoring of the destruction of the king's political body and the king's natural body along with it. The king's person could not be separated from his office or crown without his death. The appropriation of the rights of sovereignty, therefore, was both a subversion of the law and a constructive compassing of the king's death. An idea of treason more fully in keeping with Roman law could, therefore, be reconciled with the statutory foundation of the English law of treason.

The practical objective of the impeachment and attainder of the Earl of Strafford was, of course, the disposal of a hated and feared political enemy. Revisionist scholars have explained the destruction of Strafford as an event in British *political* history in terms of a broad alliance of anti-Straffordian factions. The coalescing of interests within the king's council represented in parliament with those of Pym and his junto in the Long Parliament combined to destroy the beleaguered earl.[202] Nevertheless, the task of selling the attainder to a broader political audience of possibly recalcitrant parliamentarians meant that this practical objective needed ideological definition and moral redescription in order to persuade and assure the squeamish and the faint-hearted that the course proposed was legal, legitimate, and necessary for the preservation of the king and kingdom. What makes the trial interesting both

200 St. John, *Argument of Law*, p. 27.

201 BL Harl. MS 164, fol. 993v.

202 Russell, *Fall*, pp. 274–302.

to the historian of political thought and to all readers, students, and scholars of history is not whether Strafford got a raw deal or not – even the greatest cynic will admit that he pretty obviously did. What is fascinating about an occasion of state such as Strafford's trial is the way in which existing shared political vocabularies were exploited to legitimize an extreme course of political action – the speedy and possibly illegal execution of the unfortunate earl.[203]

The theory of treason in the trial of the Earl of Strafford was not "an unprecedented theory of accumulative treason" but a clever, innovative use of pre-existing political ideas concerning the nature of public authority. If the managers of the Earl's trial did "manufacture" a novel theory of treason they were of necessity required to do so with familiar political ideas concerning the supra-personal nature of kingship and the rhetoric of necessity or "reason of state." To appropriate unlawfully the powers of the king, whether he wielded them by prerogative or in concert with parliament, was to destroy the law. The law of England, the common law, constituted the sinews of the body politic rendering the king a body politic. Its subversion entailed the destruction of his political body and subsequently his natural. Seen in continuity with a broader spectrum of political ideologies the attainder of Strafford was not an "illegal" act but an occasion of state in which the history of political ideas came to play a concrete role in public life.

[203] Quentin Skinner, "The Principles and Practice of Opposition: The Case of Bolingbroke versus Walpole," in Neil McKendrick, ed., *Historical Perspectives, Studies in English Thought and Society in Honour of J. H. Plumb* (London, 1974), pp. 93–128, esp. pp. 127–128.

4

William Laud, Archbishop of Canterbury

... there is not a more cunning trick in the world, to withdraw the people's hearts from their sovereign, than to persuade them that he is changing true religion, and about to bring in gross superstition upon them.[1]

I

The trial of William Laud, Archbishop of Canterbury has not received the same degree of attention as that of Strafford.[2] While the articles exhibited against Laud did share certain similarities with those against Strafford, Laud's trial was not simply a replaying of the events of March and April 1641. Both men stood charged for their roles in the personal rule of the 1630s and, essentially, with the unlawful usurpation of the sovereign power. However, while much of the evidence against Strafford turned on the question of the constitutional relationship between the kingdoms of Ireland and England, the crux of Laud's trial was the relationship of church and state. The bulk of the articles against Strafford, the Irish articles, charged that Strafford had taken one of the king's kingdoms and ruled it as his own – an act of usurpation consistent with Roman law conceptions of treason. The charges against Laud held that he had expanded clerical jurisdictions during the personal rule to the extent of creating an ecclesiastical state within a state.

The argument is arranged as follows. The first section considers the ideological backdrop to the trial and situates it within the ecclesiological debates of the early to mid-1640s, and in particular with respect to the rise of Erastian sentiment in the early Long Parliament. The second section analyzes the

[1] *A Speech Delivered in the Starr-Chamber, on Wednesday, the xiv. of Iune 1637 and the Censure of Iohn Bastwick, Henry Burton and William Prynne; Concerning pretended Innovations in the Church*, in *Works* VI, p. 45.

[2] For example, H. R. Trevor-Roper in his biography of Laud dismissed the trial with these words: "It is unnecessary to deal in detail with Laud's trial; for his whole life was objected against him." H. R. Trevor-Roper, *Archbishop Laud, 1573–1645*, 3rd edn. (London, 1988), p. 422.

articles themselves and the arguments presented at the trial. It demonstrates how the essentially clerical nature of Laud's usurpations led to the dependence of the prosecution's case on an almost complete conflation of treason with the lesser cause of praemunire. As Sir John Maynard remarked during the trial, Laud's principal sin was that he had labored "to exalt the Clergy above the Temporall Magistrate . . ."[3] The final section offers a brief consideration of the concluding arguments of the trial with reference to the themes and issues developed earlier in the chapter.

II

The power to alter and determine the doctrine and discipline of the Church of England constituted a mark of sovereignty. Like most marks of sovereignty in the early seventeenth century the nature of the supremacy was subject to dispute. The ideological position of Laud's prosecutors was that of Erastianism. Erastianism, according to William M. Lamont, "is now understood as the claim of the secular power to control belief; it carries with it pejorative connotations of a cynical indifference to moral questions." Unsurprisingly, it is an ideological position usually associated with that well-known seventeenth-century monster Thomas Hobbes.[4] Lamont, following J. N. Figgis, has argued that this was, in fact, an inaccurate representation of Erastus's views and that the central concern of Erastus and his followers was "with the question of how to enforce ecclesiastical discipline in a state that was uniform in religion."[5] Erastus, writing in the mid-sixteenth century, did not presume for the secular magistrate any power to define belief or doctrine.[6]

Figgis, however, allowed that the term "Erastian" meant something more expansive in the seventeenth-century, encompassing the right to define and determine doctrine as well as the enforcement of ecclesiastical discipline.[7] Thus, the working definition of Erastianism offered here is simply the view that power to determine doctrine and exercise discipline over the established church rested ultimately with the secular magistrate, whether that be king, parliament or king-in-parliament, rather than with any ecclesiastical

[3] Worcester College, Clarke MS LXXI, 16 April 1644 (the section of the manuscript relating to Laud's trial is not foliated).

[4] An important recent contribution to Hobbes's views on church and state is Jeffrey R. Collins, "Christian Ecclesiology and the Composition of *Leviathan*: A Newly Discovered Letter to Thomas Hobbes," *HJ* 43 (2000): 217–231.

[5] William M. Lamont, *Marginal Prynne, 1600–1669* (Toronto and London, 1963), p. 155; and also his study of millenarianism, *Godly Rule, Politics and Religion 1603–1660* (London, 1969), pp. 113–115.

[6] J. N. Figgis, "Erastus and Erastianism," in *The Divine Right of Kings*, ed. with intro. by G. R. Elton, (New York, 1965 [Cambridge, 1896]), p. 268.

[7] Figgis, *Divine Right*, p. 291.

body. To a parliamentary Erastian such as William Prynne – a principal chronicler and architect of Laud's demise – this meant that acts of convocation were subject to parliamentary determination and approval and that questions of doctrine, as well as discipline, were the proper province of the secular authority of king-in-parliament. This position stood opposed to one that was essentially clerical: Laud at his trial appears to have been willing to grant to the secular authority of king-in-parliament powers of discipline but reserved doctrinal questions to the clergy of the church assembled together in convocation.[8] Indeed, Erastianism in this sense stood distinct from both the pretensions of the Laudian episcopate to hold and exercise the powers of their offices *iure divino*, directly from God by apostolic descent, and with the similar *iure divino* claims made by Scottish Presbyterianism on behalf of the assembly of the kirk for a very different form of church government.[9]

For the older generation of Erastians, men such as John Selden, eschatological visions predicting the defeat of the Antichrist and the establishment of what Lamont has called "godly rule" did not necessarily inform civil magistrates' control of religious affairs. However, for the younger more "Puritan" Erastians with whom Selden allied himself in the Long Parliament – men such as Prynne and the outspoken Wiltshire barrister Robert Nicholas who prosecuted Laud – this was not so.[10] Lamont has argued that both Erastian and clericalist positions in the 1630s and 1640s shared a common set of eschatological expectations but were divided on the means of achieving "godly rule." The former sought to effect the defeat of the Antichrist and realize the millennium through the agency of the civil magistrate while the latter pursued the same end through clerical rule.[11]

Erastianism did not necessarily entail that the civil magistrates be left to their own devices in making doctrinal judgments. A printed speech of Oliver St. John dated 17 January 1642 suggested that the Erastian position was sensitive to the complications that could arise in the determination of doctrinal issues.[12] Speaking to the impeachment of the twelve bishops on charges of misdemeanor and treason St. John argued that the bishops should not have votes "concerning Religion, or any wayes to intermeddle or give

[8] *Works* IV, pp. 351–352; for this episcopal or clericalist position see Lamont, *Godly Rule*, ch. 3.

[9] Lamont, *Marginal Prynne*, ch. 7; for the *iure divino* view of episcopacy see *Works* VI, p. 43.

[10] For Prynne see Lamont, *Marginal Prynne*, *passim*; see also *New DNB*, "Robert Nicholas."

[11] Lamont, *Godly Rule*, ch. 3, 5.

[12] Interestingly, this speech was in fact made against Laud's rival, Archbishop John Williams, one of the twelve bishops impeached by the Long Parliament in 1641 and a man characterized by Nicholas Tyacke as a "Calvinist in doctrine." The Laudians did not have a monopoly on the idea of a separate clerical sphere of influence, nor were they the sole targets of the anti-clerical sentiment in the early Long Parliament: Nicholas Tyacke, *Anti Calvinists: The Rise of English Arminianism, c. 1590–1640* (Oxford, 1986), p. 209.

advise touching temporall affaires."[13] He also objected vigorously to bishops issuing writs and warrants in the ecclesiastical courts in their own names and not in that of the king.[14] Nevertheless, St. John qualified his remarks and conceded "that it may be necessary for Bishops to sit in Parliament to give their advise in points of Divinity concerning Religion" in much the same way that parliament summoned the learned judges of the law to deliver opinions on points of law during impeachments and other instances of parliamentary judicature.[15]

Late in the nineteenth century Figgis argued that in the wake of the English Reformation the idea of the divine right of kings acted to deflect the pretensions of the papacy to secular power held *iure divino* and later on to rebut the similar *iure divino* claims of Presbyterianism. The claims of monarchs to be divinely anointed served as an ideological bulwark against more clerical schemes of church government. In particular the theory answered the See of Rome's claim that the popes possessed a power to depose secular rulers and absolve subjects from their allegiance.[16] Because kings held their powers directly from God and not through the mediation of the papacy, there could not be a papal power to deprive kings of their crowns. To subject the powers of the king in church and state to that of the Pope was treasonable because it raised an earthly power, the See of Rome, above that of the king.

This idea was not new and the *State Trials* are replete with examples. In *Talbot's Case* (1613) the prosecution charged Talbot, an Irish lawyer, then Recorder of Dublin, with adhering to the doctrines of Suarez, "that he maintaineth ... a power in the pope for the disposing and murdering of kings."[17] Sir Francis Bacon's argument in *Peacham's Case* equated the deposition of the king with the compassing of his death. William Prynne, writing in opposition to the king's trial in early 1649, reiterated this construction of 25 Edward III.[18] Any act furthering the usurpations of the papacy began during Elizabeth's reign, therefore, came under the first head of 25 Edward III as a constructive compassing of the king's death. The assumption of papal power within the realm of England was necessarily treasonable by its very definition.

[13] BL TT E.200(24), *Master St. John His Speech in Parliament On Munday January the 17th An. Dom. 1641. Concerning the Charge of treason then exhibited to the Bishops, Formerly accused by the House of Commons* (London 1642), sig. A3v; for St. John and Erastianism see Valerie Pearl, "Oliver St. John and the 'middle group' in the Long Parliament: August 1643–May 1644," *EHR* 81 (1966): 500–501.

[14] *Master St. John His Speech*, sig. A3r. [15] *Master St. John His Speech*, sig. A3v.

[16] Figgis, *Divine Right*, ch. 8. [17] *State Trials* II: 779.

[18] *State Trials* II: 873–874 ; William Prynne, *A Briefe Memento To the Present Un parliamentary Iunto Touching their present Intentions and Proceedings to Depose and Execute, Charles Steward, their lawfull King* (London 1649), sig. A1r–v, pp. 3–4.

This strand of Figgis's argument has been taken up by Glenn Burgess, who has questioned the relationship of the theory to absolutist ideas. More specifically, he has questioned the claims of Johann P. Sommerville that a fully mature doctrine of royal absolutism by divine right had not only emerged in England by the early Stuart period but was in fact ubiquitous among large sections of the clergy.[19] Burgess has argued that the theory of the divine right of kings acted in the later sixteenth century not to the furthering of royal absolutism but to rebut the claims of the papacy to temporal jurisdiction over the English crown and later on against the claims of Presbyterians for an autonomous sphere of clerical action.[20] He has asserted further that the theory of divine right did not necessarily contradict the notion that the king ruled by and was bound by the customary law of the land and that the "common-law mind" remained the dominant political vocabulary of the early Stuart period. This was especially the case among the gentry who comprised the largest social stratum of early Stuart parliaments.[21] Sommerville, in contrast, has dwelt on the arguably more peripheral aspect of the theory that emphasized the subject's duty of absolute obedience to the sovereign – an emphasis intended more to secure temporal allegiance from Catholics than anything else.[22] Figgis's central concern was as much the relationship of church and state as the relationship of ruler to ruled. Indeed, what is at stake in the debate between Sommerville and Burgess appears to be largely a disputed reading of Figgis.

The picture that emerges is that of an ideological milieu in which conflict arose not from rival theories of ascending and descending power but from rival theories of descending power alone whether papal, Presbyterian, episcopal, or monarchical.[23] Furthermore, there is the claim of Conrad Russell that ascending and descending theories of power were not necessarily

[19] Glenn Burgess, "The Divine Right of Kings Reconsidered," *EHR* 107 (1992): 837–861; Glenn Burgess, *Absolute Monarchy and the Stuart Constitution* (New Haven, 1996), ch. 4.

[20] Burgess, "Divine Right": 837.

[21] Burgess, "Divine Right": 857; Glenn Burgess, *The Politics of the Ancient Constitution: An Introduction to English Political Thought, 1603–1642* (London, 1992); Burgess has essentially revised and reasserted much of the original argument of Pocock with a greater emphasis on jurisprudential issues than the historiography of the English law: J. G. A. Pocock, *The Ancient Constitution and The Feudal Law: A Study of English Historical Thought in the Seventeenth Century*, 2nd edn. (Cambridge, 1987), chs. 2, 3.

[22] I believe the term "absolutist" is employed in Sommerville's work in much the same way that Richard Tuck deploys it in his *Natural Rights Theories: Their Origins and Developments* (Cambridge, 1979); this emphasized the use of the term as requiring a subject's absolute duty of obedience. While the question of "absolutism" is largely peripheral here, I believe a better definition is that suggested by Conrad Russell, which emphasizes the king's right to exercise legal sovereignty on his own without consent of the ruled: Conrad Russell, *The Causes of the English Civil War* (Oxford, 1990), pp. 149–151.

[23] This throws into question the argument of J. B. Sanderson's *"But the People's Creatures": The Philosophical Basis of the English Civil War* (Manchester, 1989).

incompatible to the early Stuart mind: "It was . . . only if ascending and descending theories of power were compatible that the authority of king-in-parliament was conceptually possible."[24] Russell has argued that the idea of the divine right of kings was "almost universally accepted, not particularly controversial, and utterly uninformative about the extent of the king's powers."[25] The treason of Laud, therefore, had its origins not in conflicting theories of ascending and descending political power but from rival descending theories of power. Laud's prosecutors viewed his *iure divino* claims as smacking of popery and accordingly equated them to the seizure of a "papal" power greater than that of the king and his parliament. The conflict became one of godly king and parliament versus godly bishop underpinned on both sides by potentially explosive eschatological assumptions.

Johann Sommerville has argued that the *iure divino* claims of the Jacobean and Laudian episcopate did not derogate from the king's authority in spiritual matters and that clerical "absolutism" was perfectly compatible with the bishops' claim to hold the powers of their episcopal offices directly from God.[26] While Sommerville has been willing to equate the *iure divino* claims of the Stuart monarchs with absolutism he has been less willing to equate the *iure divino* claims of the bishops with clericalism – the belief in an autonomous sphere of clerical action in which the crown would not *ordinarily* interfere. However, the fears of clerical usurpation raised in the wake of convocation's continued sitting after the dissolution of the Short Parliament caused many including Pym and St. John increasingly to see the *iure divino* claims of the episcopate in a more sinister light. They constituted not merely a threat to the role of parliament and the civil magistrate but a threat to the spiritual wellbeing of the kingdom. Prynne's rhetoric did not "disguise truths" about the nature of the royal supremacy but embodied an ideologically Erastian position that was opposed both to the clericalist agenda of the Laudian episcopate and to the differing, yet in its own way equally clerical, Scottish Presbyterian model of church government.[27] Both the continued sitting of the convocation of 1640 after the Short Parliament's demise and the creation of the Westminster assembly in 1643 represented

[24] Russell, *Causes*, p.147; for the losing argument see Coke, 7 *Reports*, fols. 2b–3a.

[25] Russell, *Causes*, p. 147; and his "Divine Rights in the Early Seventeenth Century," in John Morrill, Paul Slack, and Daniel Woolf, eds., *Public Duty and Private Conscience in Seventeenth-Century England: Essays Presented to G. E. Aylmer* (Oxford, 1993), pp. 101–120, esp. 103–104; see also David L. Smith, "The Idea of the Rule of Law in England and France in the Seventeenth Century," in Ronald G. Asch and Heinz Duchhardte, eds., *Der Absolutismus – ein Mythos? Strukturwandel monarchischer Herrschaft in West- und Mitteleuropa (ca. 1550–1700)* (Cologne, 1996), pp. 167–184.

[26] Johann P. Sommerville, "The Royal Supremacy and Episcopacy '*Jure Divino*,' 1603–1640," *JEH* 34 (1983): 548–558.

[27] Sommerville, "Royal Supremacy": 558.

threats to the role of parliament and the civil magistrate in ecclesiastical affairs. Both threatened to raise an ecclesiastical assembly *above* the civil magistrate.

The central thrust of the charges against Laud was that he had during the personal rule usurped a jurisdiction greater than that properly belonging to the king or king-in-parliament and further claimed to hold this jurisdiction *iure divino*. This usurped jurisdiction was both legislative-judicial (the two were inseparable) as well as ecclesiastical. What is striking about the prosecution's arguments is that they made no significant use of radical constitutionalist arguments deriving from notions of consent and original popular sovereignty. Such arguments had already been articulated both by Prynne in his *Sovereign Power of Parliaments and Kingdomes* and by Henry Parker in his *Observations* of 1642. Later in the decade groups such as the Levellers pushed them to more populist conclusions and the same order of arguments played a foundational role in the prosecution's case against the king in 1649.[28] This scheme conceived of England as a popular state from time out of mind and reduced the king from the status of sovereign to that of chief magistrate. The king wielded magisterial power only by the consent of the governed and held his powers not directly from God but from the people who were, in the created order of things, the original of government under God. Because the king's powers were merely magisterial they were subject to revocation should he act beyond the scope of his office. Ideas of original popular sovereignty were of course not new; however, they were not necessarily dangerous to the king's throne or person. For example, according to Sommerville, they often received an "absolutist twist" in the hands of civil lawyers who combined them with the notion that under no conditions was the original grant of power to the king revocable. This made the king a sovereign in every sense of the word.[29]

Laud's defense was potent if only because, from his own recollections, he obviously understood the gravity of the charges against him. This was a man of not inconsiderable learning not only in the classics and the scriptures but in the civil law and in much of the current political theory of the day. For example, in refuting the Scots' attempts to justify their rebellion Laud cited not only the example of the early Christians but also the authorities of Bodin

[28] The conciliarist origins of early modern constitutionalism has been traced in some detail in a recent article by Francis Oakely, "'Anxieties of Influence': Skinner, Figgis, Conciliarism and Early Modern Constitutionalism," *P&P* 151 (1996): 60–110; for the king's trial and radical constitutionalism see chapter 6, below.

[29] Sommerville suggests that this was the case in instances where the king had gained his kingdom by conquest and no conditions had been imposed by the tacit consent of the governed: Johann P. Sommerville, *Politics and Ideology in England, 1603–1640* (London, 1986), pp. 68–69.

and Hugo Grotius, with whom he had a correspondence.[30] Furthermore, Laud seems to have realized from an early date in the proceedings that the idea of treason against the state, under the existing law, necessarily constituted a treason against the king and that current political theory could furnish his opponents with the idea of treason as a crime committed purely against the state. The clearest evidence of this was in his remarks to the House of Lords on 26 February 1641 when the first set of articles against him were brought up to the upper house:

> My Lords – This is a great and heavy charge, and I must be unworthy to live if it can be made good against me; for it makes me against God, in point of religion; against the King in point of allegiance; and against the public, in point of safety, under the justice and protection of the law. And though the king be little if at all mentioned, yet I am bold to name him, because I have ever been of the opinion, that the King and his people are so joined together in one civil and political body, as that it is not possible for any man to be true to the King, as King, that shall be found treacherous to the State established by law, and work to the subversion of the people; though perhaps every one, that is so, is not able to see through all the consequences, by which one depends upon the other.[31]

The case against the Earl of Strafford could not have been put better by John Pym or Oliver St. John: the king and people formed a single corporate body united by the rule of law in which the subversion of the law or the people was necessarily also a subversion of the king. This was certainly treason against the state but not the abstract state – political authority under this conception of the king's two bodies remained, in keeping with the leading precedent of *Calvin's Case*, inextricably bound up with the person of a single individual. King and state were still one.

The argument is simply this: both sides in these trials were drawing on imperfectly shared ideologies, and political vocabularies. Political ideas were like a common stock of social knowledge subject to competing strategies of appropriation and deployment. Both sides sought to frame their arguments in such a way as to *persuade* the recalcitrant party, the fence-sitters, to support a certain practical agenda. This is an attempt not to diminish the role of political ideology in the study of early Stuart and Civil-War politics but to redefine it. Political ideas can have persuasive or *rhetorical* force over a subject or subject group only if they potentially value those ideas. For example, to dismiss the Levellers' use of the idea of an ancient constitution as *merely* rhetorical is to misconstrue the relationship of political ideas and political life.[32] Political *rhetoric* – the discussion and debate of political concepts such

[30] *Works* III, pp. 367–368. [31] *Works* III, p. 396.

[32] Burgess, *The Politics of the Ancient Constitution*, p. 91; for the Levellers and the ancient constitution see R. B. Seaberg, "The Norman Conquest and the Common Law: The Levellers and the Argument from Continuity," *HJ* 24 (1981): 791–806.

as the rule of law and the liberty of the subject – was as inseparable from the actual activity of politics in the seventeenth century as contemporary debates on the nature of community and freedom of speech are from the politics of modern western liberal democracies today. To make such judgments presumes that there is some *deeper* political reality that existed beneath that constituted in the political rhetorics of the age.[33]

The events of 1642 had necessitated a move to a more impersonal conception of allegiance in which loyalty was owed to the king's crown – his corporate political body. Essentially, this was the losing argument in *Calvin's Case*.[34] This has led Conrad Russell to argue that the events leading up to 1642 saw increasing deployment of the idea of an impersonal state first by the Scots and then by parliamentary polemicists. However, this state was not abstract in the sense that Quentin Skinner has attributed to Hobbes but merely abstract in that the king's public authority, his office, became separate from his person.[35] As with the king's two bodies, the state remained a "perpetual corporation."[36] The relationship of the head and members in the political body faced a process of redefinition: the idea of the corporate body of the king was reduced to an analog for an increasingly impersonal, yet still corporate, state.

Consequently, the doctrine of the inseparability of the king's two bodies that had underpinned the theory of constructive compassing in the trial of the Earl of Strafford became by the end of the 1640s a staple of royalist polemicists and progressively inconvenient for the parliamentarian leadership. As Figgis argued, the parliamentarians "pretended that the Parliament took up arms against the person only of the King, but in support of his authority."[37] Prynne, in his *Sovereign Power of Parliaments and Kingdomes*, was at great pains to assert that treason was a crime "not onely . . . against the King, but likewise, to and against the Realm," yet clung tenaciously to the idea of inseparability: it was not the Long Parliament that had effected a treasonable separation of the king's natural person from his public authority but his evil

33 I am influenced by two approaches here. The first is that of William E. Connolly discussed in chapter 2, above, and the second is the more phenomenologically influenced approach of Charles Taylor: William E. Connolly, *The Terms of Political Discourse*, 2nd edn. (Princeton, 1983), pp. 10–44; Charles Taylor, "Interpretation and the Sciences of Man," in *Philosophical Papers 2* (Cambridge, 1985), pp. 15–57.

34 Russell, *Causes*, pp. 157–158.

35 In a paper entitled, "Hobbes and the purely artificial person of the state," delivered in Cambridge in Michaelmas term 1996, Professor Skinner argued that the abstract conception of the state that Thomas Hobbes set forth in *Leviathan* was *not* a juristic person or corporation but something else more purely abstract.

36 Marie Axton, *The Queen's Two Bodies: Drama and the Elizabethan Succession* (London, 1977), p. 12.

37 Figgis, *Divine Right*, p. 223.

counselors who had drawn him away from his "legall and regall capacitie" in parliament.[38] The prosecutors in Laud's trial, however, made little if any reference to the ideas of constructive compassing and the king's two bodies that had proved so crucial in Strafford's trial and instead concentrated on Laud's usurpation of a higher jurisdiction than that to which he had a lawful right.[39] This was reflected in the prosecution's final argument before the Lords delivered by Samuel Browne on 4 January 1645. Browne asserted (1) that there were treasons at the common law not found in 25 Edward III; (2) that some of these treasons were "Treasons against the Realm" and "That Treason may be against the Realm as well as against the King"; and finally (3) that parliament was "the only judge" of treasons at common law or against the realm.[40] There was no significant attempt to link the case against Laud to the statute of 25 Edward III by construction.

The prosecution's arguments did not explicitly address questions concerning the origins of royal power, whether by divine right or the consent of the governed. The situation of 1644 put the parliamentarians in the awkward position of attempting to prosecute a man for treason against a king with whom, or with whose person at least, they were at war. The king's authority had become abstracted from his person in practice, even though parliamentarian barristers, particularly Prynne, still clung to the notion of inseparability in theory.[41] Neither side in the Civil War was eager to identify themselves openly with the losing side in *Calvin's Case* and the treacherous Despensers of the fourteenth century. Indeed, the *legal* arguments for resistance depended heavily on the winning arguments in *Calvin's Case* and the identification of the king's party as a malignant body of conspirators drawing the king away to Oxford and away from his lawful place at the head of his parliament.[42] Yet, through all, treason remained defined as the usurpation of regal and sovereign power. The crowning irony of this situation was that the Long Parliament had by 1644 clearly (1) levied war on the king (or his person at least); (2) counterfeited the great seal after it had been removed to Oxford; and (3) adhered to the king's enemies (i.e. the rebel Scots).

Laud's trial was distinguishable from that of Strafford in two other key aspects. Firstly, there is the question of institutional context. Both men were tried by process of impeachment and ultimately attainder in the Long

38 William Prynne, *The Sovereign Power of Parliaments and Kingdomes: Divided into Fovr Parts Together with an Appendix* (London 1643), sigs. L4v–M3r, pp. 108–111.

39 Conrad Russell, "The Theory of Treason in the Trial of Strafford," *EHR* 80 (1965): 46.

40 *LJ* VII: 125.

41 D. Alan Orr, "England, Ireland, Magna Carta, and the Common Law: The Case of Connor Lord Maguire, Second Baron of Enniskillen," *JBS* 39 (2000): 403–404; and chapter 6, below.

42 I somewhat disagree with the position of Professor Russell here; see chapter 2, above – especially my discussions of Prynne and John Marsh.

Parliament. Strafford was accused, impeached, attainted, then executed in a period of roughly six months, with his trial and attainder squeezed into a hectic seven-week period from late March to early May 1641. The procurement of his speedy execution was undoubtedly *the* priority of the Long Parliament during this period. The proceedings against Laud, by contrast, were a long, drawn-out process lasting slightly over three years, taking place in what Charles Carlton has described as "a strange atmosphere of indifference and intense hatred that fed on the memory of wrongs done long before."[43] While Strafford was tried over a period of consecutive days in a marathon series of hearings, Laud's trial did not commence until 12 March 1644 and, with hearings often held weeks apart, lasted until the end of July.[44] Laud made his recapitulation on 2 September and the prosecution followed on 11 September. The archbishop's counsel spoke on point of law on 11 October.[45] On 2 November Laud learned that an ordinance of attainder had been drafted against him but that it would not be pressed against him until the charges had been summed up.[46] That same day Samuel Browne summed up for the prosecution and Laud secured time until 11 November to make his answer.[47] On 13 November Browne replied to Laud's defense and the ordinance of attainder was promptly introduced, passing the Commons on 16 November and the Lords on 4 January 1645.[48] Laud finally bowed before the executioner's axe on 10 January 1645.

After the autumn of 1642 the Long Parliament was at war and the business of running the war took priority. A combination of defections to the king at Oxford and chronic widespread absenteeism resulting from the demands of the war effort had severely depleted the judicial body of parliament, the House of Lords.[49] Laud remarked that "at the greatest presence that was any day of my hearing, there were not above fourteen, and usually not above eleven or twelve." Laud lamented further that, "of these, one third part at least, each day took [leave], or had occasion to be gone, before the charge was gone, before the charge of the day was half given."[50] While Strafford's trial had demanded the rapt attention of the Long Parliament, the parliamentarian peerage now faced the time-consuming business of "baronial revolt," which severely limited the attention that could be devoted to the archbishop's

[43] Charles Carlton, *Archbishop William Laud* (London, 1987), p. 216.

[44] *Works* IV, p. 370.

[45] *Works* IV, pp. 386–399; HMC Lords XI: 464–467.

[46] *Works* IV, p. 401.

[47] *Works* IV, pp. 401–402.

[48] *Works* IV, p. 419; C. H. Firth and R. S. Rait, eds., *Acts and Ordinances of the Interregnum* (London, 1911), vol. I, p. 608; *LJ* VI: 125–127.

[49] For the House of Lords as a court of judicature during the Civil War see James S. Hart, *Justice Upon Petition: The House of Lords and the Reformation of Justice, 1621–1675* (London, 1991), ch. 5.

[50] *Works* IV, p. 49.

cause.[51] Indeed, the trial of Laud may have not taken place were it not for pressure from the Long Parliament's Scottish allies,[52] and it was only with the formation of the Long Parliament's alliance with the Scots that the proceedings against Laud resumed in earnest.

The protracted nature of Laud's trial meshes well with the more impressionistic evidence that his defense was a better-quality effort than that of Strafford. Laud had not only more time to prepare and the lessons of Strafford's ordeal to draw on but also, in the persons of John Herne and Matthew Hale, he received a strong caliber of legal counsel.[53] Herne was an experienced barrister in high-profile trials. His past experience included serving as counsel to the barrister Henry Sherfield, Recorder of Salisbury, on a charge in Star Chamber for defacing an offending stained-glass window in St. Edmund's Church, Salisbury in 1632 and, ironically, as counsel to Prynne during his 1634 Star Chamber trial for the publication of his controversial work against female players *Histriomastix*.[54] Hale was one of the brightest young legal minds in the country and well on his way to a stellar career in the law that would culminate in his appointment as Lord Chief Justice of England under Charles II. Furthermore, while Strafford was dogged by ill health throughout his ordeal, Laud was not subject to the same fatiguing routine of daily grillings, albeit that he was over seventy years of age. (Conversely, the idle time spent in the Tower between hearings can only have worsened the already considerable stress of a man on trial for his life.) Ironically, Laud's arguably stronger defense was in an even more hopeless situation: with the Civil War raging and the Scots clamoring for his head there was no hope like that Strafford had entertained, that the king would rescue him with a dissolution. At the final hour the Long Parliament even ignored the royal pardon issued at Oxford. At best Laud could only hope

[51] For the behavior of the parliamentary peerage and their role in the first Civil War see J. S. A. Adamson, "The Baronial Context of the English Civil War," *TRHS* 5th Ser. 40 (1990): 93–120.

[52] William Palmer, "Invitation to a Beheading: Factions in Parliament, the Scots and the Execution of Archbishop William Laud in 1645," *Historical Magazine of the Protestant Episcopal Church* 52 (1983): 17–27.

[53] While Laud had originally requested Herne among his list of potential counsel, Hale was assigned by the Long Parliament. His original choices included Richard Lane, who had been Strafford's counsel, and Thomas Gardiner, the Recorder of London, both of whom were denied to him. His counsel assigned on 4 March 1641 were Herne, Hale, Newdigate, Wyndham, and Merrick. When the impeachment was resumed in October 1643 the Long Parliament assigned John Herne and Chaloner Chute on 24 October. Sir Mathew Hale was added on 28 October and Richard Gerrard was assigned later, on 16 January 1644. His counsel at the trial, by his own account, were "Mr. Hern, and Mr. Hales of Lincoln's-Inn, and Mr. Gerrard of Gray's-Inn": *LJ* IV: 174, 176; *LJ* VI: 271, 282, 381; William Prynne, *Canterburies Doome*... (London 1646), pp. 42, 46; *Works* IV, p. 386.

[54] *New DNB*, "John Herne."

for a decisive royalist military victory. This possibility dimmed considerably after news reached Westminster on 24 July 1644 of the fall of York in the wake of the combined Scots and parliamentarian victory at Marston Moor – the largest land engagement of the war.[55]

The second aspect had to do with the structure of the charges. The articles against Strafford consisted of seven general and twenty-eight specific articles. The latter were very detailed, citing specific instances where Strafford's conduct revealed a treasonable intent to subvert the law. Laud's impeachment, by contrast, proceeded in two sets of articles: one, first read to the accused on 26 February 1641, consisting of fourteen charges[56] and the second, consisting of ten additional articles, brought up on 23 October 1643, well after the commencement of hostilities in the autumn of 1642. In contrast to Strafford's trial the charges did not always specifically recount the instances where Laud's particular words and actions were interpreted as treasonable. The particulars were not always included in the charge. Another difficulty arising was that, while the original articles preferred only a charge of high treason, the second set of articles charged the prelate with "High Treason, and divers High Crimes and Misdemeanors."[57] This raised for Laud's defense the troublesome issue of linkage with a lesser cause of action.

On 31 October Laud petitioned that the articles of misdemeanor be distinguished from those of high treason.[58] This was an obvious attempt to shield himself against a charge of cumulative treason and undoubtedly reflected the input of Hale and Herne. Laud wrote at the time that "My counsel told me plainly, I were as good have no counsel, if the Articles were not distinguished; for they were so woven one with another, and so knit up together in the conclusion, that they might refer all to treason, and so they be suffered to give me no counsel at all in matter of fact."[59] Linkage meant that proofs to lesser charges were also proofs to the more general charges. Laud and his counsel resumed their call for their separation on 13 November 1643, when he entered his plea of "not guilty," but was ultimately unsuccessful in forcing the prosecution to distinguish articles of treason from misdemeanor.[60]

55 *Works* IV, p. 339.
56 The original articles represent a bibliographical conundrum as they are not present in the printed *Lord's Journal*. The copy in Laud's *Works* contains minor yet significant, omissions. Most notable is the repeated exclusion of the potentially incriminating word "procure" from Laud's copy of these articles. The Anglo-Catholic Library edition of Laud's *Works* catalogues these textual variations in great detail, establishing that the copies of the articles in Prynne and Rushworth are fairly consistent with each other: *Works* III, pp. 398–432.
57 *LJ* VI: 267.
58 *Works* IV, pp. 36–37; Prynne, *Canterburies Doome*, p. 42; *LJ* VI: 284–285.
59 *Works* IV, p. 37; *LJ* VI: 285.
60 *Works* IV, pp. 38–39, 43; *LJ* VI: 303.

The body of this chapter considers the articles of impeachment brought against Laud and analyzes the arguments advanced on either side of the debate. Certain similarities with the trial of the Earl of Strafford three years earlier become evident. This is especially the case with the early articles that concerned the counseling and procuring of extra-parliamentary taxation and the raising of proclamations above acts of parliament. However, while the religious aspects of Strafford's charges were dropped in favor of more purely constitutional concerns, in Laud's trial constitutional issues were inextricably bound up with debates on the nature of the royal supremacy. The attack on the clerical estate in the early Long Parliament, of which Laud's impeachment was a crucial part, lumped legal and constitutional perceptions of misrule together with the religious. One might expect the debate emerging from the trial to be one of a personal versus a parliamentary conception of the supremacy. However, the controversy that emerged was not one of royal prerogative versus parliament but one of parliamentary Erastianism opposing strong clerical autonomy.

There is an inherent danger in presuming an easy coherence between Laud's views as expressed at the trial and his public statements made during the personal rule – statements that his prosecutors often drew into evidence against him. Even if Laud had been the epitome of servile clerical absolutism during the 1630s, this did not preclude a shift to a more stridently clericalist position after 1642, when the king's power to protect and promote Laud's interests fell into abeyance with Laud's incarceration and the outbreak of hostilities. The picture that emerged as the trial proceeded was not one of a servile clerical absolutist sheltering under the prerogative, as Sommerville's argument would suggest, but of an ardent clericalist claiming his jurisdiction by divine right and defending it against what he saw as the usurpation of the king and state. If Laud was tried for religion, it was because his triers assumed that religion was the proper provenance of the state and civil magistrate and that the archbishop had unlawfully usurped on that ground.

III

The trial opened on 12 March 1644, at which time the managers of the commons' evidence made their opening statements with Sergeant Wilde accusing Laud of "treason in the highest altitude."[61] The committee appointed to manage the evidence consisted of John Wilde, Samuel Browne, Sir John Maynard and Robert Nicholas. A fifth manager, Robert Hill, was "Consul Bibulus" and did not speak. William Prynne, according to Laud, "was trusted

[61] *Works* IV, p. 55.

with the providing of all the evidence, and was relater and prompter, and all, never weary of anything so he might do me mischief."[62] Maynard was the only holdover from the team that had prosecuted Strafford. Nicholas, the outspoken barrister sitting for Devizes Wiltshire, had been prominent among those speaking for the earl's attainder during the debates of mid-April 1641 and would later became a Baron of the Exchequer under the Protectorate.[63] Samuel Browne, a barrister of Lincoln's Inn, was Oliver St. John's first cousin, a man that Valerie Pearl has described as St. John's "close ally" and who seems to have shared his cousin's Erastian sentiments.[64]

The following day, 13 March, the committee proceeded to the articles of impeachment. The first two articles were the first and second original articles and the second additional.[65] The first article made the general charge that Laud had "traitorously endeavoured to subvert the fundamental laws and government of the kingdom, and instead thereof to introduce an arbitrary government against law." It charged further that the archbishop had advised the king "that he might at his own will and pleasure levy and take money of his subjects, without their consent in Parliament" and that he had also affirmed that this "was warrantable by the law of God."[66] These charges of the subversion of the law and the counseling of extra-parliamentary taxation were familiar ground, bearing close similarity to those against Strafford. The second original concerned the advising and procuring of the preaching, printing, and publishing of "divers sermons and other discourses ... in which the authority of parliaments, and the force of the laws of this kingdom are denied, and an absolute and unlimited power over the persons and estates of his Majesty's subjects is maintained and defended." Significantly, Laud was charged with maintaining this power "not only in the King, but also in himself, and other bishops."[67] The charge was not only the maintenance and promotion of a power above law but the clerical assumption of that power. The second additional article bore a striking resemblance to the fourth specific article against the Earl of Strafford that he had endeavored to make acts of state, or Council Board in Ireland as binding as acts of parliament on the people of that kingdom.[68] It charged, in a similar vein, that Laud had "endeavoured to advance the Power of the Council Table, the Canons of the Church, and the King's Prerogative, above the Laws and Statutes of

62 *Works* IV, p. 47.

63 In spite of Wiltshire's well-known reputation for rottenness, Nicholas was not only a native of the region he represented but also the borough recorder: see *New DNB*, "Robert Nicholas."

64 Pearl, "Oliver St. John and the 'middle group'": 505.

65 HMC, Lords XI: 365; *Works* IV, p. 68.

66 The charge in Prynne and Rushworth reads "this kingdom of England" instead of simply "the kingdom": *Works* III, p. 398.

67 *Works* III, p. 400.

68 Rushworth, *Tryal*, p. 63.

the Realm." The article also charged specific words against the archbishop as evidence of this treasonable intent. Firstly, it was charged that "about six years last past," Laud as a privy counselor sitting in counsel had said, "'That as long as he sat there, they should know that an Order of that Board should be of equal Force with a Law, or Act of Parliament," and secondly, that at another point in time he had said "'That he hoped, ere long, that Canons of the Church and the King's Prerogative should be of as great Power as an Act of Parliament." Finally, it was charged that Laud, in an allusion to Mathew 21: 44 had said, "That those that would not yield to the King's Power, he would crush them to Pieces."[69]

This charge was aimed at the methods of the personal rule, most notably government by proclamation without parliamentary consultation. The role of the king in all this was problematic. While the Long Parliament were in reality at war with the king, managers of Laud's impeachment continued to maintain the fiction that they were acting in the king's name with the king's authority. For the Erastians of the Long Parliament, however, "king" as a legal expression clearly meant king-in-parliament, and only king-in-parliament could lawfully declare what was law in statute – not king-in-convocation. The usurpation of sovereign power remained the essence of the charge. This was similar to much of the charge against Strafford with one key difference. The charge of raising the canons of the clergy to equal the strength of acts of parliament suggested the essentially *clerical* nature of this usurpation.

The prosecution produced the deposition of Sir Henry Vane the elder in support of the charge of advising the king to levy extra-parliamentary subsidies. This asserted that on 5 May 1640 at the dissolution of the Short Parliament Laud had said at the council table "that his majesty having been refused supply from his parliament, he might lawfully now make use of his owne power, or words to that effect."[70] Laud in answer to this charge later in the day questioned the case in fact and appealed to procedural codicils rather than addressing the case in law. He questioned the validity of Vane's single testimony, alluding to the two-witness rule established by 1 Edward VI, c. 12, and cited the statute of 1 Elizabeth, c. 6 to the effect that treasonable words were to be investigated within six months of their speaking.[71] He also

[69] *LJ* VI: 267. [70] HMC Lords XI: 366.

[71] Laud in his *History* admitted that he was mistaken in citing 1 Elizabeth, c. 6, which had expired, and that he should have cited 1 Elizabeth, c. 1, which also stipulated a six-month limitation period and yet remained in force. W. R. Stacy has argued that Laud was confused by a printing error in the third part of Coke's *Institutes* where 1 Elizabeth, c. 6. was confused with 1 Elizabeth, c. 5, which also stipulated a six-month period: *Works* IV, p. 72; HMC Lords XI: 366; *SL* II: 520: W. R. Stacy, "The Bill of Attainder in English History," unpublished Ph.D. dissertation (University of Wisconsin Madison, 1986), p. 384.

made the further argument that the decision to seek extra-parliamentary revenue was the collective act of the council and "that cannot be called or accounted my counsel."[72] This would be a recurring strategy as he sought to assign responsibility for actions charged to him individually either to the body of the king's council, the courts of Star Chamber and High Commission as advisory and judicial bodies, or, in the case of the 1640 canons, the body of the convocation. He also claimed that his counsels and actions fell within the Act of Oblivion passed by the Long Parliament with regard to the Bishops' Wars, as the charges related "to the Scottish business."[73] Furthermore, he denied that there was anything pertinent in the diary that could be used as proof to his counseling of extra-parliamentary taxation.[74]

The following particulars concerned the actual collection of extra-parliamentary levies of ship money and tonnage and poundage. The first witness was one Samuell Sherman of Essex, who was "with others fetched up by pursuevant to the Counsell table for refusing to be collectors for shipping mony." Sherman had argued before council table that his town being an inland town was not a *maritime* and therefore not eligible to pay ship money. Laud disagreed and Sherman was committed to the Fleet for three weeks and eleven silver spoons of Sherman's possession were taken as payment, "which was as much as [the] 11 subsidies he was rated."[75] Laud once again asserted that this was the order of council table, not his own, and that Sherman only "believed" Laud to be the author of his misfortune and spoke "not positively."[76]

The second witness was Alderman Atkins of the City of London who, as Sherriff of London, had been reprimanded at council table for the tardy collection of ship money. He deposed that none had been "soe violent against him as the Bishop" and that Laud had pressed the Attorney-General to proceed against him in Star Chamber.[77] Alderman Adams deposed that he and another alderman, Warner, faced similar threats of Star Chamber prosecution when called to the council table concerning the slow collection of ship money.[78] Alderman Chambers deposed that Laud had been behind his Star Chamber sentence of 300*l.* fine and imprisonment for refusing to pay tonnage and poundage. The Archbishop had purportedly accused Chambers of taking away the king's bread and told him that, "if the king had many such chambers he should not have a *chamber* to putt his head in."[79]

[72] *Works* IV, p. 71.
[73] *Works* IV, p. 72; this strategy appears to have borne fruit with respect to article 13, which was dropped.
[74] *Works* IV, p. 71. [75] HMC Lords XI: 367.
[76] *Works* IV, pp. 73–74; HMC Lords XI: 367. [77] HMC Lords XI: 367.
[78] HMC Lords XI: 368. [79] HMC Lords XI: 367.

The evidence that Laud had sought to raise royal proclamations above acts of parliament derived from a Star Chamber case from May 1633. The business concerned three soap-makers hauled before Star Chamber for disobeying a royal proclamation concerning the regulation of their trade. The first of these, Edwin Griffin, deposed that Laud "used many high speeches of their *rebellion* in disobeying a proclamacion of the Kings," and then said, "If he lived and satt in that place he would make a *proclamation* as available as an act of parliament." The bishop then purportedly cited Mathew 21: 44 in describing the king's power that "on whomsoever it shall fall, it will grind him to powder."[80] His deposition was supported by two other soap-makers, one Thomas Woodsto[c]k and one John Hay.[81]

Laud's response revealed that he shared with his opponents a conception of treason as the unlawful abrogation of sovereign power. He denied explicitly speaking the words concerning proclamations and acts of parliament. As for the citation from Mathew 21: 44, he did not deny making the allusion but asserted that "He spoke it not as if the king any unlegall way should fall upon any man, but he meant it if any should take the king's just authority out of his hand, the law would fall upon him."[82] The evidence from Laud's *History* also indicates that the Archbishop was aware of the potential seriousness of this charge: "tis impossible these words should be spoken by me. For I think no man in this honourable presence thinks me so ignorant, as that I should not know the vast difference that is between an Act of Parliament and a Proclamation."[83] Strafford, when faced with similar accusations, had asserted that proclamations had equal force with acts of parliament provided they conformed to fundamental law and did not contravene statute. Laud took a safer route and simply denied the case in fact and accused his accusers of perjuring themselves.

The next witness was a Mr. Talbois concerning enclosures and depopulations. Talbois deposed, "that he was sent for to appeare before the Councell table concerning inclosures and *depopulacion*, which was pretended to be made [at] Tetbury [Salisbury] in Gloucestershire."[84] Appearing before council table Laud purportedly told him not to enclose his land and when Talbois pleaded a statute of 39 Elizabeth for enclosures "and desired he might be left to the tryall of the lawe" the archbishop responded: "*doe yee come to plead law here;* goe to your inferiour Courts and plead law there; And goe to the committee in the Country and attend them."[85] Laud responded that

[80] *Works* IV, pp. 75–76; HMC Lords XI: 368; the quotation is taken directly from the authorized King James version.
[81] HMC Lords XI: 368; Thomas Wood and Richard Hayles in *Works* IV, p. 368.
[82] HMC Lords XI: 366–367. [83] *Works* IV, p. 76.
[84] HMC Lords XI: 368. [85] HMC Lords XI: 369.

he had not acted alone in fining Talbois 50*l.* but had sat with Lord Privy Seal and Secretary Coke.[86] Laud also asserted that Talbois was but a single witness and testifying in his own cause.[87]

The next particular had to do with Laud's "printing of books, which asserted the King's prerogative above the Law, etc." mentioned in the second original article.[88] The individual texts in question were John Cowell's *Interpreter* of 1607 with its controversial definition of the royal prerogative, reprinted in 1637, and Roger Manwaring 's sermons in favor of the Forced Loan as well as works by Peter Heylin and Christopher Dove. Laud was also charged with preferring these men to livings and bishoprics in spite of their objectionable views and, in the case of Manwaring, preferring him in spite of his disablement by the 1628 parliament.[89] Laud in his defense asserted that the reprinting of Cowell's controversial legal dictionary was not at his command and was not licensed by him. He also denied that the printer Hodgkinson, who had produced the 1637 edition, was his printer but "had his whole dependence on Sir Henry Martin," the Dean of Arches.[90] Laud also argued that Cowell's *Interpreter*, while condemned "in such particulars" as its controversial definition of the royal prerogative, was "for other things ... very useful."[91] The preferment of Manwaring to St. David's, he argued, was the work of Lord Conway and the preferment of Heylin to the prebendary of Westminster was by the Earl of Danby.[92]

The charge that Laud had procured pardons and appointments rather than merely advised or recommended them was potentially very serious. Power "to graunt pardons and dispensations against the rigour of the law" was, according to Bodin, one of the marks of sovereignty as was power to appoint officers of state. Under the royal supremacy in England the king held all powers of ecclesiastical appointment – theoretically free from both clerical

86 The HMC says only "the Earl of Manchester etc.": HMC Lords XI: 369; *Works* IV, p. 77.

87 The HMC account reads with more direct reference to the second original article "That he procured diverse *sermons* and *bookes* to be made against the authority of parliament": HMC Lords XI: 367; *Works* III, p. 400; IV, p. 77.

88 *Works* IV, p. 78.

89 HMC Lords XI; *Works* IV, pp. 77–80; Prynne argued that Laud had been instrumental not only in the preferment of Manwaring and Richard Montague (censured by parliament for his supposedly Arminian views) but also in "procuring" them pardons from the king in January 1628. Manwaring was preferred to the rectory of St. Giles in 1628, the Deanery of Worcester in 1633, and finally the Welsh see of St. Davids in 1635: Prynne, *Canterburies Doome*, pp. 352–353.

90 *Works* IV, pp. 79–80; the account in the HMC reads: "Hodskin was none of his printer. He was put in by Sir H. Marten, and he put him out": HMC Lords XI: 367.

91 Being one of the first attempts to compile a comprehensive legal dictionary in England there was undoubtedly something in this claim: *Works* IV, p. 80.

92 HMC Lords XI: 368.

and papal control.[93] Laud defended his actions in approving Manwaring's appointment to St. David's, arguing that "He was bound to consecrate him, else he should have into a praemunire. The King commanded him to put him in minde of Dr. Manwaring; which he did, but withall put his majesty in minde of the sentence of this house against him."[94] By arguing that the pardon and preferment of Manwaring had been by Laud's *procurement* and not by the king's command the prosecution neatly side-stepped the question of whether the king could make commands against law. The king, of course, could do no wrong. Laud had engineered Manwaring's appointment in derogation of the king's supremacy.

Here the barrier between praemunire and treason became blurred as it understandably would when seen through an Erastian lens. Both were similar in structure: the unlawful assumption of royal jurisdiction. Praemunire concerned itself with, in Elton's words, "punishing all invasions of 'the king's regality' – especially any activity of the ecclesiastical courts that diminished the authority of the king's courts – with loss of property and imprisonment at pleasure."[95] While subject to broad definition this usually referred to the ecclesiastical courts' usurpation of the jurisdiction of the king's courts or the making of canons prejudicial to the king and the realm.[96] Laud referred to it in the sense that the refusing to grant the king's pleasure in appointing Manwaring to a bishopric would constitute a derogation of the king's spiritual authority. The threat of this legal sanction was at least as important as the law of treason in the implementation of Henry VIII's Reformation. However, in Laud's trial the instrument that the Long Parliament chose to oppose Laud's clericalism was the law of treason. For the Erastians who tried Laud the powers of defining religious doctrine and enforcing ecclesiastical discipline were both state powers, and treason was the unlawful usurpation of the powers of the state. The result was that the prosecution's case rested heavily on the almost total conflation of treason with the lesser cause of

93 Jean Bodin, *Six Bookes of a Commonweale*, trans. Richard Knolles and ed. Kenneth D. McRae (Cambridge Mass., 1962), p. 162 [161]; and for the supremacy see chapter 2, above.

94 HMC Lords XI: 368; the passage in *Works* confirms this: "That he was after consecrated by me is true likewise; and I hope tis not expected I should ruine myself, and fall into a *Praemunire*, by refusing the king's royal assent; and this for fear lest it might be thought I procured his preferment. But the truth is, his Majesty commanded me to put him in mind of him when preferments fell, and I did so; but withal I told his Majesty of his censure, and that I feared ill construction would be made of it": *Works* IV, p. 83.

95 G. R. Elton, *The Tudor Constitution: Documents and Commentary*, 2nd edn. (Cambridge, 1982) p. 339; for the relationship of the ecclesiastical and common-law courts in the century after the Reformation see R. Helmholz, *Roman Canon Law in Reformation England* (Cambridge, 1990), ch. 5.

96 See chapter 1, above, for statutory definitions.

praemunire. Indeed, the indictment of Cardinal Wolsey described praemunire as a subversion of the law and Sir Edward Coke adopted this language in the third volume of his *Institutes*, describing praemunire as a "subversion of the common law."[97]

The perceived clerical nature of this usurpation manifested itself in the inclusion of the 1640 canons and the clerical subsidy voted by the convocation of 1640 in the charges.[98] In 1641 Edward Bagshawe, a future royalist, had attacked the canons of 1640 in a printed parliamentary speech as violating the statutes of praemunire, arguing "that no Cannons can bind the Laiety and Clergy, without consent in Parliament: and therefore these Cannons made against the Laiety, as well as the Clergy, without their assent, cannot bind."[99] Convocation had passed both the seventeen canons of 1640 and the clerical subsidy at the same sitting *after* the dissolution of the Short Parliament on 5 May 1640, precluding parliamentary ratification.[100] To the Erastian faction this represented the raising of a clerical assembly above parliament. The canons of 1604 had, of course, not been ratified by act of parliament, but their status was debatable. In the Short Parliament almost four years earlier John Pym had argued that these canons "had produced ill effects[.] And therefore the Howse should nowe be more vigilant."[101] Prynne's partial and highly prejudiced account of the trial went farther than this. When Laud, defending the use of copes in cathedrals, appealed to canon 24 of 1604 to justify their use, the prosecution replied that the canon "was never any binding Law confirmed by Parliament, and expired with King *Iames*, if nor [sic] before."[102] The 1604 canons had at best the strength of a proclamation and were only valid during King James's lifetime.

While it is foolish to read such a highly tainted source as *Canterburies Doome* as an historically accurate depiction of the actual events of Laud's trial, the text still merits scrutiny as an example of the ideological position from which Laud was attacked in the Long Parliament. Read as an expression of Prynne's parliamentary Erastianism it is a valuable and historically

97 The praemunire indictment of Wolsey is cited in Sir Edward Coke, 12 *Reports*, 40; Coke, *The Third Part of the Institutes of the Laws of England: concerning High Treason, and other Pleas of the Crown, and Criminall causes* (London, 1644), p. 123.

98 *Works* IV, p. 87; HMC Lords XI: 372.

99 BL TT E.164(12), Edward Bagshawe, *Two Arguments in Parliament, the First Concerning the Cannons, the Second Concerning the Praemvnire vpon those Cannons* (London, 1641), p. 12.

100 A superb discussion of the constitutional issues involved in the continued sitting of the convocation of 1640 remains Esther S. Cope, "The Short Parliament of 1640 and Convocation," *JEH* 25 (1974): 167–184.

101 *Proceedings*, p. 175; interestingly it was canon 24 of 1604 that called for the wearing of copes.

102 Prynne, *Canterburies Doome*, p. 476.

"accurate" source consistent not only with the content of the articles of impeachment but also with other, more reliable, accounts of the trial. For example, in the suppressed "official" account of John Browne, the Clerk of Parliament, Sir John Maynard argued that the canons of 1640 were without precedent and that, "The Cannon in manner of monies cannot binde the Clergy until it be confirmed by act of parliament."[103] Objections of this order were also raised concerning the *et cetera* oath against popery stipulated in canon 6. This canon was particularly controversial because it stipulated that the oath was to be administered not only to the clergy but also to a substantial section of the laity.[104] Browne was arguably almost as hostile and "Puritan" a chronicler as Prynne; however, he can at least be relied on to report accurately the ideological position of his own faction.[105]

Similarly, Laud's *History*, first published from the original manuscript in 1694, should not be read simply as a practical journal kept as a useful device in organizing his defense. It was also a clericalist apologetic written for posterity. Accordingly, Laud's position was more complicated. He claimed that he had expressed concern to the king over the legality of convocation's continued sitting after the dissolution of the Short Parliament, especially when there was "some little exception" raised in the lower house of convocation.[106] Lord Keeper Finch, he recalled, had assured him of the legality of convocation's further sitting and he cited the written legal opinion signed by Finch and several prominent jurists to the effect that: "The Convocation being called by the King's writ, under the Great Seal, doth continue, until it be dissolved by writ, or commission under the Great Seal, notwithstanding the Parliament be dissolved."[107] Laud argued that "according to the power given us under the Broad Seal, as is requireth by the statute 25 Henry VIII, cap. 19" – the submission of the clergy – he had proceeded both to make the canons and to make up "our Act perfect for the gift of six subsidies, according to ancient form in that behalf, and delivered it under

[103] HMC Lords XI: 374 and also 372: "Subsidies to be paid by the Clergy were granted against lawe, being not confirmed by parliament."

[104] This formed the basis of the ninth additional article: see HMC Lords XI: 372; *LJ* VI: 267; St. John objected to the oath from the start of the Long Parliament, claiming that it was clearly intended to bind the laity as well as the clergy: Wallace Notestein, ed., *The Journal of Sir Simonds D'Ewes from the beginning of the Long Parliament to the opening of the Trial of the Earl of Strafford* (New Haven, 1923), pp. 153–154.

[105] Lamont, *Marginal Prynne*, p. 120.

[106] *Works* III, pp. 285–286: Clarke MS LXXI, 16 April 1644.

[107] *Works* III, p. 286; The names subscribed to the opinion were: John Finch, Lord Keeper, Henry Montague, Earl of Manchester, John Bramston CJKB, Edward Littleton CJCP, Ralph Whitfield, Sergeant at Law, John Bankes AG, and Robert Heath, Sergeant at Law.

seal to his Majesty."[108] In support of the latter practice he cited a precedent of Archbishop Whitgift's time (1586).[109]

Strictly speaking, the making of canons for the Church of England did not require an act of parliament but only the royal assent.[110] Indeed, as Esther S. Cope has shown, Pym's arguments for a parliamentary conception of the supremacy depended not on any construction of 25 Henry VIII, c. 19 but on a number of precedents from the fourteenth century when the English parliament made a number of strongly anti-clerical pronouncements. Pym and Hampden led the attack on convocation and its powers in the Short Parliament because they saw convocation as a threat to the powers of parliament.[111] Laud was probably right to balk at the legality of convocation's continued sitting. However, any attempt to impose an arbitrary and anachronistic standard of legality on Laud's and the king's actions in reasserting the legislative independence of the clergy is doomed to fail because the issue was not exactly crystal-clear to contemporaries during the Civil War. That the act for the submission of the clergy did not stipulate that canons of the church must be confirmed by parliament is less relevant than the fact that many English at the time vigorously argued that canons required parliamentary confirmation. This was the case in 1604 as it was the case in 1640 and again in 1644. The task here is not to judge the *legality* of Laud's impeachment but instead to reconstruct the myriad of shifting ideological positions from the available evidence.

The particular of the case of St. Paul's School was put forward in maintenance of the charge in the second additional article that Laud had sought to raise the canons of the church above acts of parliament. The issue was whether or not the Mercers Company "to the care of which . . . that school some way belongs" could turn out the schoolmaster, Dr. Gill, without the consent of their bishop.[112] When the mercers appeared before the archbishop

108 *Works* III, pp. 286 and 286–291, *passim*.

109 *Works* III, p. 286; HMC Lords XI: 368; Julian Davies has noted Peter Heylyn's possession of a document "which revealed that the Convocation of 1586 had granted Elizabeth I a benevolence outside parliamentary time . . . which Heylyn certainly made known as soon as Parliament was dissolved": Julian Davies, *The Caroline Captivity of the Church: Charles I and the Remoulding of Anglicanism* (Oxford, 1992), p. 254; Patrick Carter has challenged Davies's position on Charles's role in directing ecclesiastical policy, suggesting that Laud in fact played a far greater role in securing the 1640 clerical subsidy than he admitted at his trial: Patrick Carter, "Parliament, Convocation and the Granting of Clerical Supply in Early Modern England," *Parliamentary History* 19 (2000): 22–23.

110 *SL* II: 189–191.

111 Cope, "Short Parliament": 182–184; Sir Thomas Aston, *The Short Parliament (1640) Diary of Sir Thomas Aston*, ed. Judith Maltby, Camden 4th Ser. (London, 1988), pp. 28, 50–52.

112 *Works* IV, p. 80.

pleading an act of parliament for their actions they were told, according to the witness Samuel Bland, that,

> . . . nothing will doe it but an act of parliament . . . ye despise the King's prerogative; but will rescinde all acts that are against the cannons of the church[.] And I hope ere long it shall be seene, that cannons shall be of as great force or validity as an act of parliament, which ye soe much Idolyze and dote upon.[113]

Laud was quick to point out that Bland, an officer of the Mercer's company was a single witness in his own cause and denied that he had spoken the words in question.[114] Once again the tenor of the words charged against Laud were that he had endeavored the clerical usurpation of the law-giving power of king-in-parliament.

The third day of the hearing continued with more particular proofs to the second additional article that Laud had sought to raise canons and proclamations above acts of parliament. Many of the particulars concerned orders of council table in the city of London, such as the pulling down of houses around St. Paul's Cathedral, the forcing of people out of their houses in Cheapside, and the suppression of a brewery whose owners refused to enter into a bond of 1,000*l.* to desist from brewing with sea coal.[115] Other issues raised were the commitment of Burton, Bastwick, and Prynne to the island of Jersey by order of council table and the High Commission's powers of commitment exercised not only in the case of Prynne in 1629 but also, for example, in the cases of Thomas Foxily and Samuel Vassal.[116] Essentially, the day's proceedings represented an indictment of the administrative practices of the personal rule: legislation by proclamation of king-in-council and enforcement through the prerogative and ecclesiastical courts, most notably Star Chamber and High Commission.

W. J. Jones has explored the expansion of the jurisdiction of the prerogative courts during the personal rule.[117] Undoubtedly much of the impetus behind this development was driven by financial need. In the prolonged absence of a parliament the revenue derived from the fees charged and the fines imposed in the prerogative courts became invaluable. Furthermore, the courts were the only effective instruments available for administering and enforcing the policies of the personal rule, whether that was the tearing down of houses around St. Paul's or the collection of ship money. The theory of treason in the trials of Laud and Strafford bore in common the idea that the subversion of the law was the subversion of the ordinary course of justice at common law – a crime against jurisdiction. Indeed, many of the articles against Strafford and

[113] HMC Lords XI: 372. [114] *Works* IV, p. 80; HMC Lords XI: 369.
[115] HMC Lords XI: 374–375, 382–384; *Works* IV, pp. 92–99.
[116] HMC Lords XI: 377–378, 380–381.
[117] W. J. Jones, *Politics and the Bench* (London, 1971).

Laud concerned simply the denial of the ordinary course of justice at common law through the expansion of prerogative and ecclesiastical jurisdictions. As has been previously noted, because the law-giving power of the sovereign did not clearly differentiate the legislative from the judicial – power to "give law" was not simply power to command or legislate positive law but power also to judge. This disruption of the ordinary course of justice at common law constituted the erection of a sovereign jurisdiction standing apart, against, and potentially above that emanating from the crown.

Without imposing an anachronistic conception of legality on the particular cases cited in both trials it becomes clear that the role of the early modern state was largely juristic, arbitrating disputes between subjects and maintaining civil order. The contact that ordinary citizens had with the authority of the "state" was usually mediated through the magistrate, whether this was through the administration of the electoral process, serving on juries, holding office, involvement in a civil suit, or even being subject to criminal sanction. This is a comparatively weak conception of the "state." The early modern state may have been, at least potentially, "abstract," as Skinner has asserted, but it was a far cry from Hegel. It was certainly not secular. The picture of the early modern state that emerges from these impeachments was simply the constitutional order that defined ruler and ruled as a single corporate body constituted through fundamental law.

The third and fourth original articles, prosecuted on 22 and 28 March, were similar in that they both charged Laud with subverting the ordinary course of justice, identifying this with the subversion of the laws of the kingdom in general. The former charged that Laud "by letters, messages, threats, promises, and divers other ways, to judges and ministers of justice, interrupted and perverted, and ... hath endeavoured to interrupt and pervert, the course of justice, in his Majesty's Courts at Westminster." The article was, like many against Laud, vague on particulars. The fourth article was a more straightforward corruption charge. However, it was equally vague on particulars, asserting that Laud had "traitourously and corruptly sold justice to those that had causes depending before him, by colour of his ecclesiastical jurisdiction, as Archbishop, High Commissioner, Referee, or otherwise."[118]

The particulars to the third article were many and were concerned mainly with the jurisdictional issues arising from conflicts between the common-law and ecclesiastical courts and, in particular, writs of prohibition. Writs of prohibition, when obtained from the appropriate common-law judge, removed causes of action from ecclesiastical courts into the common-law courts. The

[118] *Works* IV, p. 401.

ecclesiastical courts were bound to give way when the writ was presented. Professor Helmholz has argued that common lawyers saw five instances in which writs of prohibition were warranted: (1) as a means of policing the jurisdictional boundaries between the ecclesiastical and common-law courts; (2) when the cause involved the interpretation of a statute – the exclusive right of the common-law courts; (3) matters involving the customary rights of the laity (to many common lawyers this included the lay impropriation of tithes); (4) when the common-law courts could provide a remedy and the ecclesiastical courts could not; and (5) as a means by which the king's judges "could legitimately supervise the exercise of ecclesiastical jurisdiction."[119] Civil Lawyers, according to Helmholz, "gave a limited kind of assent to the second and the fourth of these positions."[120]

The first particular concerning the case of the town of Colchester illustrated the problems of jurisdiction arising from disputes over the administration of the sacraments. The first witness, Samuel Burroughs, deposed that because he had refused to "*come up to the rayles* to receive the Sacrament" it was denied to him by his pastor, Thomas Newcomen.[121] Burroughs in response preferred an indictment against Newcomen and found himself promptly attached, imprisoned, and his goods attached by order of the High Commission.[122] When he requested he be set at liberty the mayor of Colchester "tould him no, he had received a letter from the Archbishop to the contrary; and he would obey that before the king's writt sealed with the King's seall." Burroughs was held for a number of weeks in the gatehouse and when he moved for a prohibition "a letter came to the Judges from the Archbishop and he was sent abacke againe to Colchester." Burroughs' testimony was undoubtedly heavily stage-managed but even so the alleged remarks of the mayor of Colchester represented a clear attempt to portray Laud as assuming a forensic jurisdiction above that emanating from the king. Laud, in response, suggested that the mayor had shown "no obedience to his majesty in saying those words," accusing Burroughs and the supporting witnesses of being "refractory . . . to the law and Government of the Church."[123]

Another example, more explicitly concerning prohibitions, was the case of George Combs. The particular arose from the refusal of Combs and others to pull down a pew in Austen Church in London as part of the "beautification" of the church according to the Laudian pattern.[124] Laud,

119 Helmholz, *Roman Canon Law*, pp. 172–173.
120 Helmholz, *Roman Canon Law*, p. 173.
121 HMC Lords XI: 385; "Newcommin," in *Works* IV, pp. 118–120.
122 The warrants for his commitment were under the archbishop's hand: HMC Lords XI: 385–386.
123 HMC Lords XI: 385.
124 HMC Lords XI: 393; Laud could not recall the name of the church in question: *Works* IV, p. 137.

then Bishop of London, had objected that the pew stood above the communion table. The offending parties were brought before the High Commission and, when they threatened to bring a prohibition, Laud was purported to have "wondered who should dare to bring a Pro[hi]bition to this Court," and said that "He would breake the backe of Prohibitions, or else they should breake his."[125] While Laud responded that he could not remember the speaking of these words, they were well witnessed by three different individuals.[126] Laud was also purported to have said that anyone bringing a prohibition into the High Commission "deserved to be layd by the heele."[127]

In his *History* Laud offered a fuller and more sophisticated explanation of his views on ecclesiastical jurisdiction since the Reformation and the role of writs of prohibition:

> there is a great difference touching prohibitions, and the sending of them, since the time of the Reformation and before. For before, the Bishops Courts were kept under a foreign power, and there were then weighty reasons for prohibitions, both in regard of the King's power, and the subjects indemnity. But since the Reformation all power exercised in the spiritual courts is from the King, as well as the temporal; so that now there neither is, nor can be, so much cause as formerly was.[128]

Laud, in spite of the prosecution's best efforts, never denied at his trial that his *forensic* jurisdiction was held of the king and not held *iure divino*. Laud distinguished between the bishops' jurisdiction *in foro contentioso*, their forensic jurisdiction held from the king, and their jurisdiction *in foro conscientiae*, which was held "from god, and from Christ, and by divine and apostolical right" yet exercised only by the king's leave. When Laud had sat as a judge in High Commission he did so by the jurisdiction granted to him under broad seal by the king but when he exercised the spiritual powers of his episcopal office he did so *iure divino*.[129] The denial of writs of prohibition could not be an affront to regal jurisdiction because the ecclesiastical courts themselves derived their jurisdiction from the king.

The idea that the jurisdiction of the ecclesiastical courts derived wholly from the crown and not from any other power was not new. Tudor and early Stuart civilians had argued this position to counter charges of praemunire. For example, the Tudor statesman and civil lawyer Sir Thomas Smith, writing

[125] HMC Lords XI: 393; by Laud's own account the words charged were "You desire and order of the court that you may have it to show, and get a prohibition: but I will break the back of prohibitions or they shall break mine": *Works* IV, p. 138.

[126] John Pococke, Rowland Tompson, and Samuel Langham: HMC Lords XI: 393.

[127] HMC Lords XI: 393–394. [128] *Works* IV, p. 141.

[129] *Works* IV, p. 196; Laud appears to have formulated this argument in response to allegations by Burton and Bastwick that Laud had remarked on the occasion of Bastwick's censure in High Commission "that *he did not* [sai –del.] *hold his Bishoprick from the King but from God.* That Bishops were afore Christian kings. *That Bishops anoynted Kings.* [and] That the Imperiall state could not stand without Bishops." HMC Lords XI: 408.

in the mid-1560s argued that the ecclesiastical courts had their "force, power, authoritie, rule, and jurisdiction, from the royall majestie and the crowne of England and from no other forren potentate or power under God" and that, as a result, the praemunire statute of 16 Richard II, c. 5 "hath nowe no place in England."[130] John Cowell took up this line of argument in his controversial *Interpreter* of 1607 and it seems also to have influenced the common lawyer John Selden.[131] If the articles of impeachment against Laud resembled charges of praemunire, Laud at least had the knowledge to respond with an appropriate strategy.

The managers of the evidence, however, were common lawyers with little sympathy for civilians or the jurisdictions in which they operated. Professor Helmholz has argued that the ecclesiastical courts were under constant threat of encroachments from the common-law courts to the point where the threat of a writ of prohibition entered into the calculations of both jurists and litigants in the ecclesiastical courts.[132] Laud was probably not far from the truth when he remarked that it was more likely that prohibitions would break his back first.[133] The attack on the powers and jurisdiction of the High Commission was lent additional force by the views of Coke, published by the order of the Long Parliament in the same year as Laud's trial. Coke, always the champion of the common-law courts against the jurisdictions of both equity and the church courts, reiterated the argument of Nicholas Fuller (1607) that the powers conferred to the High Commission under the Elizabethan settlement did not include powers of fining and imprisonment.[134]

The main particular to the fourth original article concerned the case of the Chester men fined by the High Commission at York. Laud was accused of accepting a bribe of wine from the Chester men's creditor, a Mr. Thomas Stone, to mitigate their fine of 2,000*l.* down to 200*l.*[135] Laud protested that the wine had been accepted from Stone against his commands to return it and without his knowledge (his steward having died three years previous, Laud was at a loss to substantiate this).[136] Other particulars concerned

130 Sir Thomas Smith, *De Republica Anglorum*, ed. Mary Dewar (Cambridge, 1982), pp. 142–143.

131 John Cowell, *The Interpreter: or Booke Containing the Signification of Words* (Cambridge, 1607), sig. Ddd2v; John Selden, *The Table Talk of John Selden, A New Edition with a Biographical Preface* (Chiswick, 1818), pp. 138–139.

132 Helmholz, *Roman Canon Law*, p. 183.

133 HMC Lords XI: 393.

134 "...by this Act [1 Elizabeth, c. 1] no power of fining or imprisoning in Ecclesiastical causes is given by this Act": Sir Edward Coke, *The Fourth Part of the Institutes of the Laws of England Concerning The Jvrisdiction of Courts* (London, 1644), p. 326; Coke largely reiterated the position of Nicholas Fuller in *The Argument of Nicholas Fuller of Grayes Inne Esquire, in the Case of Thomas Lad, and Richard Mansell his Clients* (London, 1607; reprinted London, 1641).

135 *Works* III, pp. 402–403, IV, pp. 141, 143; HMC Lords XI: 395.

136 *Works* III, p. 403, IV, p. 145; HMC Lords XI: 395.

the sequestration of fines in the High Commission toward the renovation St. Paul's.[137]

After a series of delays the hearings resumed on 16 April, with Robert Nicholas proceeding to the fifth and sixth original articles and the ninth additional article. The fifth original and the ninth additional concerned themselves with the legality of the 1640 canons and reflected, once again, the conflation of praemunire and treason in the charges against Laud. The fifth charged Laud with the composition and execution of the "pretended canons" in which were contained "many matters . . . contrary to the King's prerogative, to the fundamental laws and statutes of the realm, to the right of Parliament, to the propriety and liberty of the subjects, and matters tending to sedition, and of dangerous consequence; and to the establishment of a vast, unlawful, and presumptuous power in himself and his successors."[138] The latter part of the article concerned itself with the controversial oath against popery stipulated in canon 6. This oath was to be administered to all of the clergy and *all* the members of the universities, be they doctors of law, divinity, or physic, as well as all masters and bachelors of arts.[139] This, of course, included a substantial section of the laity, putting the canons in direct conflict with Pym's argument in the Short Parliament. Pym and his allies St. John and Hampden had insisted that in order for canons of the church to be binding on the laity they must be confirmed by parliament.[140]

The ninth additional article was almost identical in content to the fifth original. However, it made no mention of the canons being contrary to the king's prerogative, asserting only that the canons were "made and established, by [Laud's] Means and Procurement" and were "contrary to the Laws of this Realm, the Rights and Privileges of Parliament, and Liberty and Property of the Subject, tending also to Sedition and dangerous Consequence."[141] Laud was quick to pounce on the inconsistency between the two articles, asking how he could be accused both of advancing the king's prerogative above law and yet making canons contrary to it.[142] Indeed, as Lamont has remarked, the charge that Laud sought to destroy the king's prerogative appears from John Browne's account of the trial to have been "quietly dropped" from the prosecution's argument.[143] In the case of Strafford, accusing the earl of usurping the king's prerogative powers was as good as accusing him of

137 *Works* IV, pp. 142–149; HMC Lords XI: 394–397. 138 *Works* III, pp. 404–405.

139 *Works* III, p. 405; *Constitutions and Canons Ecclesiasticall; Treated upon by the Archbishops of Canterbury and York, Presidents of the Convocations for the respective Provinces of Canterbury and York, and the rest of the Bishops and Clergie of those Provinces; And agreed upon with the Kings Majesties Licence in their severall Synods begun at London and York, 1640* (London, 1640), sigs. E1v–E2v.

140 Cope, "Short Parliament": 181–182. 141 *LJ VI*: 267.

142 *Works* IV, pp. 156–157. 143 Lamont, *Godly Rule*, p. 63; HMC Lords XI: 398–402.

derogating from the rights and privileges of parliament. King and parliament were still together sitting as a single body corporate at Westminster. This was the context in which the fifth original article had been drawn up. The outbreak of the first Civil War and the de facto if not de jure severing of the king's authority from his person had reduced the king to a juristic abstraction, effectively removing the prerogative from the equation and making any further mention of it uncomfortable for the prosecution. Strafford could be accused of taking upon himself the king's prerogative power of war and peace but, by 1644, so too could every individual member of the Long Parliament.

The prosecution's position was that canons in matter of doctrine, like canons concerning clerical subsidies, should be subject to parliamentary confirmation. The canons of 1640 were in their content a confirmation of Laud's program of reforms of the 1630s. For example, canon 7 had confirmed the communion table's status as an altar, ordered its setting altarwise and the erection of railings around it.[144] The oath against popery decreed in canon 6 also enjoined the subject to swear that they approved "the Doctrine and Discipline, or Government, established in the Church of England, as containing all Things necessary to Salvation" and that they will never give consent "to alter the Government of this Church, by Archdeacons, etc. *as it stands now established*, and as by Right it ought to stand."[145] For any opposed as a matter of conscience to the ecclesiastical innovations of the 1630s these passages would have been more than a mere political setback. They were a real and imminent threat to the spiritual wellbeing of the commonwealth.

Laud, in his defense alluded to the legal opinion of Finch and the other learned counsel that, according to the Act for the Submission of the Clergy (25 Henry VIII, c. 19), the convocation, summoned by a separate writ, might continue to sit after the dissolution of parliament.[146] He also alluded to the 1604 canons which had not received the assent of parliament yet remained in force.[147] With respect to the particular charged concerning the oath in canon 7 Laud, in his *History*, remarked that the 1604 canons had made several oaths including one against simony (canon 40), one to be administered to churchwardens (canon 118), an oath concerning marriage

[144] *Constitutions and Canons Ecclesiasticall*, sigs. E3r–F1r; this was a significant departure from the canons of 1604; J. P. Kenyon, *The Stuart Constitution, 1603–1688: Documents and Commentary*, 2nd edn. (Cambridge, 1986), pp. 113, 125–126.

[145] *Constitutions and Canons Ecclesiasticall*, sig. E2r; *LJ* VI: 267; italics added.

[146] *Works* IV, p. 153; HMC Lords XI: 399; see also Clarke MS LXXI, 16 April 1644: "My Lords. The Cannons was [sic.] by the broadseale of England according to the statute of 25 Hen. 8. [25 Henry VIII, c. 19] to sitt after the parliament was ended."

[147] HMC Lords XI: 399.

licenses (canon 103), and an oath for judges in ecclesiastical courts (canon 127).[148] Furthermore, Laud argued that he did not procure the canons but that the whole body of the convocation had freely enacted them.[149] The prelate protested that the making of the cannons was "an Act of the whole Convocation" and that he could "bee no more accused of itt neither criminally nor traiterously then all the rest of the Convocation House."[150]

We have argued previously that the 1604 canons were of questionable validity to the Erastian faction in the Long Parliament. Indeed, Pym had questioned their validity in the Short Parliament, complaining that "they have bred great Confusion in church & Kingdome" and that their precedent ought not to be followed.[151] To a parliamentary Erastian the continued sitting of convocation after the dissolution of the Short Parliament and the subsequent making of canons was nothing less than a clerical usurpation of the law-giving power of the king-in-parliament in ecclesiastical matters. The sixth original article, composed before the outbreak of hostilities, made it clear that from the outset Laud's accusers saw his actions as a subversion of the royal supremacy. To Pym and his allies – a group that included Maynard and St. John – this was popery.[152] The article charged that Laud had

> ... traitorously assumed to himself a Papal and tyrannical power, both in Ecclesiastical and temporal matters, over his Majesty's subjects in this realm of England, and other places; to the disinhersion of the Crown, dishonour of his Majesty, and derogation of his supreme authority in ecclesiastical matters. And the said Archbishop claims the King's ecclesiastical jurisdiction, as incident to his episcopal and archiepiscopal office in this kingdom; and doth deny the same to be derived from the Crown of England; which he had accordingly exercised, to the high contempt of his royal majesty, and to the destruction of divers of the King's liege people in their persons and estates.[153]

For the prosecution, the reassertion of the legislative autonomy of the clerical estate in making canons that bound the laity was the assumption of a "popish" power.

The assumption of papal power was not just treasonable but in Laud's trial the idea became fused with the eschatological expectations of the godly. The Antichrist would, like Pope Boniface VIII, attempt to assume the power

148 *Works* IV, p. 155: Clarke MS LXXI, 16 April 1644.
149 *Works* IV, p. 157; Clarke MS LXXI, 16 April 1644.
150 Clarke MS LXXI, 16 April 1644. 151 Aston, *Short Parliament*, pp. 151–152.
152 For example, see Maynard's remarks to the Long Parliament on 15 December 1640: "... those who would binde us by the Canons of his clergie doe use the very arguments the Pope did to raise his owne power": Notestein, *D'Ewes*, p. 155.
153 *Works* III, p. 406.

of both swords.[154] The comparison with this particular pope was highly significant. Boniface VIII (1294–1303) had made one of the strongest claims of the papacy to secular power in the Middle Ages. In 1302, at the height of his conflict with Philip IV of France, he issued the decree *Unam Sanctam* which asserted that both the temporal and spiritual swords were in the power of the church, the latter being exercised by the church and the former being exercised for the church "by the hand of kings and soldiers, though at the will and sufferance of the priest."[155] Nor was this the first time the specter of Boniface VIII appeared in an English treason trial. Bacon had cited the example of Boniface in *Talbot's Case* as an example of how the papacy had sought to derogate from the sovereignty of not only Protestant monarchs but also from Catholic kings such as Philip.[156]

A key particular to the sixth article concerned Laud's alleged expansion of the jurisdiction of the High Commission through the procurement of a new commission conferring powers of fining and imprisonment and a *non obstante* clause restricting appeals from that court. Burton, who witnessed the particular, recounted that his attempt to appeal a decision of the High Commission to the king was denied.[157] Laud was successful in demonstrating that the commission of 9 Carolus was identical to the former under which the court had operated.[158] However, the issue of High Commission's powers to fine and imprison was a long-standing controversy and the abuses of the personal rule had served only to intensify an already embittering debate. Nicholas Fuller, in his 1607 *Argument*, had openly questioned the statutory basis from which the High Commission drew its powers, arguing that the statute of 2 Henry IV, c. 15, made for the suppression of Lollardy, had been "procured by the *Popish prelats*" and parliament had passed the statute "in time of darknesse (if not without the full consent of the commons yet to their great dislike)."[159] Furthermore, the Elizabethan settlement (1 Elizabeth, c. 1) had merely restored "to the Crowne the ancient Iurisdiction over Ecclesiastical and Spiritual Estate" and "the power to imprison subjects, to fine them, or to force them to accuse themselves upon their own enforced oaths . . . was no part of the ancient Ecclesiastical jurisdiction, nor used in England by any spirituall Iurisdiction, before the Statute of 2 Hen. 4 cap. 15."[160] The High Commission did not enjoy the power to imprison, fine, or administer an *ex-officio* oath that compelled

154 *Works* IV, p. 180; HMC Lords XI: 405; Clarke MS LXXI, 4 May 1644. (Note that this entry is misdated as 30 April in the MS.)

155 Brian Tierney, ed., *The Middle Ages I: Sources of Medieval History*, 4th edn. (New York, 1983), p. 313.

156 *State Trials* II: 780–781.

157 *Works* IV, p. 180; HMC Lords XI: 405–406.

158 *Works* IV, p. 179.

159 Fuller, *Argument*, sig. A2r, p. 3; *SL* I: 415–418.

160 Fuller, *Argument*, sigs. A1v–A2r, pp. 2–3.

the accused to testify against themselves. Significantly, this tract was reprinted in 1641 amid the heightening debate on church government in the Long Parliament.

Previously we noted that Laud never denied during his trial that his forensic jurisdiction was derived from the crown. However, the wording of the charge and the prosecution's arguments suggested that not only were Laud's actions as a High Commissioner not within the court's jurisdiction but that his jurisdiction was illegally obtained. The use of the word *procure* – often conveniently missing from Laud's account of the trial and charges – was significant. Fuller had made ample use of it over three decades before in arguing against the statutory basis of High Commission. The term connoted *agency* and its inclusion suggested that Laud as a counselor to the king had done more than simply advise and in so doing had encroached on the kingly office.[161] In Filmer's words "counsellors have no power to command their consultations to be executed, for that were to take away the sovereignty from their prince."[162] The power to give law and appoint magistrates was, of course, a mark of sovereignty and the allegation that Laud had procured the Commission brought his actions within the definition of treason as the unlawful assumption of sovereign power.

The charge of denying appeal from the High Commission was potentially serious. Both the power to mitigate the severity of the law and right of final appeal were marks of sovereignty and the latter by its very definition could not be imparted to any inferior magistrate. Either the sovereign held this right or they were not the sovereign. Analytically there could not be two final appeals. Sir John Maynard in summing up for the prosecution on 4 May 1644 argued that Laud's actions were tantamount to "taking royall power out of the Kinge" in his denying the king's power to pardon and mitigate against ecclesiastical sanctions.[163] The charge was roughly analogous to the sixteenth specific article against the Earl of Strafford that had charged him with the denial of appeals to England. Where Strafford had taken one of the king's kingdoms, that of Ireland, and ruled it as his own fiefdom, Laud stood charged with having erected a rival center of sovereignty emanating from the clerical estate – an autonomous sphere of clerical action tantamount to an ecclesiastical state within a state. Since it was inconceivable that the king would willingly divide his sovereignty and unmake himself any more

[161] The *OED* identifies the word "procure" with agency: one definition offered for "procuring" is "The action of causing or contriving to bring about; the fact of being the prime agent; = PROCUREMENT 1. Now *rare*." This is clearly the sense in which the prosecution were using the term: *OED Compact Edition*, vol. II, p. 1416.

[162] Sir Robert Filmer, *The Freeholder's Grand Inquest*, in Johann P. Sommerville, ed., *Patriarcha and Other Writing* (Cambridge, 1991), p. 94.

[163] Clarke MS LXXI, 4 May 1644. (Note that this entry is misdated as 30 April in the MS.)

than he would cut off his own head, the prosecution argued in the cases of both Strafford and Laud that the authorization for their actions was illicitly obtained by their own procurement and not through any fault of the king.

The seventh original and seventh additional articles followed on 20 May. They concerned primarily the ecclesiastical innovations of the personal rule and would occupy the court for the better part of four days (20, 27 May and 6, 11 June). The seventh original charged that Laud had "traitorously endeavoured to alter and subvert God's true religion by law established in this realm; and instead thereof to set up Popish superstition and idolatry" and that in printed books and speeches he had "declared and maintained ... divers Popish doctrines and opinions contrary to the Articles of Religion established by law." The article charged further that Laud had "urged and enjoined divers Popish and superstitious ceremonies, without any warrant of law" and abused his powers of ecclesiastical discipline in punishing those who opposed his program of ecclesiastical innovation.[164] The seventh additional struck a similar tone. It charged that Laud had "endeavoured to advance Popery and Superstition within the Realm" and to that end had received and harboured popish priests, in particular "One called Sancta Clara alias Damport," author of a book entitled *Deus Natura Gratia*, "wherein the Thirty-nine Articles of the Church of England, established by Act of Parliament, were much traduced and scandalized ..."[165] It charged further that Laud had had conference with Sancta Clara during the writing of this book and that Laud had patronized and maintained a popish priest, a Monsieur St. Giles, at Oxford.[166] The seventh additional article was closely linked to the tenth original article that the prosecution did not press until 17 July. Indeed, the proofs were at times largely indistinguishable. This article charged that Laud had "traitorously and wickedly endeavoured to reconcile the Church of England with the Church of Rome." To this end Laud had allegedly conspired with priests and Jesuits, keeping "secret intelligence" with the Pope. More heinously he had "permitted and countenanced a Popish hierarchy, or ecclesiastical government, to be established in this kingdom."[167]

The particular proofs to the seventh original and seventh additional articles were voluminous and read like a laundry list of grievances flowing from the ecclesiastical innovations and abuses of the personal rule. It is not necessary for our purposes here to consider them closely. The detailed investigation of any single particular could potentially yield material sufficient for a brief scholarly article and the use of iconographic evidence in the trial, particularly, is a subject that is on its own worthy of deeper investigation. There is also the troublesome historiographical question of the broader significance

[164] *Works* IV, p. 407. [165] *LJ* VI: 267. [166] *LJ VI*: 267. [167] *Works* III, p. 411.

of the Laudian program – more specifically, whether Laud should be seen as a Counter-Reformation figure attempting to re-Catholicize the church of England or, more plausibly, as a Reformation figure presenting his own vision of reform competing with both the model of Scottish Presbyterian church government and alternately undermining the "Calvinist consensus" that had predominated in the Jacobean church. Irrespective of the position one takes, it is clear that Laud at his trial assumed a position of episcopal and clerical supremacy that would be exercised at the king's leave but, for the most part, independently of lay control. This position may, as Lamont has argued, have been informed by a similar set of eschatological expectations to those advocating godly king and godly parliament. However, with respect to the simple question of who was supreme in the Church of England, Laud was deeply hostile to the Erastian vision of a godly parliament that Pym, St. John, Prynne and their ilk were advocating. The key question here is not whether Laud was, as his tormentors claimed, a closet papist – he clearly was not. The key issue in the trial was whether Laud enjoyed the legal and legitimate authority in the state to undertake the program of ecclesiastical reforms that he did during the 1630s. The point of contact between the law of treason and the ecclesiastical practices and policies of the 1630s was the question of the supremacy.

The particular ecclesiastical innovations of the personal rule included the setting of the communion table altarwise, the wearing of copes, the deployment of images and crucifixes in places of worship, the practice of bowing to the altar, the reading of the Book of Sports, and the use of a credential or side table after the pattern of Lancelot Andrewes' own chapel. Evidence was drawn from a diverse number of instances including, for example, the arrangement of Laud's own chapel and the Chapel Royal, his attempts to impose this pattern of worship on cathedrals and parish churches, and the practices of certain Cambridge college chapels, most notably Peterhouse. There were also numerous cases where individuals had been disciplined in both Star Chamber and High Commission for opposing these innovations or simply failing to comply with the Laudian program.[168] Most notable of these was the celebrated case of the barrister Henry Sherfield (d. 1634), onetime Recorder of Salisbury, fined in Star Chamber for the breaking of a stained-glass window in a church in Sarum. The prosecution contended that this image had been idolatrous, portraying "God the Father" as an old man, "pulling Addam & Eve out of his pouch."[169]

[168] The evidence to these articles took up four full days of the trial (20, 27 May and 6, 11 June) as well as part of a fifth (17 June): HMC Lords XI: 409–433; *Works* IV, pp. 197–280: for a most pedantically complete summary of these particulars see Prynne, *Canterburies Doome*, *passim*.

[169] HMC Lords XI: 419; see also *Works* IV, pp. 237–239.

The charge of harboring seminary priests and Jesuits was potentially very serious, but not treasonable. The Jesuit Act of 1585 had stipulated that the receiving and aiding of Jesuits and seminary priests was punishable by death as a felony but fell short of imposing the pains and forfeitures of high treason.[170] In any event, Laud vehemently denied the prosecution's contention that St. Giles and Sancta Clara were in fact the same man as well as any hint that he was in any way inclined towards popery.[171] With respect to the Habernfeld Plot he confirmed that he had at one point been offered a Cardinal's hat but denied any conference with priests and said that he had reported the offer to the king immediately as the law required.[172] While Laud acknowledged patronizing St. Giles when he was at Oxford, he had been forbidden to stay in college or exercise his priestly office.[173] Citing the authority of Coke's newly published third installment of his *Institutes*, Laud argued further that St. Giles as a Frenchman was not within this statute of 27 Elizabeth and subsequently his patronizing of the priest was in no way treasonable.[174]

The status of images in churches was also problematic. Similarly the statute cited by the prosecution of 4 & 5 Edward VI, c. 10, entitled "An Act for the abolishing an putting away of divers Books and Images," did not prescribe the punishment of high treason for offenders but only fines and imprisonment.[175] Furthermore, as Laud pointed out in his *History*, the statute did not mention "glass-windows nor the images that are in them."[176] Laud also made the argument that Calvin himself had allowed historical images for didactic purposes "provided they did not themselves become objects of idolatry."[177] Laud defended the practices of bowing to the altar and the wearing of copes as consistent with the canons of 1604.[178] This was a problematic line of argument because these canons, unlike, for example, the Thirty-nine Articles, had not received parliamentary confirmation.[179]

The eighth, ninth, tenth, eleventh, and twelfth original and the sixth additional articles continued in a similar vein, focusing on the ecclesiastical policies of the personal rule and Laud's alleged actions in promoting them.[180] The eighth accused Laud of "procuring" to himself the power of nominating "sundry persons to ecclesiastical dignities, promotions, and

[170] *SL* II: 633. [171] *Works* IV, p. 331; HMC Lords XI: 446.
[172] *Works* IV, pp. 331–332; HMC Lords XI: 447.
[173] *Works* IV, pp. 327–331. [174] *Works* IV, p. 331. [175] *SL* II: 434.
[176] *Works* IV, p. 199. [177] *Works* IV, p. 199; HMC Lords IX: 410.
[178] Canons 18 (bowing) and 24 (copes); *Works* IV, p. 221; HMC Lords XI: 210.
[179] Originally passed by convocation in 1563, the parliament confirmed the Thirty-nine Articles in the wake of Elizabeth's excommunication in 1571: Claire Cross, *The Royal Supremacy in the Elizabethan Church* (London, 1969), pp. 75–76.
[180] These articles comprised most of the proceedings for 17 and 27 June and 5, 17, and 24 July 1644.

benefices, belonging to his Majesty, and divers of the nobility, clergy and others" and in particular of preferring chaplains to the king's service that were "popishly affected, or other wise unsound and corrupt both in doctrine and manners."[181] The ninth article similarly charged Laud with employing popishly affected chaplains and licensing the printing of "divers false and superstitious books."[182] The tenth article, charging that Laud had harbored Seminary priests and Jesuits, has been previously discussed. The eleventh original article concerned the suppression of preaching and hindering "the preaching of God's word" through the use of such sanctions as suspension, degradation, deprivation, and even excommunication.[183] The sixth additional article concerned the attempts of the Laudian church to buy in impropriations from their lay impropriators and the alleged misappropriation of ecclesiastical revenues towards this end.[184] The twelfth concerned Laud's attempts to bring Dutch and Huguenot "visitor" churches into conformity with the Church of England in contravention of the privileges and immunities previously granted them by the king and his predecessors. This had caused "division and discord between the Churche of England and other reformed Churches."[185]

Once again, the proofs, accurate or inaccurate, were voluminous.[186] Detailed consideration of them is not necessary for our purposes here, although such an investigation would be invaluable to any study attempting to evaluate fully the impact of the ecclesiastical policies of the 1630s on English politics and society. The purpose here is rather to establish a point of contact between ecclesiastical policy and the marks of sovereignty and to demonstrate that legal-constitutional concerns did not, as John Morrill has argued, constitute "a distinct and separable" perception of misgovernment from the religious in the early 1640s.[187] In order for the Long Parliament to claim competence over ecclesiastical affairs the two perceptions of misrule came together. Erastianism was the agent behind this convergence, constituting an ideological position that, if not completely opposed to an independent clerical sphere of action, depended on containing and subordinating the powers and influence of ecclesiastical bodies such as convocation and the Westminster assembly. That Laud's intentions and motives were driven by a general inclination toward Rome is highly questionable and at best controversial. The long-term goal of the Laudian program was not the re-Catholicization of the English Church but the reform of the Roman Church

[181] *Works* III, pp. 408–409. [182] *Works* III, p. 410. [183] *Works* III, p. 420.
[184] *LJ* VI: 267. [185] *Works* III, p. 421; Prynne, *Canterburies Doome*, p. 389.
[186] HMC Lords XI: 425–430, 433–453.
[187] J. S. Morrill, "The Religious Context of the English Civil War," in Richard Cust and Ann Hughes, eds., *The English Civil War* (London, 1997), p. 161.

according to the English episcopal pattern. However, that not only Prynne and company but a number of ordinary English perceived him as intending a reconciliation with Rome is less problematic. That he sought to expand and preserve the powers of convocation and those of its upper house in particular is even less so.

Unsurprisingly, the managers laid aside the thirteenth original article relating to Laud's alleged role in Scottish affairs in the years 1637–40. The Act of Oblivion relating to the recent Scottish conflagration passed early in the Long Parliament had made much of the contents moot and Laud was quick to take shelter in its provisions in his answers to Lords of 22 January 1644.[188] Nevertheless, the article is worthy of note because it struck a note of continuity with the twentieth particular article against the Earl of Strafford, charging that Laud had "maliciously and traitorously plotted, and endeavoured to stir up war and enmity betwixt his Majesty's two kingdoms of England and Scotland" by attempting "to introduce into the kingdom of Scotland divers innovations both in religion and government, all or the most part tending to Popery and superstition, to the great grievance and discontent of his Majesty's subjects of that nation." When the Scots resisted these innovations Laud had treacherously advised the king "to subdue them by force of arms; and by his own authority and power, contrary to law, did procure sundry of his Majesty's subjects, and enforced the clergy ... to contribute towards the maintenance of that war."[189]

The fourteenth original article was the last pressed. It charged that Laud, in order to avoid answering for his actions, had "laboured to subvert the rights of Parliament, and the ancient course of parliamentary proceedings; and by false and malicious slanders to incense his Majesty against Parliaments." Echoing the seven general articles against Strafford, the article charged further that Laud had, "traitorously and contrary to his allegiance, laboured to alienate the hearts of the King's liege people from his Majesty, to set a division between them, and to ruin and destroy his Majesty's kingdoms."[190] Laud's treason was against both king and kingdom, dividing ruler from ruled at the peril of the whole body politic. The particulars, supported by letters and notes seized from Laud's study, went as far back as 1626, when Laud was purported to have advised the young king to dissolve parliament.[191] There was undoubtedly some truth in Laud's alleged hostility to parliaments. Unlike Wentworth, who continued to believe in the value of parliaments and their place in the constitution, Laud is legitimately counted as one of the "new counsels" who questioned the usefulness and necessity of regular

[188] *Works* IV, pp. 44–45; for a text of the Act of Oblivion see John Rushworth, *Historical Collections*, vol. III (London, 1692), pt. 1, pp. 370–372, 374–375.

[189] *Works* III, p. 425.

[190] *Works* III, p. 432.

[191] HMC Lords XI: 454.

parliaments.[192] At stake was not merely the future law-giving role of parliament, its continued importance with respect to the "first and chiefest" mark of sovereignty, but also parliament's role as the guardian of the reformed religion in England and a bulwark against "popery."

The substance of the articles of impeachment against Laud was that, like Strafford, he had unlawfully assumed to himself the marks of sovereignty. Laud was charged with expanding the law-giving jurisdictions of not only king-in-council, but also those of convocation and the ecclesiastical courts at the expense of parliament, the common-law courts, and ultimately the king himself. In short, he denied and subverted the royal supremacy. However, the nature of Laud's usurpations, unlike those of Strafford, was clerical. While Strafford had allegedly seized one of the king's kingdoms and ruled it as his own in derogation of the king's sovereignty, Laud was charged with creating an ecclesiastical state within a state.

IV

The case against Laud rested heavily on an almost complete conflation of treason with the lesser cause of praemunire. The making of canons prejudicial to the king and his realm, the deciding in ecclesiastical courts of issues usually determined in common-law courts and other similar invasions of the king's regality were offenses consistent with the law of praemunire, not treason or misdemeanor – the offenses with which Laud had been charged. The predominant Erastian tendency to see the royal supremacy, and more generally power over ecclesiastical affairs, as a mark of sovereignty led the prosecution inevitably to this position.

The argument in law of Laud's counsels delivered by John Herne on 11 October revealed an awareness of the extent to which the case against the prelate depended on the charge's conflation with the lesser charge of praemunire. Herne asserted that there was no treason but that contained in 25 Edward III made to contain mischiefs and uncertainties in the law, in particular the definition of treason as "accroaching the royal power" by which "every excess was subject to a construction of treason."[193] In other words, consistent with Bellamy's interpretation of the late medieval period, the statute prohibited the emergence of a more fully fledged Roman-law conception of treason. With respect to the cases of Wolsey and Lingham during the reign of Henry VIII, Herne acknowledged that they had in fact

[192] Anthony Milton, "Thomas Wentworth and the Political Thought of the Personal Rule," in J. F. Merritt, ed., *The Political World of Thomas Wentworth, Earl of Strafford, 1621–1641* (Cambridge, 1996), p. 142.

[193] *Works* IV, p. 389.

been charged with endeavoring to subvert the ancient laws of the kingdom but denied that this had been "imputed to be treason, but ended in a charge of a praemunire."[194] The arguments of both Laud and his counsel revealed an understanding of the extent to which the prosecution's case depended on a hidden linkage with a lesser cause of action. Both causes of action were utilized to preserve the role of the civil magistrate in ecclesiastical affairs from both popish and other forms of clerical depredation, whether episcopal or Presbyterian.

The relationship of church and state during the 1630s provided the flashpoint over which conflict eventually erupted in early Stuart Britain: first in Scotland in 1637, then in Ireland in 1641, and finally in England in 1640–42. By the outbreak of the Civil War, power over the doctrine and discipline of the established church in England had, for many leading public men, achieved the status of a mark of sovereignty and its unlawful assumption and exercise was as much an act of treason as unlawfully seizing power to give law or make war. Laud, like Strafford, defended his actions by claiming the king's warrant and leave for his actions. The prosecution denied this and claimed, as they had in Strafford's trial, that the accused had *procured* the treasonable actions by misinforming the king. In the end it matters little to our purposes whether it was Charles or Laud who was ultimately responsible for the ecclesiastical innovations of the 1630s. The prosecution in laying the blame for the ecclesiastical policies of the personal rule at Laud's feet appealed to the king's authority in parliament over ecclesiastical affairs. The legitimacy of the prosecution's case still rested on their claim to be acting in the king's name and in the king's interest. This was in spite of the reality that they had been at war with him for two years. The king could still, at least in theory, do no wrong.

[194] *Works* IV, p. 394; Clarke MS LXXI, 11 October 1644. In the case of Empson, tried shortly after Henry VIII's accession to the throne, Herne was forced to acknowledge that the charge had in fact identified the subversion of the law with treason but that Empson's subverting of the laws had been actual rather than simply endeavored: *Works* IV, pp. 394–395; the indictment of Empson and Deadly was printed in Coke, *The Fourth Part of The Institutes*, pp. 198–199; Russell, "Theory of Treason": 31; for Wolsey and Lingham see Coke, 12 *Reports*, fol. 40; 77 *Eng. Rep.* 1322 (KB).

5

Connor Lord Maguire, Second Baron of Enniskillen

I

The treason trial of Connor Lord Maguire, Second Baron of Enniskillen, in February 1645 brought into focus competing conceptions of the constitutional relationship of England and Ireland. Maguire stood implicated in the plot to seize Dublin Castle on 23 October 1641 during the Irish Revolt of that year and was tried in early 1645 before a Middlesex jury. The key issue of the trial was whether Maguire, as a peer of Ireland, having committed treasonable acts in Ireland and elsewhere, and being brought "into England against his will, might be lawfully tryed . . . in the King's Bench at Westminster by a Middlesex Jury, and outed of his tryal by Irish Peers of his condition by the statute of 35 Henry VIII c. 2."[1] In the Earl of Strafford's trial almost four years earlier the defense had consistently assumed a position of Irish constitutional "exceptionalism." Both Strafford and other apologists for his rule as Lord Deputy in Ireland during the 1630s adopted this constitutional stance in response to proceedings against them in both the English and Irish parliaments during 1641. This position held that, while Magna Carta and the common law generally held sway in Ireland, because of circumstances unique to that kingdom, significant exceptions existed with regard to the legal rights and privileges that these legal instruments conferred on the king's Irish subjects. In contrast, the case for Maguire rested on a view of the constitutional relationship of England and Ireland that emphasized a closely shared heritage of legal privileges for both commoners and peers as guaranteed

[1] William Prynne, *The Subjection of all Traytors, Rebels, as well Peers, as Commoners in Ireland, to the Laws, Statutes, and Trials by Juries of good, and lawfull men of England, in the Kings Bench at Westminster, for Treasons perpetrated by them in Ireland, or any foreign Country out of the Realm of England. Being An Argument at Law made in the case of Connor Magwire, an Irish Baron* (London, 1658), sig. A2v; Bodl. Lib. Tanner MS 418, fol. 29; IT Petyt MS 511, v. 23, fol. 120v.

by Magna Carta and the common law – a position best characterized as "constitutionalist."[2]

The argument consists as follows. The first section defines the term constitutional "exceptionalism" and examines its role in legitimating the policies and practices of the Straffordian rule in Ireland during the 1630s.[3] The second section considers the arguments of the opposing counsels in Maguire's trial, William Prynne and Henry Rolle for the prosecution, Matthew Hale and Thomas Twysden for the defense. The third section discusses the decision of Justice Bacon. Each section addresses the question of how competing conceptions of the relationship of not just England and Ireland but of all three kingdoms underpinned the issues of the trial. *Calvin's Case* had purportedly provided an authoritative statement of Stuart Britain's constitutional character as a "composite" or "multiple" monarchy consisting of three kingdoms united by a single personal allegiance, but its legacy was uncertain.[4] Ireland was a distinct kingdom separate from both England and Britain; however, Magna Carta and the common law held sway there. Scotland, while governed by laws and customs other than those of England, was anciently part of one "British" kingdom.[5] In religion, Ireland remained predominantly Catholic, while the Protestant Reformation had made greater inroads in Scotland and England. Maguire's fate was inextricably bound up with the need to reconcile these tensions and clarify the place of Ireland within the fledgling imperial "British" state system.

Historians of political thought, in particular Quentin Skinner, have emphasized the emergence of an abstract conception of the state in early modern Europe.[6] Under this conception of public authority subjects owed their

[2] The definition offered here differs somewhat from that offered by Michael Perceval-Maxwell with respect to the parliamentary opposition in the Irish House of Lords in 1641. It is exemplified both by the arguments of Patrick Darcy in response to the Queries and by those of the prosecution in Strafford's impeachment: Michael Perceval-Maxwell, *The Outbreak of the Irish Rebellion of 1641* (Montreal and Kingston, 1994), pp. 123–124.

[3] The best account of Strafford's administration in Ireland remains, arguably, H. F. Kearney's *Strafford in Ireland 1633–1641: A Study in Absolutism* (Manchester, 1959).

[4] H. G. Koenigsberger, "Monarchies and Parliaments in Early Modern Europe: Dominium Regale or Dominium Politicum et Regale," *Theory and Society* 5 (1978): 191–217; H. G. Koenigsberger, *Early Modern Europe, 1500–1789* (London, 1987), pp. 48–49; Conrad Russell, "The British Problem and the English Civil War," *History* 72 (1987): 395–415; Conrad Russell, *The Fall of the British Monarchies 1637–42* (Oxford, 1991; reprinted Oxford, 1995). Russell's argument is essentially an attempt to assimilate the British Isles to the "composite monarchy" model that has been suggested for European states. In Britain as on the continent the destabilizing agent is religious change or "passions," whether it be the spread of the Counter-Reformation or militant international Protestantism.

[5] The belief that England and Scotland were anciently one kingdom was something of a commonplace in the sixteenth century and was reiterated by Sir Edward Coke in his *Institutes*: Sir Edward Coke, *The Fourth Part of the Institutes of the Laws of England Concerning the Jvrisdiction of Courts* (London, 1644), p. 345.

[6] See Introduction and chapter 2, above; Quentin Skinner, *The Foundations of Modern Political Thought*, vol. I: *The Renaissance* (Cambridge, 1978), pp. ix–x; Quentin Skinner, "The State,"

allegiance to the impersonal, abstract entity of the "state" as a freestanding constitutional order and not to the reigning monarch and the monarch's corporeal heirs. However, in the aftermath of the Personal Union of 1603, and under the constitutional compromise of *Calvin's Case* (1608), the three kingdoms of England, Ireland, and Scotland stood under the personal allegiance of the Stuarts. As David M. Jones has remarked, "Innovative schemes of government, new modelling of the state, the abstract speculations of a Hobbes, Harrington or Locke had little appeal to the conservative legal-mindedness of the English governing classes."[7] England and Ireland may have shared the common law, but the crowns of England and Ireland became united in the person of the king. Furthermore, the position of Irish constitutional exceptionalism preached alternately by Strafford in his defense and by Prynne and Rolle in their prosecution of Maguire allowed for substantial departure from normal English practice in the administration of justice. For example, lord deputies enjoyed broad, de facto if not de jure, discretionary powers relating to the equitable jurisdiction of the lord-deputy-in-council and to the exercise of martial law. The concept of an abstract state was undoubtedly available, but it found only limited purchase within the composite monarchy of the Stuarts envisioned in *Calvin's Case*. The case against Maguire depended not on the reinterpretation of his treason as a crime against the abstract state but in the continuing and increasingly strained claim of parliamentarian jurists after 1642 that they acted in the king's name for the maintenance of his regal estates and the safety of his person.

II

In defending the policies and practices of his rule in Ireland (1633–40), Strafford in his 1641 trial adopted a constitutional position best characterized as "exceptionalist."[8] While affirming that the common law and Magna

in Terence Ball et al., eds., *Political Innovation and Conceptual Change* (Cambridge, 1989), pp. 90–131; Quentin Skinner, *Liberty Before Liberalism* (Cambridge, 1998), pp. 4–5. For a competing view, see Gaines Post, *Studies in Medieval Legal Thought: Public Law and the State* (Princeton, 1964), pp. 241–309.

[7] David M. Jones, "Sir Edward Coke and the Interpretation of Lawful Allegiance in Seventeenth-Century England," *HPT* 7 (1986): 321.

[8] The term is borrowed here from Louis Hartz's *The Liberal Tradition in America* with some modifications. Hartz's argument was that American liberalism could be distinguished from its European counterpart because it developed in an atmosphere completely free of a feudal past. It therefore did not come into conflict with feudal institutions, in particular that of a politically hegemonic, landed aristocracy. This situation meant that a genuinely conservative political ideology could not develop because it lacked institutional norms that a feudal past provided. Because liberalism did not come into conflict with feudalism, socialism, the logical outcome of that conflict, failed to emerge. Post-revolutionary America was dominated by a liberal consensus characterized by an ideology of equality, inalienable rights, and social atomism that cut across regional as well as class lines. It is this author's contention that

Carta were in force in Ireland, this position allowed for exceptions to their rules because circumstances peculiar to that realm demanded it. Ireland was the first line of westward colonial expansion for the fledgling empire of the Tudor monarchs, and the need to establish a shared antiquity with England created difficulties in determining the status of the English common law in Ireland. J. G. A. Pocock, in his seminal discussion of the "ancient constitution," argued that the English common lawyers of the late Tudor and early Stuart period, exemplified by Sir Edward Coke, viewed the common law as immemorial custom existing "time out of mind."[9] The claims of English common lawyers and old English lawyers in Ireland that the common law was in force in Ireland and that English laws and customs applied there "time out of mind" could not be backed up by historical argument, except possibly in the narrow, technical sense that "time out of mind" meant prior to 1189. The immemorial past of Ireland outside the pale was one of native Irish customs, tanistry and Brehon law, not feudal tenures and primogeniture, as was that of the pale before the Norman Conquest in the twelfth century.

The arguments of English common lawyers such as Coke for the antiquity of the common law in England did not then necessarily have the same purchase in Ireland. Not surprisingly, the legal thinking of Sir John Davies, the Attorney-General in Ireland early in the seventeenth century, emphasized not the immemorality of the common law like Coke but the *rationality* of the common law as the basis of both its binding authority and its superiority over native Irish customs.[10] Davies offered a common-law jurisprudence that was more amenable to the difficulties of colonial expansion and the legal maintenance of imperial authority than that of Coke. For example, primogeniture was superior to the Irish form of gavelkind, tanistry, even though the latter

Hartz was probably more successful in explaining the failure of America to develop a genuine conservative ideology than in characterizing the nature of American liberalism. Louis Hartz, *The Liberal Tradition in America* (New York, 1955; reprinted New York, 1991).

[9] J. G. A. Pocock, *The Ancient Constitution and the Feudal Law: A Study of English Historical Thought in the Seventeenth Century*, 2nd edn. (Cambridge, 1987), chs. 2, 3.

[10] Sir John Davies, *Le Primer Report des Cases & Matters in Ley resolues & adiudges en les Courts del Roy en Ireland. Collect et digest per Sr. John Dauys Chiualer Atturney Generall del Roy en cest Realme* (Dublin 1615), Intro. Glenn Burgess has suggested that Coke's emphasis on the immemorality of the common law was based on his appropriation of Fortescue and that this was atypical for the early-Stuart period. The majority of common-law writers, according to Burgess, emphasized like Davies the rationality of the common law, with custom being simply a mode for determining natural reason as positive law: Glenn Burgess, *The Politics of the Ancient Constitution: An Introduction to English Political Thought, 1603–1642* (London, 1992), ch. 2; Glenn Burgess, "Common Law and Political Theory in Early Stuart England," *Political Science* 40 (1988): 5–17; see also J. W. Tubbs, "Custom, Time and Reason: Early Seventeenth-Century Conceptions of the Common Law," *HPT* 19 (1998): 363–406.

was a long-standing custom in Ireland, because "a custom which is contrary to the publick good . . . or injurious and prejudicial to the multitude, and beneficial only to some particular person is repugnant to the law of reason, which is above all positive laws and no prescription of time can make it good."[11] The rationality of a particular custom and not its immemoriality gave it the force of law.

Hans Pawlisch has argued that Davies and his contemporaries borrowed heavily from civil-law sources, particularly in asserting "an English title to Ireland by right of conquest," and has questioned Pocock's argument for the emergence of an insular "common-law mind" among early Stuart jurists.[12] Davies, like Coke, was undoubtedly familiar with civilian writers, as were many common lawyers of the early Stuart period.[13] Pocock has advanced Coke as the champion of common-law insularity. However, Coke also possessed a library that included no fewer than fifty-six volumes on the civil and canon laws, including not only continental editions of Justinian but also the civil lawyer John Cowell's controversial *Interpreter* of 1607.[14] However, the relationship of political thought to political action is more complicated than simply establishing "hidden" influences – an enterprise supported by the identification of unacknowledged appropriations of civil-law principles in common-law writings. That common lawyers often borrowed from the civil law is undeniable. The insufficiency of common-law authorities, especially with regard to public law, made such borrowings a necessity. For example, Sir Frederick Pollock once argued that Coke's famous maxim in *Bonham's Case* that "when an act of parliament is against common right or reason, or repugnant, or impossible to be performed, the common law will control it and adjudge such act to be void" derived from his study of the canonists.[15] Unable to appeal to the written authority of statute, Coke, consciously or unconsciously, redescribed this principle as a maxim at common law in order to legitimate his appropriation of a non-common-law source. Origins were often less relevant than usage and attribution.

[11] Sir John Davies, *A Report of Cases and Matters in Law, Resolved and Adjudged in the King's Courts in Ireland. Collected and Digested by Sir John Davies, Knight, The King's Attorney-General in that Kingdom. Now first Translated into English* (Dublin, 1762), p. 89.

[12] Hans S. Pawlisch, *Sir John Davies and the Conquest of Ireland: A Study in Legal Imperialism* (Cambridge, 1985), pp. 168–169; Hans S. Pawlisch, "Sir John Davies, The Ancient Constitution and the Civil Law," *HJ* 23 (1980): 689–702.

[13] Pawlisch, *Sir John Davies*, pp. 161–166.

[14] W. O. Hassall, ed., *A Catalogue of the Library of Sir Edward Coke, with a Preface by S. E. Thorne* (New Haven, 1950), pp. 38–41; for Coke and Roman law see also Richard Helgerson, *Forms of Nationhood: The Elizabethan Writing of England* (Chicago, 1992), ch. 3.

[15] Sir Frederick Pollock, *The Expansion of the Common Law* (London, 1904), p. 122; J. W. Gough, *Fundamental Law in English Constitutional History* (Oxford, 1955), pp. 31–32.

The question of influence is an important one but it does not adequately explore the question of why political actors might choose to redescribe their actions in one way and not the other. The reception of the Roman and civil laws in England had been ongoing at least from the time of Glanvill.[16] For the common lawyers this was essentially a twofold process, first of appropriation and secondly of redescription as rational or, alternatively, immemorial custom. Statute and custom constituted the law of England. Thus, for civil-law principles to have purchase in common-law courts they had to be either attributed to a relevant statute or redescribed as custom. Measured not only by modern standards of historical scholarship but by the best antiquarian researches of the day, the common law's alleged insularity from Roman-law based legal systems was an increasingly difficult contention to maintain by the early seventeenth century. The issue that scholars should be addressing, however, is whether this myth continued to exert influence over the shape of political argument and language in early Stuart England. In spite of the ongoing efforts of Johann P. Sommerville to discredit Pocock's original interpretation of the ancient constitution, the model of common-law discourse first posited in 1957 remains, with subsequent revisions, highly relevant to the study of early Stuart political thought and culture. It cannot be easily dismissed either on the grounds of establishing that other bodies of law exerted influence on the common law or, as Sommerville has so ably demonstrated, by establishing the availability of non-historical modes of political argument based on natural law, contract, and consent.[17]

The status of the common law and Magna Carta in Ireland was not a novel concern in 1645.[18] The majority of the charges against Strafford in 1641 pertained to the administration of justice and in particular to the law-giving function of the lord-deputy-in-council. The prosecution argued that Strafford had expanded and abused these functions during his tenure as Lord Deputy. Of particular concern was the perceived expansion of the equitable

[16] F. W. Maitland, *The Constitutional History of England*, ed. H. A. L. Fisher (Cambridge, 1908; reprinted 1965), p. 14; J. H. Baker, *An Introduction to English Legal History*, 3rd edn. (London, 1990), p. 33.

[17] Sommerville has questioned not only the existence of a "common-law mind" or mentality but also its alleged ubiquity in early Stuart political thought and culture: see Johann P. Sommerville, "History and Theory: the Norman Conquest in Early Stuart Political Thought," *Political Studies* 34 (1986): 249–261; Johann P. Sommerville, *Politics and Ideology in England, 1603–1640* (London, 1986); and Johann P. Sommerville, "The Ancient Constitution Reassessed: The Common Law, the Court and the Languages of Politics in Early Modern England," in Malcolm Smuts, ed., *The Stuart Court and Europe: Essays in Politics and Political Culture* (Cambridge, 1996), pp. 39–64.

[18] For the medieval background see R. Dudley Edwards, "'Magna Carta Hiberniae,'" in John Ryan, ed., *Essays and Studies Presented to Professor Eoin MacNeill on the Occasion of His Seventieth Birthday* (Dublin, 1940), pp. 307–318.

jurisdiction of Council Board at the expense of the common-law courts and the status of "acts of state" – legislative orders of the lord-deputy-in-council roughly analogous to royal proclamations in England. In defending his actions Strafford assumed the exceptionalist line, arguing that, while English laws and customs were generally in force in Ireland, the particular customs and practices by which lord deputies had governed Ireland differed from those in England. This left him a great deal of discretion with regard to conciliar justice, martial law in time of peace, and the making of executive orders or "acts of state." Those who prosecuted Strafford in March and April 1641, unsurprisingly, emphasized his rough handling of the common law and Magna Carta in both England and Ireland as part of his general endeavor to subvert the fundamental laws of those kingdoms.[19]

Strafford's constitutional position was very similar to that taken by the Irish judges in their response to the Queries of the Irish parliament in February, 1641.[20] The first and perhaps the most revealing of these questions asked: "Whether the Subjects of this Kingdome [of Ireland] be a free people, and to be governed, only by the Common Lawes of England, and Statutes of force in this kingdome."[21] The judges' response was exceptionalist in tone and bore a strong resemblance to Strafford's attempts to defend his record in Ireland:

> that the subjects of this kingdome are a free people and are, for the generall to bee governed only by the Common-lawes of *England*, many statutes are growen *obsolete*, and out of use, and some particular ancient Lawes (as well in criminall as in Civill causes) have been changed by interpretation of the Iudges there, as they found it most agreeable to the generall good of the Common-wealth, and as the times did require it; So our predecessors the Iudges of this kingdome as the necessitie of the times did move them, did declare the law in some particular cases otherwise than the same is practised in *England*...[22]

The jurisprudence probably owed more to Ellesmere than to Coke: the body of the common law was subtly altered and changed as the necessity of situations required it, with new laws being accreted and old ones being discarded – the ship may have needed a few planks but it essentially remained the same ship.[23]

[19] See chapter 3, above.

[20] Perceval-Maxwell, *Outbreak*, pp. 172–176; Aidan Clarke, *The Old English in Ireland, 1625–42* (Worcester and London, 1966), pp. 141–145.

[21] Patrick Darcy, *An Argument Delivered by Patricke Darcy Esquire; by the Expresse Order of the House of Commons in the Parliament of Ireland, 9. Iunii 1641* (Waterford, 1643; reprinted Dublin, 1764), p. 5.

[22] Darcy, *An Argument*, p. 22.

[23] Richard Tuck, *Natural Rights Theories: Their Origin and Development* (Cambridge, 1979), p. 83.

Question 7 was also illuminating. It concerned the validity and force of acts of state or proclamations "to bind the libertie, goods, possession or inheritance" of the natives of Ireland and "to alter the Common Law."[24] It raised essentially the same issue as the fourth particular article against Strafford: could an act of state have equal force to an act of parliament?[25] The judges evaded the thorny question of the relationship of acts of state to the common law, responding that "although acts of State, are not of force to bind the goods, or inheritance of the subject, yet they have beene of great use for the setling of the estates of very many subjects in this kingdome..."[26] In response to the judges' answers, the Irish Catholic lawyer Patrick Darcy, later a prominent figure in the Confederacy of Kilkenney, took a position akin to that of Coke in the *Case of Proclamations* of 1610: "an act of state or Proclamation cannot alter the Common-law, nor restrayne the old, nor introduce a new law, and that the same hath no power, or force to bind the goods, lands, possessions, or inheritance of the subject..."[27]

Like the articles against Strafford, the Queries were concerned largely with the administration of justice during the Straffordian regime in Ireland. For example, the issue of the legality of martial law in peacetime that had formed the basis of the fifth specific article against Strafford recurred in the eighth question to the Irish justices.[28] The judges, unlike Strafford, were evasive, saying only that they conceived that "the granting of authority and Commission for the execution [of martial law]... [was] derived out of his Majesties Regall and prerogative power, for suppressing of suddaine and great inconveniencies and insurrections, among armies or multitudes of armed men lawfully or unlawfully convented together..."[29] As with the sixteenth article of his impeachment, Strafford's attempts to limit judicial appeals from Ireland to the king and his courts in England also drew fire, forming the basis of the thirteenth question.[30] Darcy assumed a position similar to that of the managers in Strafford's trial, arguing that "no man can affirme that *England*

[24] Darcy, *An Argument*, p. 6.

[25] John Rushworth, *The Tryal of Thomas Earl of Strafford* (London 1680; 2nd edn. London 1700), p. 63.

[26] Darcy, *An Argument*, p. 30.

[27] Darcy, *An Argument*, p. 95; *State Trials* II: 725 (reprinted from the *Twelfth Part of the Reports*). While Coke's opinion did not appear in print until the publication of the *Twelfth Part of the Reports* in 1656, it is entirely possible that Darcy had access to a manuscript copy of the opinion. The surviving manuscript copies of this opinion have been traced by Esther S. Cope and often pre-date the publication of the *Twelfth Part of the Reports* by a number of years: Esther S. Cope, "Sir Edward Coke and Proclamations 1610," *AJLH* 15 (1971): 215–216.

[28] Darcy, *An Argument*, p. 7; Rushworth, *Tryal*, p. 63; for Darcy see also Aidan Clarke, "Patrick Darcy and the Constitutional Relationship between Ireland and Britain," in Jane H. Ohlmeyer, ed., *Political Thought in Seventeenth Century Ireland: Kingdom or Colony?* (Cambridge, 2000), pp. 35–55.

[29] Darcy, *An Argument*, p. 31.

[30] Darcy, *An Argument*, p. 8.

is *pars extera* as to us, Ireland is annexed to the Crowne of England, and governed by the lawes of England..."[31] Darcy's conception of the judicial system in Ireland was, as Aidan Clarke has commented, interlocked with that of England.[32] Darcy's reply to the judges rejected the exceptionalist position that had underpinned Strafford's defense and appealed to a shared heritage of the rule of law between the two realms:

> The King is the fountaine of Iustice, and as his power is great to command, so the Scepter of his Iustice is as great, nay the Scepter hath the priority, if any be, for at his Coronation, his Scepter is on his right Side, and his Sword in on his left Side to his Iustice he is sworne, therefore if any writ, Commandment or proclamation bee obtayned from him, or published contrary to his Iustice, it is not the act of the King, but the act of him that misinformed him... as said before in the case of a writ of error in the Kings Bench of *England*, or in the Parliament of England, which are remedies given by the law, therefore the Common-law doth not hinder any man to prosecute those remedies which are given to everie subject by the same.[33]

Darcy echoed the managers of Strafford's impeachment: the Lord Deputy's letter from the king authorizing the restraint of appeals to England was invalid because Strafford had obtained it by misinformation contrary to the king's justice.[34] Accordingly, in keeping with the commonplace maxim that the king could do no wrong, it was accounted an act of the ill-fated Strafford and not of the king.[35]

Darcy pushed his argument further, citing the statute 10 Henry VII, c. 22, by which "all the generall statutes of *England* were received in *Ireland*... such as were for the Common and publicke weale, etc." Darcy argued that it could not be "for the weale of this kingdome, that the subjects here be stayed from obtayning of Iustice or following other lawfull causes in *England*."[36] The *Argument* offered a vision of the two kingdoms in which the administration of justice in both kingdoms was institutionally linked by a right of appeal to a common sovereign judiciary whether King's Bench in England, the king-in-council, or the English parliament. Strafford's position, by contrast, had uncoupled the administration of justice in Ireland from the English judicial system to the extent that, as Perceval-Maxwell has observed, it was almost as if he were governing a separate kingdom.[37]

[31] Darcy, *An Argument*, p. 108. [32] Clarke, *Old English*, p. 146.

[33] Darcy, *An Argument*, p. 109.

[34] Rushworth, *Tryal*, p. 486; Robert Baillie, *Letters and Journals of Robert Baillie*, 2 vols., ed. D. Laing (Edinburgh, 1841–1842), vol. I, pp. 336–337; BL Harl. MS 164, fol. 953v.

[35] For a recent discussion of this maxim's role in seventeenth-century constitutional debate see Joyce Lee Malcolm, "Doing No Wrong: Law Liberty, and the Constraint of Kings," *JBS* 38 (1999): 161–186.

[36] Darcy, *An Argument*, p. 111.

[37] Perceval-Maxwell, *Outbreak*, p. 163; Michael Perceval-Maxwell, "Ireland and the Monarchy in the Early Stuart Multiple Kingdom," *HJ* 34 (1991): 289.

These issues corresponded closely with the content of the specific articles against the Earl of Strafford. Strafford's impeachment represented a catalogue of grievances relating to the administration of the personal rule in Ireland. These were in many cases the same grievances that the Queries were intended to illuminate. The irony is that Strafford, like "old English" constitutionalists such as Patrick Darcy, affirmed that there was an independent legislative power in Ireland. However, the defenders of the Straffordian rule in Ireland necessarily conceived of this coordinate power in conciliar as well as parliamentary terms. As Aidan Clarke remarked over thirty years ago, on the eve of the October 1641 revolt "It was not the relationship of the Irish and English parliaments which was at issue, but the relationship of executive government to the law."[38] Where Strafford and the judges were forced to diverge from Darcy was not the relationship of the legislative bodies and their powers but over issues concerning the rule of law and the administration of justice. Darcy's constitutional position presumed as a matter of course that Magna Carta was in force in Ireland and the king's Irish subjects were under the same legal protections as the king's English subjects, *without exception*. In questioning the judicial role of council table during Strafford's tenure in Ireland Darcy cited Magna Carta cap. 29, asserting that "No Freeman shall be taken imprisoned, put off his freehold, liberties and free customes, etc. other then by the lawfull judgement of his Peers, as by the law of the land."[39] By the late 1630s the old English themselves had come under threat of plantation, and Darcy's approbation of Magna Carta undoubtedly reflected the need to defend the rights of Catholic subjects in Ireland with respect to not only their persons but also their estates.

Maguire's trial played out over this ideological landscape. At stake was both the status of the common law and Magna Carta in Ireland and, more broadly, the ambiguous place of Ireland within the emerging British state system. The exceptionalist position opposed the extension of legal rights and privileges on the grounds that, while the common law and Magna Carta were in force there, Ireland was a separate and distinct kingdom and its particular customs and practices had developed of necessity in ways divergent from those of England. The alleged abuses of Strafford's rule in Ireland (conciliar justice, martial law etc.) were justified as consistent with the past conduct of lord deputies.[40] The opposing "constitutionalist" position presumed a closely shared heritage of legal rights and privileges between the two kingdoms in keeping with the common law and confirmed by Magna Carta. Among these privileges was the right to trial by peers.

[38] Clarke, *Old English*, p. 149. [39] Darcy, *An Argument*, p. 80.

[40] Sir Ralph Verney, *Verney's Notes of the Long Parliament*, ed. J. Bruce (Camden Series 31, 1845), pp. 15–17; BL Harl. MS 162, fols. 362r, 368r; chapter 3, above, *passim*.

The constitutional character of Stuart Britain and Ireland rested heavily on the precedent of *Calvin's Case*. Maguire's trial evolved largely over conflicting interpretations of Coke's report of the case (1608) and dealt with the same key issue of the definition and transferability of the subject's legal rights from one of the Stuarts' three kingdoms to another. The central issue of *Calvin's Case* was whether Robert Calvin, a Scot born at Edinburgh after the accession of James I to the English throne, a *post-nati*, was entitled to inherit land in England and enjoy the benefit of English law. In Coke's report of the case the decision of the judges was framed in terms of the theory of the king's two bodies.[41] According to this theory, the king had in him two capacities, a body politic or corporate for each of his three realms and a single body natural.[42] The case against Calvin rested on the contention that, because Calvin was a Scot by birth, he was solely under the allegiance of the king's political body of Scotland and not entitled to the benefit of English law. The judges insisted that Calvin's allegiance was owed not only to the monarch's particular crowns, English, Irish, and Scottish – that is, corporate bodies, or bodies politic – but also to his or her natural person as well. Calvin could therefore receive the protection of the king's justice and the English common law in England, being subject to the king there also. This was in spite of the fact that the king governed his realm of Scotland according to the laws of that realm and not according to the common law of England. *Calvin's Case* thus offered a vision of Britain in which the kingdoms of England, Ireland, and Scotland were united under the personal allegiance of James Stuart and the heirs of his body with each of the three kingdoms constituting distinct bodies politic.[43]

Calvin's Case was distinguishable from that of Maguire on three particulars. First, it concerned the constitutional relationship of England to Ireland, which, unlike Scotland, was also, at least in theory, governed by the common law. This was crucial because *Calvin's Case* was considerably more vague concerning this relationship. Secondly, it raised the issue of the privileges of the Irish peerage in England and not that of commoners. Thirdly, it concerned a charge of high treason and not simply the legal right to maintain a suit for title to landed estates. This second issue was particularly relevant considering the remarkable inflation in the size of the Irish peerage under the early Stuarts. Lawrence Stone has observed that between 1603 and 1641 the Irish peerage grew from twenty-five to 105, with approximately fifty of the new creations being Englishmen, "at least 30 of whom had no connection with Ireland

[41] For a fuller discussion see chapter 2, above. [42] Coke, 7 *Reports*, fol. 10a–b.

[43] Brian P. Levack, *The Formation of the British State: England, Scotland and the Union, 1603–1707* (Oxford, 1987), p. 53.

whatever."[44] The privileges of the English peerage were, according to Stone, well defined by the Elizabethan period. They were free from arrest "except for treason, felony, or breach of the peace ... could not be outlawed ... were free of various writs designed to force men to appear in court" and "were not obliged to testify under oath."[45] Furthermore, and more crucial to our discussion here, they had a right to legal judgment by their peers either before the court of the Lord High Steward or, after the revival of parliamentary judicature in 1621, before the Lords assembled in parliament with the Lord High Steward presiding. In the case of the Earl of Strafford this right had gone largely unquestioned; however, the legal rights of the Irish peerage were not so clearly defined.

III

Connor Maguire, Second Baron of Enniskillen, stood implicated in what has been referred to as the "Colonels' plot" – an abortive attempt to seize Dublin Castle on 23 October 1641 during the outbreak of the Irish rebellion of that year.[46] He was first imprisoned and tortured in Dublin and from June 1642 incarcerated in the Tower of London. At the time of his trial he had, with the exception of a brief period of escape from the Tower of London in August 1644, been constantly imprisoned for a period in excess of three years.[47]

Maguire, unlike Strafford and Laud, was tried not by process of parliamentary impeachment and attainder but by a jury before a commission of *oyer* and *terminer*. The events of the actual trial itself on 10 and 11 February 1645 were of relatively little interest, and the manuscript reports pay scant attention to them. The court was in no doubt of Maguire's guilt, and Maguire's attempts to obstruct proceedings first by challenging the entire jury and then, more legitimately, by questioning the validity of the new parliamentary seal, ultimately failed.[48] The preliminaries, however, proved a different issue entirely. Having pleaded not guilty to the allegations in the indictment Maguire

[44] Lawrence Stone, *The Crisis of the Aristocracy, 1558–1641*, abridged edn. (Oxford, 1967), p. 52.

[45] Stone, *Crisis*, p. 29.

[46] Perceval-Maxwell, *Outbreak*, p. 208.

[47] William Prynne et al., *The Whole Triall of Connor Lord Macguire, with The perfect copies of the Indictment, and all the evidences against him* (London, 1645), sig. Aa4r, p. 15; Brendan Fitzpatrick, *Seventeenth Century Ireland* (Dublin, 1988), pp. 133–150.

[48] A full narrative of this is in the official printed account of Prynne, Rolle and Newdigate: Prynne et al., *The Whole Triall*, sigs. B2r–C2v, pp. 3–10; see also BL Sloane MS 3828, fols. 73v–74r; and Bodl. Lib. Tanner MS 418, fols. 89–91; for Maguire's questioning of the Long Parliament's newly forged seal see HLS MS 113, fol. 221 and Prynne et al., *The Whole Triall*, sig. E2v, p. 28; the creation of the new seal had been necessitated by the removal of the old one to Oxford: Stephen F. Black, "The Courts and Judges of Westminster Hall During the Great Rebellion 1640–1660," *JLH* 7 (1986): 26–29.

was asked by what manner he would be tried. In response he pleaded not "by the country," as was customary, but instead "he pleaded the statute of Magna Carta made in England" to the effect that no free man be seized, imprisoned, disfranchised, etc. but only by the lawful judgment of his peers "and the statute of 10 H[enry] VII Poynings Law,[49] by which Magna Carta is made parcell of the Lawes of Ireland."[50] The issue was argued before Justice Francis Bacon by Prynne and Rolle for the prosecution and Hale and Twysden for the defense, each speaking in turn.[51]

The indictment against Maguire was printed in English in the official account after his trial. It charged that Maguire

> At Dublin in Ireland . . . as well . . . as elsewhere, falsely, maliciously and traiterously did conspire imagine and compasse utterly to deprive and disinherit the Kings Majesty of His Royall Estate and Kingdome of Ireland. To bring His Majesties Person to death and destruction, To raise sedition and breed and cause miserable slaughter and destruction amongst the kings Subjects, throughout all the whole Kingdom, To make an insurrection and Rebellion against the King His Soveraigne, To levy Publique open bloody and fierce War against the King in that Kingdome, To change and alter according to their own wills, the government of the Kingdome, and the Religion there established, and totally to subvert the well ordered State of the Common wealth, To procure and bring in divers strangers and forreiners (not being, the Kings Subjects) in a Warlike manner to invade that Kingdome of Ireland, and to levy Warre there.[52]

The indictment is worthy of note for two reasons. Firstly, it made mention of the destruction of the king's person. This was in keeping with the first head of Edward III's foundational treason statute of 1352, according to which it was high treason to compass or imagine the death of the king. More importantly, it suggested a persistence of ideas of constructive compassing of the king's death over two years after the outbreak of open hostilities with the king – ideas that, according to Conrad Russell, had largely fallen out of use by the time of Laud's trial in 1644.[53] Secondly, the charge that Maguire had

[49] The statute usually referred to by historians as Poynings' Law is the Irish statute of 10 Henry VII, c. 4 entitled "An Act that no Parliament be holden in this Land until the Acts be certified into England"; however, counsels for both sides in Maguire's trial appear to have followed Coke's usage when referring to Poynings' Law as the statute of Poynings' Parliament 10 Henry VIII, c. 22: Coke, *The Fourth Part of the Institutes*, p. 351; Bodl. Lib. Tanner MS 418, fols. 41–42, 48–49; IT Petyt MS 511, v. 23, fol. 117v; BL Sloane MS 3828, fols. 65r, 67v; HLS MS 113, fols. 187, 194, 198, 207; see also Aidan Clarke, "The History of Poynings' Law, 1615–41," *IHS* 18 (1972): 207–222.

[50] BL Sloane MS 3828, fol. 65r. Prynne's own account in the Inner Temple library reads: "after he had pleaded Not guilty; he had pleaded yt hee is a Peer of Ireland so h[e] ought to be tried there by Peers of Peers and not by an Ordinary Iury[.]": IT Petyt MS 511, v. 23, fol. 120v.

[51] Bacon, not to be confused with his famous namesake, was at this time the only sitting judge in the King's Bench: Black, "Courts and Judges of Westminster Hall": 28–29.

[52] Prynne et al., *The Whole Triall*, sigs. Aa2v–Aa3r, pp. 12–13.

[53] Conrad Russell, "The Theory of Treason in the Trial of Strafford," *EHR* 80 (1965): 46.

sought to alter government and the established religion to the total subversion of "the well ordered State" of the commonwealth of Ireland suggested that treason was not simply a crime against the king's natural person but against the state established by law. The charge against Maguire was not simply a breach of personal allegiance to the king but an offense against the legal-constitutional order of the state in both temporal and spiritual affairs – the latter being a clear reference to the accused's Catholicism. However, this conception of state was not fully impersonal or abstract and still paid lip service at least to the idea of the king's two bodies, their inseparability, and subsequently to the idea of constructive compassing. The king's office, his crown, his dignity, and his "state" were, at least theoretically, inseparable from his body natural and to compass the destruction of one was to compass the death of the other. Thus, the notion of constructive compassing persisted in Maguire's trial and along with it the notion of personal allegiance.

Central to the debate in the trial was the question of whether the English statute of 35 Henry VIII, c. 2, made for the trying of treasons committed outside of the realm of England, applied to the Irish peerage. This statute, entitled "An Act for the Trial of Treasons committed out of the King's Dominions," declared

> That all manner of Offences, being already made and declared, or hereafter to be made and declared by any of the Laws and Statutes of this Realm to be Treasons, Misprisions of Treasons, or Concealments of Treasons, and done perpetrated or committed, or hereafter to be done, perpetrated or committed, by any Person or Persons out of this Realm of England, shall be from henceforth enquired of, heard and determined before the King's Justices of his Bench, for Pleas to be holden before himself, by good and lawful Men of the same Shire, in like Manner and Form to all Intents and Purposes as if such Treasons, Misprisions of Treasons, or Concealments of Treasons had been done, perpetrated and committed within the same Shire where they shall be so enquired of, heard and determined as is aforesaid.

The statute added the further proviso concerning the trial of peers, "That if any Peers of *this* Realm shall happen to be indicted of any such Treasons, or other Offences aforesaid, by the Authority of this Act" they were to be tried "by their Peers, in such like Manner and Form as hath heretofore been accustomed."[54]

In his report of *Calvin's Case* Coke had framed the constitutional relationship of England and Ireland, perhaps not unintentionally, in ambiguous terms. He cited a charter of Henry III to the effect that "as now the laws of England became the proper laws of Ireland."[55] He also, however, affirmed that it was "evident from our books" that "Ireland is a dominion separate

[54] *SL* II: 361, italics added. [55] Coke, 7 *Reports*, fol. 23a.

and distinct from England."[56] He conceded as well that Ireland "because they have Parliaments holden there ... they retain unto this day divers of their ancient customs ... [and] that Ireland is governed by law and customs, separate and diverse from the laws of England."[57] At other places, however, the report stated "That albeit Ireland was a distinct dominion, yet the title thereof being by conquest, the same by judgement of law might by express words be bound by act of the Parliament of England."[58]

From a passage such as this it is tempting to see Coke as a conquest theorist, as Johann Sommerville has interpreted him.[59] This was, of course, not nearly as controversial an assertion as the contention that England had been conquered in 1066 and that the current English law was the corrupt product of the Norman Conquest – a position which Christopher Hill has associated with the radicals of the 1640s and 50s.[60] Early Stuart jurists appear to have been fairly comfortable with the idea that Ireland had been conquered. Ellesmere, for example, in his speech on the *post-nati* did not shrink from the idea that Ireland had been conquered and English law imposed there by King John.[61] Davies in the *Case of Tanistry* was willing to advance the proposition that Ireland had gradually been "conquered and reduced to the subjection of the crown of England." At the same time, however, he asserted that in England "the common law ... was not introduced by the conqueror" and that this had been "observed and proved very learnedly by lord *Coke* in the preface to the third part of his reports."[62]

While potentially troublesome and certainly intriguing, the question of the authorial intent is not particularly relevant in dealing with these authorities. Coke had been dead since 1634, and how he would have dealt with the issues raised in Maguire's trial remains as much a matter of speculation today as it was in the 1640s. More central to our purposes here is to inquire into how the authority of key texts such as Coke's report of *Calvin's Case* was subject to appropriation and exploitation by competing interests. It should be evident that Coke and the other authorities in question could be read in such a way as to support either an exceptionalist conception of the relationship between England and Ireland or one like that of Darcy that emphasized a shared heritage of Magna Carta and the common law.

The status of Magna Carta and other English statutes in Ireland was problematic. The Irish statute of 10 Henry VII, c. 22, "Poynings' Law" to

56 Coke, 7 *Reports*, fol. 22b. 57 Coke, 7 *Reports*, fol. 23a.
58 Coke, 7 *Reports*, fols. 17b–18a. 59 Sommerville, "History and Theory": 252–253.
60 J. E. Christopher Hill, "The Norman Yoke," in Hill, *Puritanism and Revolution* (London, 1958), pp. 50–122; Pocock, *Ancient Constitution*, pp. 125–127, 318–321.
61 Louis Knafla, ed., *Law and Politics in Jacobean England: The Tracts of Lord Chancellor Ellesmere* (Cambridge, 1977), p. 232.
62 Davies, *Report of Cases*, pp. 101, 109.

Coke and his contemporaries, had decreed "That all statutes, late made within the said realm of England, concerning or belonging to the common and publique weal of the same, from henceforth be deemed good and effectuall in the law, and over that be acceptyd, used, and executed within this land of Ireland in all points at all times requisite according to the tenor and effect of the same ..."[63] In the Earl of Strafford's trial difficulty arose concerning the fifteenth article when the prosecution had sought to pursue the impeachment not only under 25 Edward III for levying war but under the Irish treason statute of 18 Henry VI, c. 3. Strafford was able to argue that the act of 1 Henry IV, c. 10 made in England for the repeal of all treasons not contained in 25 Edward III, had been brought into force by the Irish Act of 10 Henry VIII, c. 22 effectively repealing 18 Henry VI, c. 3.[64] Sir Edward Coke, in *The Fourth Part of The Institutes*, published on the eve of Maguire's trial, affirmed that 10 Henry VII, c. 22 "extendeth to Magna Carta, and to all Acts of Parliament made in England before this Act ..."[65] However, Coke reserved a level of independence for the Irish parliament, asserting that "it is to be observed that such Acts of Parliament as have been made in England since 10. H[enry] 7. wherein Ireland is not Particularly named or generally included, extend not thereunto, for that albeit it [Ireland] be governed by the same law, yet is it a distinct Realm or kingdom and ... hath Parliaments there."[66] This was in keeping with his earlier report of *Calvin's Case* except that in this later work he made no mention of a title by conquest.

The published authorities were divided on the issue of the privileges of the Irish peerage. Sir James Dyer, writing during the reign of Elizabeth, reported a case in which the Chancellor of Ireland, Sir William Gerrard, had moved the question to the queen's learned counsel of "Whether an Earl or Lord of Ireland, who commits treason in Ireland by open rebellion, shall be arraigned and put to this trial in England by the statute of 26 Henry VIII, c. 13, 32 Henry VIII, c. 4, 35 Henry VIII, c. 2 or 5 Edward VI, c. 11." The resolution of Gerrard and justices Wray CJKB and Dyer CJCP was that an Irish peer could not be so tried because "he cannot have his trial here by his peers nor by any jury of twelve because he is not a subject of England, but of Ireland; and therefore his trial shall be there." The common usage of trying Irish peers, Dyer's *Abridgment* stated, was by attainder in the Irish parliament and "not by peers."[67]

Richard Crompton in his treatise on the jurisdiction of courts confirmed Dyer's authority in this matter.[68] These authorities were in turn followed by

[63] *Irish Statutes*: 56. [64] BL Harl. MS 164, fol. 950r; Rushworth, *Tryal*, p. 452.
[65] Coke, *The Fourth Part of the Institutes*, p. 351.
[66] Coke, *The Fourth Part of the Institutes*, p. 351.
[67] 3 Dyer 360b, 73 *Eng. Rep.* 807 (KB).
[68] Richard Crompton, *L'Avthoritie et Ivrisdiction des Covrt de la Maiestie de la Roygne:*

Oliver St. John in his printed *Argument* in the Earl of Strafford's case. Scottish or French peers, St. John argued, were triable in England as commoners "because those Countries are not governed by the Lawes of England" and, therefore, "the Law takes no notice of their Nobility." However, Ireland, because it was governed by the same laws as England, was a different matter: "the Peers there are triable according to the Law of England, onely *per pares*." Strafford, being an English and not an Irish peer, was "not triable by the Peers of Ireland."[69] St. John, conceding that Irish peers had a similar right to be tried *per pares*, simply developed the counter-argument to Strafford's constitutional exceptionalism. Because Magna Carta was in force in Ireland, Strafford's actions in exercising conciliar justice and administering martial law in time of peace were of questionable legality. Like Darcy he presumed a shared legal heritage between the two kingdoms.

Against the authority of Dyer was that of the later writings of Sir Edward Coke. In *The First Part of the Institutes of the Lawes of England,* published in 1628, Coke argued that Wray had subsequently at the trials of Brian O'Rourke (1591) and Sir John Perrot (1592) "utterly denied" the opinion of Dyer.[70] In *The Second Part of the Institutes of the Lawes of England*, published posthumously in 1642 on the order of the Long Parliament, Coke asserted with respect to Magna Carta that "Only a Lord of Parliament of England shall be tried by his Peers being Lords of Parliament: and neither noblemen of any other Country, nor others that are called Lords, and are no Lords of Parliament, are accounted Pares, Peers within this Statute."[71] In *The Third Part of the Institutes,* published before Maguire's trial in 1644 by order of the Long Parliament, Coke reaffirmed his earlier stance, stating that "albeit a man be Noble, and yet no Lord of the Parliament of this Realm (as if he be a Nobleman of Scotland, or of Ireland, of France, etc.) he shall be tried by knights, Esquires, or others of the Commons." The sons of peers, while they may style themselves lords, not being lords of the English parliament did not enjoy the right to trial by peers and were to be tried "as one under the degree of a Peer, and Lord of Parliament." Ecclesiastical peers were also to be tried "by the countrey, that is, by free-holders, for that they are not of the degree of Nobility."[72]

Nouelmant collect & compose, per R. Crompton del milieu Temple Esquire, Apprentice del Ley (London, 1637), fol. 23a.

69 BL TT E.208(7), Oliver St. John, *An Argument of Law concerning the Bill of Attainder of High Treason of Thomas Earle of Strafford: At a Conference in a Committee of both Houses of Parliament* (London, 1641), p. 63.

70 Sir Edward Coke, *The First Part of the Institutes of the Lawes of England. Or A Commentarie vpon Littleton, not the name of a Lawyer onely, but of the Law it selfe* (London, 1628), fol. 261b.

71 Sir Edward Coke, *The Second Part of the Institutes of the Lawes of England* (London, 1642), p. 48.

72 Sir Edward Coke, *The Third Part of the Institutes of the Laws of England: concerning High Treason, and other Pleas of the Crown, and Criminall causes* (London, 1644), p. 30.

The role of these authorities in early modern legal argument was problematic not only because of the variety and ambiguity of these texts but because of the nature of early modern reading practices themselves. Roger Chartier has argued that the act of reading is essentially an act of appropriation.[73] "Readers," he argues, "use infinite numbers of subterfuges to procure prohibited books, to read between the lines, and to subvert the lessons imposed on them." The intention in producing a text is considered distinct from its reception and this reception "without fail . . . invents, shifts about, distorts."[74] Moving beyond the banal post-structural truism that texts are infinitely readable, Chartier's project of a history of reading suggests a far more compelling set of questions: why does it become advantageous for historical actors to read a text one way and not another?

In the case of state treason trials the evident answer is that legal authorities were read in whatever way was deemed most convincing for the counsel's argument. It is clear that barristers formed a community of professional readers who included among their reading practices the performative citation and quotation aloud in court of authoritative writings. Furthermore, there can be little doubt that many legal writings were composed with an eye to this purpose.[75] These writings could be published or unpublished treatises, histories, statutes, yearbooks, or reports, or could include material usually unpublished such as writs, deeds, and charters. When a legal text was openly cited in court its authority was appropriated with it. These authorities were exploited through strategies of truncation, selective quotation, and quite simply the offering of disputed readings of the same text. For example, with regard to the aforementioned treason statute of 25 Edward III, what did "compassing the death of the king" entail? In short, treason trials were fought out through the appropriation of sometimes shared and sometimes competing authoritative texts. Seen in this light the publication and reception of the remaining three volumes of Coke's *Institutes* on the eve of Maguire's trial were of crucial importance.[76]

Printed on the order of the Long Parliament, the second, third, and fourth volumes of Coke's *Institutes* had something of a quasi-canonical status and

[73] Roger Chartier, "Texts, Printing, Readings," in Lynn Hunt, ed., *The New Cultural History* (Berkeley, Calif., 1989), pp. 154–175 and his *The Order of Books*, trans. Lydia G. Cochrane (Cambridge, 1994), Preface and ch. 1.

[74] Chartier, *Order of Books*, pp. vii, x.

[75] This aspect of early-modern legal argument has been explored by Adam Fox in "Custom, Memory and the Authority of Writing," in Paul Griffiths, Adam Fox, and Steve Hindle, eds., *The Experience of Authority in Early Modern England* (London, 1996), pp. 89–116.

[76] The second part containing Coke's commentaries on Magna Carta was published in 1642 with the third part concerning pleas of the crown and the fourth part dealing with the jurisdiction of the courts both appearing shortly before Maguire's trial in 1644. Only the first volume, his commentaries on Littleton, appeared during his lifetime, in 1628.

were read and cited by such divers individuals as the Welsh royalist Judge David Jenkins and the Leveller John Lilburne.[77] Disputes concerning interpretation aside, the authority of statutes as the approved declarations of king, lords, and commons was relatively unproblematic. Legal treatises also enjoyed a certain authority, whether by virtue of their antiquity, the good reputation of their authors, or, in the particular case of Coke, quasi-official status. In Maguire's trial the opposing counsels appealed to a number of shared, disputed, and competing authorities consisting of statutes, legal reports, and treatises offering a variety of rival readings. Indeed, the forensic rhetoric of the day placed a premium on voluminous citation and quotation of the written authorities.

Prynne was the first to present his argument. He denied that Maguire's Irish peerage was within the final proviso of 35 Henry VIII, c. 2 and countered the objection that Maguire's trial was contrary to Magna Carta by questioning its status in Ireland. Prynne established first that it was beyond doubt that Irish commoners were comprehended within the act. To this effect he cited first the trial of Brian O'Rourke, a Gaelic lord tried late in the reign of Elizabeth, then that of Sir John Perrott, an English commoner, one-time Lord Deputy of Ireland, also tried late in Elizabeth's time, and, finally, that of Maguire's alleged co-conspirator Hugh MacMahon, who was tried in November 1644 shortly before Maguire's own trial.[78] He rebutted the authority of Dyer by arguing that it was simply an opinion given in response to a "question demanded by the Chancellor of Ireland in a private discourse" and that, "the reason rendered as the ground of this opinion" was "utterly

[77] This should not come as a surprise as the two men were prisoners together in the Tower of London during the late 1640s: D. Alan Orr, "John Lilburne and the Ancient Constitution, 1646–1649," unpublished MA dissertation (Queen's University, 1993), ch. 3.

[78] IT Petyt MS 511 v. 23, fol. 120v: "It is as cleare yt a treason committed in I[reland] by and Irish subiect may be [by?] his or hers [peers?] in England by virtue of this Act though triable in Irl[and] and yt a com[m]oner of Irland brought prisoner ther against his will is triable her [heer?] for such a treason by this law, as was adiudged by a[ll] the iudges of England in Orourkes case; 33 Eliz[abeth]; as in S[i]r John Perrott @ 34 Eliz: contrary to the opinion of Dyer... 42 Eliz. f. 360:b resolved to be no law... now admitted resolved in the case of Hugh MacMahon, condemned for this very treason of w[hi]ch Maguire stands indicted." I have used Prynne's own manuscript report in the Inner Temple in preference to his printed argument published in 1658 and other manuscript reports when attempting to characterize his position in the trial. For the trial of O'Rourke see 1 Anderson 262, 123 *Eng. Rep.* 463 (CP); *The Annales, or Generall Chronicle of England, begun first by maister Iohn Stow and after him continued and augmented with matters forreyn and domestique, auncient and moderne, unto the ende of this present yeare 1614* (London, 1615), sigs. Sss2v–Sss3r, pp. 763–764; for the political background to the trials of both Perrott and O'Rourke see Hiram Morgan, "Extradition and Treason-trial of a Gaelic Lord: The Case of Brian O'Rourke," *Irish Jurist* 22 (1987) 285–301; for the trial of MacMahon see Bodl. Lib. Tanner MS 418, fols. 5–16; although the first four leaves of this manuscript are missing the account of MacMahon's trial is fairly complete.

false and erroneous."[79] He also argued that historically there was no right of trial *per pares* for Irish peers, asserting that he had "sought to fynde whether any Peere in Ireland had been tryed per pares" and claimed that he could "neither in history nor elswhere find any."[80] Prynne conceded only the sole precedent of the case the Lord Slane, but was unwilling to accept it as binding precedent as "it was confessed by the Judges there [that] they never heard or read of any one such tryal used in Ireland."[81]

Against Dyer he summoned the authority of Coke's *Institutes* and also the late Lord Chief Justice's reports of *Calvin's Case* and of the *Lord Sanchar's Case*.[82] With respect to the Scottish nobility Coke's report of *Calvin's Case* stated that, "albeit a postnatus in Scotland, or any of his posterity, be the heir of a nobleman of Scotland, and by his birth legitimated in England, yet he is none of the peers or nobility of England; for his natural ligeance and obedience due by the law of nature, maketh him a subject and no alien within England: but that subjection maketh him not noble within England; for that nobility had his original by the King's creation, and not of nature."[83] The argument was clear: the legal privileges to be enjoyed by the *post-nati* were not to extend to the privileges of peerage.

This position was further clarified in *Lord Sanchar's Case*. Robert Crichton, Lord Sanchar, was a Scottish baron who had procured through intermediaries the murder of one John Turner within the city of London during the reign of James I. The case dealt primarily with the law of accessory, but the question of Sanchar's Scottish peerage also arose. When it was inquired how Sanchar "being an ancient Baron of Scotland should be tried," the Chief Justices replied "that none within this realm of England is accounted a peer of the realm, but he who is a lord of the Parliament of England; for every subject either is a lord of the Parliament, or one of the Commons, and the Lord Sanchar was not a lord of the Parliament within this kingdom, and therefore

[79] IT Petyt MS 511 v. 23, fol. 117v; the manuscript is bound upside-down so that the foliation is backwards.

[80] Bodl. Lib. Tanner MS 418, fol. 40; this argument is repeated and developed at length in the printed version of Prynne's argument: *The Subiection of all Traytors*, sigs. G2v–G3v, pp. 28–30.

[81] Bodl Lib. Tanner MS 418, fol. 41: "... But making inquiry I confesse I was informed that the Lord Slany was tryed by his Peeres But the truth of that I know not, however una hiuernuo non facit ver"; Prynne in his printed argument asserted that at Lord Slane's trial held "much about 20 years since" the judges had confessed that "*they never heard or read of any one such tryal used in Ireland*" (Prynne's italics): Prynne, *The Subiection of all Traytors*, sig. G 3r, p. 29; I quote here from Prynne's printed argument, the accuracy of which is confirmed by the independent manuscript account under the provenance of Sir Arthur Turnour (d. 1651) in the Harvard Law School, which noted of Lord Slane's trial "... mes les Iudges disont qe ft vn nouell case": HLS MS 113, fol. 193.

[82] Bodl. Lib. Tanner MS 418, fols. 31, 38, 42, 44, 48; IT Petyt MS 511 v. 23, fol. 119v.

[83] Coke, 7 *Reports*, fol. 15a.

should be tried by the Commons of the realm viz. Knights, Esquires, or others of the Commons..."[84]

With Scotland, of course, the exceptionalist model was easier to apply because it was not only a separate and distinct realm but, unlike Ireland, it was governed *per aliam legem* – by a law other than that of England.[85] St. John's argument against exceptionalism, that the common law would recognize the peerage, was therefore not available.

Prynne's response to the objection that Maguire's trial by a Middlesex jury composed of commoners would contravene Magna Carta, and that acts of parliament made contrary to the great charter were void, revealed not just a constitutional exceptionalism, but also a position more in keeping with legal positivism than the jurisprudence of Coke. Prynne argued first that Magna Carta had been "originally made for England and not for Ireland" and that it was not brought into force by the Irish statute 10 Henry VII, c. 22. The words of the statute "all statutes late made" did not comprehend Magna Carta because Magna Carta, having been made over two centuries previously, could not be taken as within the word of the statute "late."[86] Even admitting that Magna Carta was intended for Ireland and brought into force by 10 Henry VII, c. 22, Prynne was unwilling to concede that this invalidated Maguire's trial by a common jury. Magna Carta, asserted Prynne was "but an Act of Parliament and no Doubt may be repealed..." To this Prynne added that "Magna Charta hath been repealed and the com[m]on Law altered in sundry p[ar]ticulars since the making of it." There were "sundry causes" for which a man could now be incarcerated or imprisoned which he could not have been according to the common law and the great charter, "by virtue of subsequent Acts." Pushing his point further he argued that "now by the Act of 35 Henry VIII [c. 2] Magn[a] Ch[arta] and the com[mon] law are both altered in the p[ar]ticular..."[87] If an Irish commoner could be tried in England by virtue of this act so too could an Irish peer, a peer having "no mean [more?] interest in his Peerage that a Com[m]oner in his liberty, priviledge and birth right, the com[m]on law and Magna Charta..."[88] Prynne, however, stopped short of arguing for a general repeal of Magna Carta and it is unclear from this evidence if he saw the fundamental principles behind the great charter as subject to repeal.

[84] Coke, 9 *Reports*, fol. 117a–b.

[85] For Coke's views on Scotland see *The Fourth Part of the Institutes*, pp. 345–349.

[86] Bodl. Lib. Tanner MS 418, fol. 42.

[87] IT Petyt MS 511 v. 23, fol. 117v; see also Bodl. Lib. Tanner MS 418, fol. 43 and especially HLS MS 113, fol. 195, which reads: "Mes es sans question qe M: Charta in cet point repeale" and that "M: Ch: in cet realm est change in mults particulars."

[88] IT Petyt MS 511 v. 23, fol. 119r; see also 117v: "so the Peerage of a Peere may as well be taken away by this Act, as the priviledge of a Com[m]oner."

Prynne was, of course, one of the most slippery political polemicists of the period and his prolixity makes him difficult to pin down on anything particular for more than a single occasion on a single issue. His argument did, however, closely resemble the exceptionalist position of the Irish Judges in their response to the queries of 1641. Prynne also made appeal to the rhetoric of *necessity* in arguing his case. In its particulars, at least, the common law was mutable and the particular circumstances of Ireland had *necessitated* changes in order to settle the governance of that kingdom. In the case of the Irish peerage, Prynne argued, this divergence from English practice in the trial of peers had been rendered necessary by the prominent role played by the Irish peerage in previous rebellions as captains and heads.[89] The contention was that the Irish peerage were "allyed in Blood . . . and will not bee forward to try him" and that the Irish peerage would without doubt acquit the prisoner.[90] Furthermore, it was asserted that "for necessity sake" Maguire must be tried in England because were he kept at Dublin his confederates there would attempt to rescue him.[91]

Thomas Twysden was the first to speak for the defense.[92] He answered the objection that Magna Carta was not comprehended within 10 Henry VII, c. 22 by referring to the shared (and disputed) authority of Coke.[93] While Coke's authority could be invoked by the prosecution on the issue of the validity of foreign peers' privileges there can be little doubt that on this particular issue Coke was uncharacteristically clear. The exceptionalist arguments of the prosecution demanded that the status of Magna Carta in Ireland be thrown into question. While Coke's authority supported the prosecution on the question of privilege of peerage, *The Fourth Part of the Institutes* made it clear that the Irish statute 10 Henry VII, c. 22 included the great charter.[94]

With respect to the continued status of Magna Carta in Ireland Twysden was quite willing to concede that it could be altered by subsequent acts of parliament. Magna Carta, he argued, "by expresse words may be repealed

89 Bodl. Lib. Tanner MS 418, fols. 35–36; HLS MS 113, fols. 190–191; the appeal to necessity is brought out most strongly in these two manuscript accounts.

90 Bodl. Lib. Tanner MS 418, fol. 35; HLS MS 113, fol. 191.

91 Bodl. Lib. Tanner MS 418, fol. 37.

92 I have relied extensively on the Bodleian Library manuscript Tanner MS 418 in characterizing the arguments of Twysden, Rolle, and Hale. BL Sloane MS 3828, an account in the hands of Heneage Finch, is obviously a much later transcription and has the disadvantage of conflating the argument of Prynne with that of Rolle and that of Twysden with that of Hale. This is unsurprising as, according to Tanner MS 418, there is much repetition in the second arguments.

93 I assume that the citation "Inst 351" in Bodl. Lib. Tanner MS 418, fol. 49 means *The Fourth Part of the Institutes* as this is the exact page of that volume on which Coke addresses the issue; see also Bodl. Lib. Tanner MS 418, fol. 53.

94 Coke, *The Fourth Part of the Institutes*, p. 351.

but not by implyed."[95] 35 Henry VIII, c. 2 did not mention the great charter explicitly as an act of repeal but merely affirmed that peers of *this* realm were to be judged always by their peers. Furthermore, the statute did not create "a new kinde of tryall not heertofore used in the Com[m]on Law but only enlarged their power..."[96] In support of this Twysden cited Coke's report of *Foster's Case,* in which it was decreed that "a statute in the affirmative shall not take away a former statute in the affirmative."[97] To the authority of Dyer he added that of St. John's *Argument of Law* which he cited "not as the opinion of a privat man – but as the Censure of the whole house of Commons delivered by him that this Statute [35 Henry VII, c. 2] extends not to Peeradge in Ireland."[98] Coke may have believed in a shared legal heritage between the two realms of England and Ireland, but he was unwilling to extend this to the privileges of peerage. With St. John's *Argument* there was no such reticence – because Ireland was governed by the common law, the common law would recognize an Irish peerage and thus assure Irish peers of trial by their peers. The presumed shared heritage of legal rights and privileges that had underpinned the attack on Strafford became the bulwark of Maguire's defense.

Rolle's argument for the prosecution followed much the same pattern as Prynne's. He affirmed the precedents of O'Rourke and Perrot, citing the first volume of Coke's *Institutes* in support of the contention that, as commoners (both English and Irish) were bound by 35 Henry VIII, c. 2, so too were peers.[99] He cited also the disputed passages of *Calvin's Case* as evidence that a statute made in England could bind subjects in Ireland with respect to their persons "without particular words."[100] With regard to the status of Magna Carta in Ireland, Rolle conceded that the great charter had been confirmed in Ireland but, because the defense had not shown "that Custome of tryall of Peeres in Parliament in Ireland[,] the confirmacon of Magna Charta of the lawes of England ther will not helpe."[101] St. John's *Argument* was dismissed in much the same way as Prynne had dismissed Dyer 360b as "but his privat opinion."[102]

The argument of Hale which followed was a vehement rejection of the exceptionalist position based on two premises. The first was that the right of peers to trial by their peers pre-dated the Norman Conquest in England.

[95] Bodl. Lib. Tanner MS 418, fol. 53. [96] Bodl. Lib. Tanner MS 418, fols. 52–53.

[97] Bodl. Lib. Tanner MS 418, fol. 57; see also BL Sloane MS 3828, fols. 66v, 68r ; Coke, 11 *Reports*, fol. 6a. This case concerned the relationship of the several Elizabethan recusancy statutes to each other.

[98] Bodl. Lib. Tanner MS 418, fols. 56–57. [99] Bodl. Lib. Tanner MS 418, fol. 60.

[100] Bodl. Lib. Tanner MS 418, fol. 61; by the disputed passages I mean fols. 17b–18a and 22b–23a.

[101] Bodl. Lib. Tanner MS 418, fol. 65. [102] Bodl. Lib. Tanner MS 418, fol. 66.

To this effect was cited the precedent of "Goodwyn Earl of Kent in the time of the Saxons [who] was Tryed by the Earls and Barons."[103] Magna Carta, therefore, did not create a new manner of trial but simply confirmed an existing privilege at common law.[104] The second was that "The Com[m]on Law of England is prima facie, the Com[m]on Law of Ireland for that [realm] was Conquered by England and soe the Com[m]on Lawe made of force there."[105] Ellesmere had argued in his speech on the *post-nati* that the English law had come into force in Ireland in the time of King John and Hale took a similar line, citing the case of the Prior of Dublin from the thirteenth year of Edward I's reign.[106] The right of Irish peers was therefore a privilege at common law which had been confirmed both by the Irish statute of 10 Henry VII, c. 22 and, consequently, by the great charter.[107] Ireland as a subordinate kingdom to England, argued Hale, was "intituled to the preservacon of such priviledge as the Com[m]ons introduced thereupon the Conquest."[108] While he conceded that these legal rights and privileges could be revoked or limited by statute, he argued that this could only be the case if Ireland was specifically named.[109]

Hale was, of course, on familiar ground in claiming the common law and its attendant liberties and privileges for Ireland. St. John and his colleagues in Strafford's trial made much the same argument as had the old English lawyer Patrick Darcy in condemning Strafford's administration in Ireland.[110] Hale affirmed the common law's pre-conquest origins and the attendant right to trial by peers in England. Like Sir John Davies he envisioned the extension of English rights and liberties to Ireland by conquest and seems to have had no problem reconciling this to the pre-Norman conquest pedigree of the English common law. Unsurprisingly the defense did not hesitate to bring Davies's authority in the *Case of Tanistry* in support of their constitutional posture.[111]

This section has demonstrated that the competing claims of the prosecution and the defense in Maguire's trial reflected differing stances on the

[103] BL Sloane MS 3828, fol. 67r; while the arguments of Hale and Twysden are conflated into a single text in this report there can be no doubt that this is Hale's argument. Both Tanner MS 418, fol. 67 and HLS MS 113, fol. 206 attribute the use of this precedent to Hale.

[104] Bodl. Lib. Tanner MS 418, fol. 68; BL Sloane MS 3828, fol. 67r.

[105] Bodl. Lib. Tanner MS 418, fol. 68; HLS MS 113, fols. 206–207.

[106] Knafla, ed., *Law and Politics*, p. 232; Bodl. Lib. Tanner MS 418, fol. 68; BL Sloane MS 3828, fol. 67r.

[107] Bodl. Lib. Tanner MS 418, fols. 68, 70; BL Sloane MS 3828, fol. 67v.

[108] Bodl. Lib. Tanner MS 418, fol. 70.

[109] Bodl. Lib. Tanner MS 418, fol. 69.

[110] Perceval-Maxwell, *Outbreak*, pp. 164–165.

[111] BL Sloane MS 3828, fol. 67r; this is most likely Twysden's argument as Bodl. Lib. Tanner MS 418, fol. 55 has Twysden citing "Davies rep. 29[39?]" and HLS MS 113, fol. 200 has Twysden citing the *Case of Tanistry* as well.

constitutional relationship of England and Ireland. The defense seeking to uphold Maguire's right to be tried by Irish peers in Ireland adopted a constitutionalist position that emphasized the shared legal heritage of England and Ireland. This heritage of legal privileges was grounded in the common law and was confirmed by Magna Carta and the Irish statute of 10 Henry VII, c. 22 called Poynings' Law. In response the prosecution erected an exceptionalist position that emphasized the differences between the laws and customs of England on the one hand and Ireland on the other. The two sides endeavored to legitimate these positions through the presentation of competing interpretations of alternately shared and competing textual authorities. It was from these competing visions that Justice Bacon fashioned his decision.

IV

The decision of Justice Bacon was, unsurprisingly, in favor of the prosecution, affirming that Maguire was triable by a Middlesex jury composed of knights and esquires. Bacon's position, however, represented a softening of the hard exceptionalism of Prynne and Rolle. Bacon considered the central issues of the previous manner of trial for Irish peers, the status of Magna Carta in Ireland, and, concomitantly, the power of the English parliament to bind Irish subjects. The decision he reached was based on his own particular interpretation of the central disputed text of *Calvin's Case*. Maguire, like Calvin, *did* have legal rights and privileges in England to enjoy property and to hold suit in the king's courts there, but this privilege did not extend to his peerage. The exceptionalist position represented certain dangers in that it could be used to justify an autocratic style of executive government characterized by the abuse of martial law and an unusually liberal conception of the equitable and other prerogative jurisdictions. Because it was by the same policy of common law that Ireland was made a body politic, what could legally be done there might also be done in England. Bacon's argument sought to justify Maguire's trial by commoners in England in such a way as would not lend too much approbation to the exceptonalist position.

The most obvious precedent that Bacon examined was that of Gerald Fitzgerald, Ninth Earl of Kildare, attainted by the Irish parliament in 1536 along with his son, the notorious "Silken" Thomas Fitzgerald.[112] Kildare's career had been plagued by accusations of treason and at his death in 1534 he had been, once again, under suspicion of high treason.[113] The problem here was that Kildare had died before being brought to trial, necessitating

[112] Bodl. Lib. Tanner MS 418, fols. 76–77. [113] *DNB* VII, pp. 118–120.

a bill for his attainder in 1536.[114] Silken Thomas also presented difficulties as a precedent. The histories available to the jurists in Maguire's trial were divided on his fate.[115] Stow in his *Annales* named Thomas as Earl of Kildare and described the manner of his execution by beheading as befitted a peer.[116] Holinshed, by contrast, vehemently denied that Thomas had ever been confirmed as Earl of Kildare but made no mention of his manner of execution.[117] Bacon cited also the precedent of O'Rourke's trial to the effect that Ireland was comprehended within 35 Henry VIII, c. 2 because, although it was within the king's dominions it was, in accordance with the words of the statute, "out of the Realme of England."[118]

With respect to the status of Magna Carta in Ireland Bacon affirmed that it was possible for parliament to revoke privileges guaranteed by the great charter and that this could be done by general words.[119] He affirmed also that an English statute could bind the king's Irish subjects "by express words or generall," justifying Maguire's removal to England.[120] However, he denied that there was anything in 35 Henry VIII, c. 2 that had repealed the privilege of trial by peers guaranteed by Magna Carta.[121] The great charter had not been repealed by 35 Henry VIII, c. 2 but stood in force because "the quality of the Prisoner is altered by his bringing over for his Peeres ther are not Peeres heer . . . but knights and esq[uire]s."[122] Maguire had not lost

[114] He was in fact not attainted until his son was in 1536. Silken Thomas according to the *DNB* was attainted in *both* the English and Irish parliaments and executed as a commoner. I have, however, found no mention in the sources relating to Maguire's trial or the index to *SR* of either an English bill of attainder or evidence that Thomas was executed as a commoner: *DNB* VII, pp. 149–150.

[115] Bacon appears to have made use of Stow in his decision and the defense counsels of Holinshed: for Bacon see HLS MS 113, fol. 212 and the defense BL Sloane MS 3828, fol. 70r.

[116] Stow, *The Annales*, sig. Bbb4v, p. 573; Kildare's five uncles were executed as commoners by hanging, drawing, and quartering.

[117] Raphael Holinshed, *The Chronicles of Ireland*, in *Holinshed's Chronicles: England, Scotland and Ireland with a New Introduction by Vernon F. Snow*, 6 vols. (New York, 1965; reprinted New York, 1976), vol. VI, p. 304.

[118] Bodl. Lib. Tanner MS 418, fol. 80; HLS MS 113, fol. 212.

[119] Bodl. Lib. Tanner MS 418, fols. 84–85; Sloane MS 3828, fol. 72v.

[120] Bacon cited Coke's *The Fourth Part of the Institutes* in support of this contention. The exact words of Coke are, however, ". . . such Acts of Parliament as have been made in England since 10 Henry 7 wherin Ireland is not particularly named or generally included, extend not thereunto . . ." The assumption that Ireland was to be "generally included" in the words "out of the Realm of England" appears to be Bacon's and the prosecution's interpretation: Coke, *The Fourth Part of the Institutes*, p. 351; Bodl. Lib. Tanner MS 418, fol. 77; see also BL Sloane MS 3828, fol. 72r, which asserts that Bacon held that although an English peerage could "not be taken away by Generall words" other foreign peerages (including Irish and Scottish) could.

[121] Bodl. Lib. Tanner MS 418, fol. 85.

[122] Bodl. Lib. Tanner MS 418, fol. 85; see also BL Sloane 3828, fol. 72v.

his right to trial by his peers but his legal status had been redefined by his removal to England. Like Lord Sanchar he still enjoyed the right of trial by twelve freeholders. In response to the defense's objections that Maguire as a sitting member of the Irish House of Lords enjoyed privilege against his removal to England, Bacon answered that parliamentary privilege did not hold in cases of high treason.[123]

Earlier it was argued that the significance of Maguire's trial was that it raised the issue of the constitutional relationship of the three kingdoms. In a sense it was a retrying of *Calvin's Case* and much of the debate in the trial hinged on disputed interpretations of Coke's printed report of that trial. Dyer 360b's contention was that an Irish peer was not triable in England, "for he cannot have his trial here by his peers, nor by any jury of twelve because he is not a subject of England, but of Ireland; and therefore his trial shall be there."[124] These words smacked of impersonal allegiance – the idea that allegiance was owed first to the political body of the realm and not to the natural person of the king. This doctrine may have been fashionable during the uncertain years of the Elizabethan succession crisis but it quickly became anathema after the Personal Union of 1603. Bacon accordingly marshaled the authority of *Calvin's Case* against Dyer, claiming that: "Now it is resolved in Calvins Case 7 Co[ke's Reports] 9 that Legiance and subiection extend to the Realme of Scottland and by the same reason to Ireland, for the Protection and Government of the King is to all his dominions and Realmes and all are under his obedience and soe that if protection draw allegiance then the Allegiance may not bee Locall or confined within the Lymitts of one Realme..."[125] Conrad Russell has argued that the parliamentarian position depended upon an impersonal conception of allegiance that separated the king's authority from his natural person, his natural from his political capacities – essentially the losing argument in *Calvin's Case*.[126] Bacon's reading of *Calvin's Case* conveniently side-stepped this potentially thorny issue and emphasized instead how the king's law and protection extended to all corners of his three realms. However, just as the indictment had continued to make allusion to constructive compassing, Bacon's decision depended ultimately on the winning argument in *Calvin's Case*. While Coke was preoccupied with asserting that allegiance was owed to the king in both his capacities,

123 BL Sloane MS 3828, fol. 72v; objections made on behalf of Sir George Radcliffe who had been sitting in the Irish House of Commons at the time of his removal by the Long Parliament had received a similar response: *CJ* II: 28.

124 3 Dyer 360b, 73 *Eng. Rep.* 807 (KB).

125 Bodl. Lib. Tanner MS 418, fols. 82–83; see also HLS MS 113, fol. 216: "... accordant al Calvins case, le allegiance de ascun subiect le roy, in Ireland England ou Scotland est eadem et nemy seuerable ..."

126 Russell, *Fall*, p. 55; Russell, *Causes*, pp. 157–158.

natural and political, Bacon laid stress on the ubiquity of the king's majesty in all three realms. He could not do so, however, without reaffirming the nature of the Personal Union as defined in *Calvin's Case.*

Ultimately Justice Bacon's decision affirmed the contention of the prosecution that Irish peers were triable in England by the statute of 35 Henry VIII, c. 2 by juries composed of commoners. Bacon's position represented a compromise. He did not swallow whole the exceptionalist position that had played such a prominent role in the attempts to legitimate the abusive practices of Strafford's administration in Ireland. He did not deny that Magna Carta was in force in Ireland and, while he accepted that a repeal of the great charter was possible, he denied that the statute of Henry VIII had done so. He affirmed, however, that an English statute could bind Irish subjects and that 35 Henry VIII, c. 2 had bound Maguire to come into England for trial. In England his condition was altered to that of a mere commoner. Maguire may have been outed of his peerage but, like Robert Calvin, he would still have his day in court, enjoy the benefit of English law, and suffer its gruesome penalties – in this case death as a commoner by hanging, drawing, and quartering.

V

Maguire's trial reflected a prevailing uncertainty over the constitutional relationship of the three kingdoms – an uncertainty raised to prominence by a prolonged period of crisis. The right to try treason was subsumed under the rubric of power to give law, whether by legislation or judgment from the bench. The trial raised the question of the nature of English sovereignty over Ireland. Ireland was a separate and distinct yet subordinate kingdom but in the eyes of early modern jurists, both English and Irish, it was rendered a body politic by the same fundamental policy of law as England, that of the English common law. This situation was, needless to say, highly ambiguous. In order to reconcile these issues it was necessary to establish firmly the status of Magna Carta and the common law in Ireland. Strafford and the Irish judges had sought to legitimate their perceived rough handling of Magna Carta and the common law through the position of Irish constitutional exceptionalism: while the common law was generally in force in Ireland, circumstances particular to that realm had necessitated departures from the accepted English practice. Thus, a position that might be characterized as "separatist" was marshaled in defense of Strafford's autocratic style of government. This is, of course, highly ironic as Strafford, while arguably uniting the Irish people in their distaste for his government, can hardly be described as an Irish nationalist. The prosecution in Maguire's trial exploited this position in support of the contention that Maguire could be tried in England contrary to Magna Carta. The defense in response assumed a constitutionalist position that emphasized a shared legal heritage of Magna Carta and the common law. Justice Bacon's decision sought to legitimate Maguire's trial in England by commoners without showing too much approbation for the exceptionalist position and the potentials for arbitrary government that it held. Magna Carta remained unrepealed in Ireland, but Maguire, being no peer in England, was triable by commoners there.

Under English law in the early modern period, treason was not merely a breach of allegiance but the unlawful assumption of sovereign jurisdiction. Such usurpations were also necessarily a constructive compassing of the king's death. In an ideal unitary state where the powers of the sovereign body are clearly defined and the territorial boundaries of the state are indisputable the issue of sovereign jurisdiction is relatively unproblematic. Such a state may in fact only exist in political-science texts. Stuart Britain and its dominions was definitely not such a state in the early modern period; nor was it, in terms of constitution or practice, fully abstract. It was rather an empire – a haphazard agglomeration of kingdoms and dominions held together by a single personal allegiance and highly vulnerable to the same religious divisions that afflicted both France and the Habsburg Empire in the sixteenth and seventeenth centuries.[127] Seen in this light, the mature political theories of Bodin and Hobbes, respectively, were as much prescriptive remedies to prolonged periods of political instability as attempts to distill the essence of political power and statehood. However, in February 1645, with regicide still unthinkable to most, the parliamentarian lawyers who tried Maguire sought to present a picture of a well-ordered constitution deriving from the leading precedent of *Calvin's Case* that would see the British Isles through the present troubled times. In spite of the more radical theories of parliamentary sovereignty that writers such as Henry Parker were developing in the parliamentarian cause, the moral redescription of political action in Maguire's trial still adhered to customary forms of law and the courts remained, at least in name, the king's courts and the law the king's law. Political practice and thought may have been intertwined, but there was no obligation to make use of the latest and most fashionable of political theories.

Britain in early 1645 was an empire that had, at least since 1638, been embroiled in a religious, constitutional, and military crisis – a crisis that would be resolved only by the sword with the brutal and systematic reduction of Ireland and Scotland by parliamentarian armies in the period 1649–51.[128] *Calvin's Case* had left a legacy of legal and constitutional uncertainties as

[127] I have been somewhat influenced by Richard Mackenny's survey study, *Sixteenth-Century Europe, Expansion and Conflict* (New York, 1993).

[128] Russell, "British Problem": 397.

to the nature of Britain. During the deepening crisis of the 1640s, lawyers, politicians, and polemicists on all sides ruthlessly exploited its ambiguities in often incredulous ways. Parliament waged war against the personal commands of the king in the name of his authority while trying traitors like Maguire for constructively compassing his death. These ambiguities allowed the opposing counsels in Maguire's case to redescribe the constitutional relationship of the three kingdoms in a fashion most favorable to winning their case, farming sources such as *Calvin's Case* for authoritative evidence. Jurisdictions were ill defined and, in the context of the three kingdoms, the crime of high treason was bound up with questions of disputed jurisdictions and the faultlines emerging between them. Strafford's crime was not simply a breach of allegiance but that he took possession of one of the king's realms and ruled it as his own sovereign jurisdiction above and against that of the king. Maguire's misfortune was that he fell into a crack dividing two of three kingdoms, perishing between them.

6

Charles Stuart, King of England

I

The trial of Charles Stuart, King of England in January 1649 attempted to legitimate the claims of the Rump Parliament on behalf of the emerging Commonwealth to be the sole wielders of sovereign power in England. The trial of the king was just one stage in what J. P. Kenyon has described as a "ragged and haphazard" process of constitutional revision beginning with the army's purge of the Long Parliament in December 1648 and culminating on 19 May 1649 with the passage by the Rump of an act declaring England "to be a Commonwealth and Free State."[1] This act stated further that England was "henceforth [to] be governed . . . by the supreme authority of this nation, the representatives of the people in Parliament, and by such as they shall appoint and constitute as officers and ministers under them for the good of the people . . . without any King, or House of Lords."[2] The redescription of England as a popular state in which the people were, according to the Commons' resolution of 4 January 1649, "under God, the original of all just power" was essential to the Commonwealths-men's endeavors to legitimate their actions.[3]

Concomitantly, the king's status in relation to the body politic changed. He was no longer a sovereign king but merely an inferior magistrate administering his office in accordance with the sovereign will of the people as expressed by their representatives and, both in theory and in practice, answerable for the maladministration of his office and any abuses of his authority. The state remained a perpetual corporate entity but, in contrast to the commonplace notion of the king's two bodies, the political body of the whole state was no longer irrevocably tied to the king's natural person and the heirs of his body. This was an idea of the state that was abstract in the sense of

[1] J. P. Kenyon, ed., *The Stuart Constitution, 1603–1688: Documents and Commentary*, 2nd edn. (Cambridge, 1986), p. 296; S. R. Gardiner, ed., *Constitutional Documents of the Puritan Revolution, 1625–1660*, 3rd edn. (Oxford, 1906), p. 388.

[2] Gardiner, *Constitutional Documents*, p. 388.

[3] Kenyon, *Stuart Constitution*, p. 292.

the whole people forming, in the words of George Garnett, "a corporation (*universitas*), a single, abstract, juristic person."[4] One could conceive of a corporate conception of public authority in terms of a popular state as well as a monarchical one. With the king's two bodies, the state was the corporate body of the king and inseparable from his person and the heirs of his body. In this scheme, however, the king was not sovereign but merely a magistrate forming part of the government. It was not the immortality of the kingly dignity but that of the corporate body of the whole people that lent continuity to the constitutional order.

A notable precursor of this development was the sixteenth-century Huguenot tract, the *Vindiciae Contra Tyrannos*, translated and reprinted in English in 1648 on the eve of the regicide. The anonymous author[5] observed that, "although kings die, the people meanwhile, just like any other corporation, never dies. Like the perpetual flow of a river, the people is made immortal by the cycle of birth and death."[6] Similarly, Sir Cheney Culpeper in the postscript of a letter to Samuel Hartlib on the day following the king's execution asserted that "The [*King*] is noe partie to but a parte of the gouernment; The People cannot be called a party, but a body consultinge its owne good."[7] Culpeper was not a public man. He played no part in the trial and execution of the king and never sat in the Long Parliament.[8] He was, however, in the words of M. J. Braddick and Mark Greengrass, "a committed Parliamentarian with a developed and radical political agenda."[9]

This chapter is structured as follows. The first section considers the legislative and ideological contexts of the king's trial. The regicides' actions strongly suggest that they were less concerned with justifying their resistance to the king than with asserting their title to govern and exercise control over the marks and rights of sovereignty. They did this through a series of statutes passed from early January 1649 onwards, the first of which erected the High Court of Justice for the trying of the king. The second section deals with the charge against the king and the actual events of the trial itself. The principal concern is the king's challenge to the High Court's jurisdiction and the court's counter-claim to be a sovereign jurisdiction exercising right of final appeal. The third section concerns with the argument of John Bradshaw,

[4] Stephanus Junius Brutus [Philippe Mornay? Hubert Languet?], *Vindiciae Contra Tyrannos: or concerning the legitimate power of a prince over the people, and of the people over a prince*, ed. and trans. George Garnett (Cambridge, 1994), p. xxiii.

[5] Scholarly opinion is divided on whether the tract was the work of Philippe Mornay or Hubert Languet: Brutus, *Vindiciae Contra Tyrannos*, Intro., p. 2.

[6] Brutus, *Vindiciae Contra Tyrannos*, p. 90.

[7] Sir Cheney Culpeper, *The Letters of Sir Cheney Culpeper, 1641–1657*, in M. J. Braddick and Mark Greengrass, eds., *Seventeenth-Century Political and Financial Papers* Camden Society 5th Ser. (London, 1996), p. 349.

[8] *Letters of Cheney Culpeper*, p. 115. [9] *Letters of Cheney Culpeper*, p. 137.

Lord President of the court and his redescription of the English polity as a popular state.

II

The transition of England from monarchy to republic was unprecedented. English monarchs had been successfully deposed – Edward II, Richard II, Henry VI, and Richard III being the most prominent examples. However, in each case it was a rival claimant to the throne or, in the case of Edward II, his own son and heir who replaced the reigning monarch.[10] In contrast, the events of early 1649 consisted not simply in replacing the tenant of the throne but constituted an attack on hereditary kingship itself. On 1 January the House of Commons declared "That by the fundamental Laws of this Kingdom, it is treason in the King of *England*, for the Time being, to levy War against the Parliament and Kingdom of *England*."[11] On 4 January the Commons passed a further resolution that they were "the supreme power in this nation" and had the power to declare and enact laws independently of the House of Lords or the king.[12] The erection by unicameral "act" of parliament of a high court for the king's trial followed two days later, with the actual trial in Westminster Hall taking place between 20 and 27 January and the king punctually going to the scaffold on 30 January.[13] On the day of the king's execution the Rump passed a further statute entitled "An Act prohibiting the proclaiming any person to be King of England or Ireland, or the Dominions thereof."[14] The regicide was not simply an assault on a particular king but on the very notion of hereditary monarchy.

The declaration of 4 January marked the initial claim of the Rump to exercise in their own name the first and most crucial mark of sovereignty – the power to give law. In the trials of Strafford, Laud, and Maguire the Long Parliament's servants had maintained the fiction that they were acting in the king's name and in his interest. The "Act of the Commons of England Assembled in Parliament, for Erecting of a High Court of Justice for the Trying and Judging of Charles Stuart, King of England" of 6 January was the first significant attempt to exercise this mark of sovereignty independently of the king's authority.[15] The regicides would repeat this claim to sovereign power and jurisdiction during the king's trial. These events occurred well before both the Rump's resolutions of 6–7 February to abolish the kingly office

[10] I do not consider Simon de Montfort's deposition of Henry III to have been successful.

[11] *CJ* VI: 107. [12] Kenyon, *Stuart Constitution*, p. 292; *CJ* VI: 111.

[13] Gardiner, *Constitutional Documents*, p. 357.

[14] C. H. Firth and R. S. Rait, eds., *Acts and Ordinances of the Interregnum* (London, 1911) vol. I, p. 1263.

[15] Firth and Rait, *Acts and Ordinances* I, pp. 1253–1255.

and House of Lords and the subsequent legislative actions to this effect on 17 March and that of 19 March establishing a commonwealth or free state.[16]

The ideological position from which the king was attacked was both, broadly speaking, republican and radically constitutionalist. Scholars such as Jonathan Scott and Blair Worden have argued that a distinctively English republican tradition was conspicuously absent from England before 1649 and developed only in response to the actual experience of republican government in 1649–53 and its failure. For example, the mature works of the leading English republican thinkers John Harrington and Algernon Sidney did not appear until the Commonwealth had passed into memory.[17] For Sidney, at least, the experience of republican government was hands-on, he having been a naval administrator during the Commonwealth.[18] In contrast, the political theory of the regicides was "improvised and limited" in content[19] and the early republican works of 1649–50 were "limited" and "defensive" with an eye only to the objectives of "justification and submission."[20]

It is more than credible, however, to speak of a "classical republican" tradition, language, or mode of civic consciousness before 1649. This tradition, based on Greek and Roman models of political society, was definitely available to the humanist learning cultures of early Stuart England via the writings of such classical authors as Aristotle, Cicero, and Tacitus. As Scott has observed, the materials with which to construct a uniquely English republicanism were certainly to hand.[21] Markku Peltonen has recently offered a useful thumbnail sketch of the term "classical republicanism":

> The term "classical republicanism"... embraces a cluster of themes concerning citizenship, public virtue and true nobility. But it also refers to a more specific constitutional stance. Virtue was closely linked with the distinctively republican character of classical republicanism: to ensure that the most virtuous men governed the commonwealth and to control corruption, magistracy should be elected rather than inherited. In this sense republicanism (in the narrow sense of a constitution without a king) could be an anti-monarchical goal: civic values required concomitant republican institutions, but monarchical arrangements were said to suppress these. Arrangements usually favoured by classical republicans were those of the mixed constitution, and the term republic was also used in the wider and more general sense of referring to good and just constitution.[22]

16 Kenyon, *Stuart Constitution*, p. 296; Gardiner, *Constitutional Documents*, pp. 384–388.
17 Harrington's *Oceana* first appeared in 1656 and Sidney's *Discourses Concerning Government*, while written in 1681–3, did not actually see print until 1698.
18 Jonathan Scott, "The English Republican Imagination," in J. S. Morrill, ed., *Revolution and Restoration: England in the 1650s* (London, 1992), p. 53.
19 Blair Worden, "English Republicanism," in J. H. Burns and M. Goldie, eds., *The Cambridge History of Political Thought, 1450–1700* (Cambridge, 1991), p. 444.
20 Scott, "English Republican Imagination," p. 40.
21 Scott, "English Republican Imagination," p. 36.
22 Markku Peltonen, *Classical Humanism and Republicanism in English Political Thought, 1570–1640* (Cambridge, 1995), p. 2.

Kingship was at best an elected office, an inferior magistracy, to be administered in the interest of the public good and at its worst, tyranny – a single individual governing without the restraint of law promoting private interest ahead of the common good. Monarchical arrangements were bad and hereditary monarchies were worse because they provided no constitutional safeguards for ensuring either that the most virtuous citizens held places of public office or that those lacking virtue were excluded from office. For classical republicans the institution of hereditary monarchy was irrational because it was far from clear that the heirs of the king's body would prove to be the most capable of virtue in the state.[23] Political participation was valued as an end in itself because only through an active role in political life, the *vita activa*, could an individual citizen's virtue be realized. Virtue could be understood both in the sense of virtuous actions and as a quality inherent in the constitutional arrangement that promoted such actions.

While there can be no doubt that monarchical arrangements predominated in England before 1649, current scholarship has suggested that the appropriation of classical republicanism was well advanced in England at the dawn of the 1640s. Authors such as Patrick Collinson and Peltonen have argued that the bifurcation of republican modes of civic consciousness and those of territorial and jurisdictional monarchy before the outbreak of the Civil War, suggested by J. G. A. Pocock in his *The Machiavellian Moment*, was too severe. The former was an "ideology of civic activism" in which the individual was a citizen expected to exercise virtue through participation in political life while in the latter individuals were subjects rather than citizens and "took on positive being primarily as the possessor of rights – rights to land and to justice affecting [their] tenure of land."[24] Pocock's original interpretation of the birth of English republicanism posited that before the Civil War the latter mode predominated in England largely to the exclusion of the former. The events of the 1640s were a catalyst, mulling together these two hitherto distinct modes of civic consciousness.[25] The result was, by the second half of the seventeenth century, the beginnings of a distinctly English republicanism. The two modes were not mutually exclusive.

Recent criticisms of Pocock have focused on the extent to which republican values had become conflated with those of jurisdictional and territorial monarchy during the late Tudor and early Stuart periods. Employing the term "monarchical republicanism," Collinson has made the case that, while

[23] Blair Worden, "Classical Republicanism and the Puritan Revolution," in Hugh Lloyd-Jones, Valerie Pearl, and Blair Worden, eds., *History and Imagination: Essays in Honour of H. R. Trevor-Roper* (London, 1981), pp. 193–194.

[24] J. G. A. Pocock, *The Machiavellian Moment: Florentine Political Thought and the Atlantic Republican Tradition* (Princeton, 1975), pp. 334–335.

[25] Pocock, *Machiavellian Moment*, chs. 10, 11.

Elizabethan parishioners "were taught by the Homily of Obedience that rebellion was worse than the worst government of the worst prince," there remained in late Tudor political ideology "an anti-monarchical virus which was part of the legacy of early sixteenth century humanism."[26] The uncertainties of the Elizabethan succession served to promote conceptions of monarchy, "not as an indelible and sacred anointing but a public and localised office, like any other form of magistracy."[27] More recently, Peltonen has argued that "A partial embracing and employment of republican themes in England was not entirely dependent on a complete and dramatic change in the political context." The absence of full-blown republicanism as a specific constitutional stance did not, for example, preclude "the development of civic consciousness."[28] Attitudes toward magistracy and the value of office-holding did not fall exclusively within the paradigm of jurisdictional and territorial monarchy before the conflagrations of the 1640s but reflected a limited seepage of classical republican values. While it is absurd to say that republican ideas caused events of 1640–60, the ground was not unbroken. The restatement of "the terms on which Englishmen as civic beings lived with one another" in the vocabulary of classical republicanism was well advanced at the outbreak of the Civil War.[29]

Aside from classical republicanism another ideological strand that the regicides drew on was radical constitutionalism. Broadly speaking radical constitutionalism had the following identifying features: (1) in keeping with the Rump's declaration of 4 January, that all political power resided originally and naturally in the people immediately under God their creator; (2) that the power of kings and princes was secondary and derivative from that of the people under God and committed to them for their protection and the promotion of the common good; (3) that regal or princely power was merely magisterial, held in trust from the people and subject to their consent; and (4) that, if kings and princes did not fulfill their trust or acted contrary to that trust, both active and passive resistance was justified.

Radical constitutionalism was a compatible position with classical republicanism. Worden has argued that the classical republicans of the Long Parliament, men such as Henry Marten, Thomas Challoner, Algernon Sidney, and Henry Neville, were "proudly independent" and "offered automatic support neither to the event – regicide – nor to the institution – the purged Long Parliament – which gave them power."[30] Indeed, of the four individuals

[26] Patrick Collinson, "The Monarchical Republic of Queen Elizabeth I," *Bulletin of the John Rylands Library*, 69 (1987): 406.
[27] Collinson, "Monarchical Republic": 412.
[28] Peltonen, *Classical Humanism and Republicanism*, p. 7.
[29] Pocock, *Machiavellian Moment*, p. 348.
[30] Worden, "Classical Republicanism," p. 193.

mentioned above only Marten and Challoner were regicides, with Sidney absenting himself early in the proceedings.[31] However, as Worden has noted, there was one principle "behind which republicans in the Long Parliament could unite." This was the maxim identified with radical constitutionalism, "that all power derived originally from the people and could be resumed by the people."[32]

This is, of course, a general sketch and individual authors differed on many particulars. For example, the Levellers were a group clearly belonging under the rubric of radically constitutionalist but not necessarily republicans on principle. Their leader John Lilburne asserted that the commons of England were "the originall and fountaine of power" and pushed these premises to a far more populist conclusion than the more oligarchic regicides.[33] Thomas Hobbes, an intellectual figure of an altogether different order, began from a similar premise of the popular origins of government in attempting to rebut the claims of radical constitutionalists such as the Levellers. The boundaries of consent and what, in practice constituted consent were imperfectly shared at best. For example, in a Hobbesian scheme where the barest physical safety of the subject formed the basis of political obligation, it was only in the event of the sovereign directly attempting to kill the subject that they were justified in resisting. The grant of power to the sovereign was almost total.

Furthermore, the elements of these schema, both republican and constitutionalist, did not, either individually or in combination, automatically lead to active resistance, let alone regicide. As Johann P. Sommerville has noted, the idea of original popular sovereignty was nothing new, having been articulated in the early Stuart period by a number of civil lawyers without any ill consequences to King James's health.[34] These ideas did not cause the trial and execution of the king any more than they caused the Civil War. They did, however, when recombined and redeployed, provide the regicides with a vocabulary for redescribing their actions in an ultimately vain hope to legitimize them. In hindsight this effort can only be seen as a failure. Rather than legitimizing the actions of the regicides the events of the trial and execution allowed Charles to recast his image both as a Christian martyr and as a tragic hero worthy of Sophocles or Shakespeare. If his ability as a ruler

31 PRO SP 16/517/46; John Nalson, *A True Copy of The Journal of The High Court of Justice for the Tryal of King Charles I as it was Read in the House of Commons, and Attested under the hand of Phelps, Clerk to that Infamous Court* (London 1684), sig. Ffv, p. 110; C. V. Wedgwood,*The Trial of Charles I* (Glasgow, 1964; reprinted Harmondsworth, 1983), p. 99.

32 Worden, "Classical Republicanism," p. 193.

33 BL TT E.341(12), John Lilburne, *The Free-mans Freedome vindicated* (London 1646), p. 6.

34 Johann P. Sommerville, *Politics and Ideology in England, 1603–1640* (London, 1986), p. 61.

remains questionable, the doomed king's thespian talents were put beyond reproach by his performance on the scaffold.[35]

The intellectual origins of radical constitutional ideas remain the subject of some debate. Skinner in his *Foundations of Modern Political Thought* took up a position similar to that of J. N. Figgis in suggesting the centrality of late medieval conciliarist theories, particularly that of Jean Gerson in the development of early modern constitutionalism.[36] With respect to Gerson, Skinner has written that, according to his theory, "no ruler can be *maior* or greater in power than the community over which he rules." Concomitantly, ultimate political power in the polity remained "at all times within the body of the community itself, and ... the status of any ruler in relation to such a community must in consequence be that of a *minister* or *rector* rather than that of an absolute sovereign."[37] Princely power was therefore magisterial and limited by a commission granted by the consent of the governed. More recently Francis Oakley has examined the influence of late-medieval conciliarist thought on both seventeenth-century English parliamentarians and their sixteenth-century Scottish and Huguenot predecessors, noting that "The range of proto-conciliarist and conciliarist literature cited by the English writers of the late sixteenth and seventeenth centuries is admittedly quite broad."[38] Indeed, in 1642 Henry Parker saw fit to appropriate the time-worn maxim popularized by conciliarist writings in the king as *singulis major* yet *universis minor*, affirming that "power is but secondary and derivative in Princes" and that "the fountaine and efficient cause is the people."[39] The Lord President of the High Court of Justice, John Bradshaw, invoked the same maxim in his speech at the king's trial on 27 January.[40] While this is not in itself evidence of direct influence, it is less problematic simply to assert that both the apologists for the Long Parliament and the regicides deployed ideas meeting the criteria

[35] For the royalist appropriation of the tragic mediums see Nancy Klein Macguire, "The Theatrical Mask/Masque of Politics: The Case of Charles I," *JBS* 28 (1989): 1–22; Franco Moretti, "The Great Eclipse: Tragic Form as the Deconsecration of Sovereignty," in Franco Moretti, *Signs Taken for Wonders: Essays in the Sociology of Literary Forms*, trans. Susan Fischer et. al. (London, 1983; revised edn. London, 1988), pp. 43–82.

[36] Quentin Skinner, *Foundations of Modern Political Thought*, vol. II: *The Age of Reformation* (Cambridge, 1978), pp. 114–123.

[37] Skinner, *Foundations* II, p. 117; all italics are Skinner's.

[38] Francis Oakley, "'Anxieties of Influence': Skinner, Figgis, Conciliarism and Early Modern Constitutionalism," *P&P* 151 (1996): 107–108.

[39] Henry Parker, *Observations upon some of his Majesties late Answers and Expresses* (London, 1642), in William Haller, ed., *Tracts on Liberty in the Puritan Revolution* (New York, 1933), vol. II, p. 2 [167].

[40] PRO SP 16/517/38; BL TT E.545(4), Gilbert Mabbot, *King Charls his Tryal or A perfect Narrative of the whole proceedings of the High Court of Iustice* (London 1649), sig. D4v, p. 32.

established above for the term "radical constitutionalist" in defense of their actions.

One consequence of this was the redefinition of the king's status vis-à-vis the body politic. He was no longer a sovereign but an inferior magistrate. As the work of Skinner and Oakley has demonstrated, this idea was current before the king's trial and subject to appropriation by a number of competing interests. While ultimately opposing the actions of the regicides, the Levellers in their Humble Petition of 11 September 1648 asserted that the House of Commons was "the supreme authority of England, as chosen by and representing the people, and entrusted with absolute power for the redress of grievances and provision for safety."[41] The king, by contrast, "was at most the chief public officer of this kingdom, and accountable to this House (the representative of the people, from whom all just authority is or ought to be derived) for the discharge of his office."[42] Indeed, Leveller objections to the trial of the king may have flowed more from the irregular manner of the king's trial without a conventional jury than from issues of principle.[43]

John Milton was both a republican and a radical constitutionalist. He was also a friend of John Bradshaw, president of the High Court of Justice and later also of the Commonwealth's Council of State.[44] In his *The Tenure of Kings and Magistrates*, appearing on 13 February 1649, he defended the actions of the regicides arguing

> ... that the power of Kings and Magistrates is nothing else, but what is onely derivative, transferred and committed to them in trust from the people to the Common good of them all, in whom power yet remaines fundamentally, and cannot be taken from them, without a violation of thir natural birthright ...[45]

Milton asserted further that, according to Aristotle and "the best of the Political writers," a king was only "him who governs to the good and profit of his people, and not for his owne ends"; accordingly, "the titles of Sovran Lord, naturall Lord, and the like" were dismissed as "either arrogancies, or flatteries, not admitted by Emperors and Kings of best note."[46] The kingly office and dignity was not the birthright or entail of the ruling monarch but an

[41] Kenyon, *Stuart Constitution*, pp. 276–277. [42] Kenyon, *Stuart Constitution*, p. 277.

[43] D. Alan Orr, "John Lilburne and the Ancient Constitution, 1646–1649," unpublished MA dissertation (Queen's University, 1993), pp. 125–126; this thesis emphasizes the increasing extent to which Lilburne operated within the conventions of common-law discourse in his pamphlets of 1646–9. For a contrasting view see Samuel Dennis Glover, "The Putney Debates: Popular versus Elitist Republicanism," *P&P* 164 (1999): 47–80.

[44] Worden, "Classical Republicanism," p. 191.

[45] John Milton, *The Tenure of Kings and Magistrates*, in *The Prose of John Milton, Selected and Edited from the Original Texts with Introductions, Notes, and Translations*, ed. J. Max Patrick (Garden City, N.Y., 1967), p. 353.

[46] Milton, *Tenure*, p. 353.

office of public trust that the people bestowed upon him and subject to their ongoing consent. Milton's republicanism reduced kingship from sovereignty to magistracy.

Earlier, in our discussion of the trial of Archbishop Laud, we advanced the proposition that ideological conflict in the early Stuart period arose not from conflict between ascending and descending theories of power but from rival descending theories of power.[47] In was not a question of popular sovereignty versus the divine right of kings but a question of rival divine rights. The divine right of kings was not *necessarily* a theory of royal absolutism but an attempt to rebut the *iure divino* claims of the papacy to absolve subjects from their bonds of allegiance and depose kings. Similarly, James VI's approbation of divine-right kingship was aimed largely at rebutting the *iure divino* claims of Scottish Presbyterians for the assembly of the kirk. At issue was not the relationship between subject and sovereign but the relationship between the sovereign and rival claimants to any of the marks of sovereignty. As Conrad Russell has observed, "Divine right, like democracy today, covered a multitude of sins because it was the basic currency of legitimacy."[48] Of particular concern was the power over the doctrine and discipline of the established church. To those of an Erastian frame of mind, a category that included both James VI and I and the likes of William Prynne, the *iure divino* claims of pope and Presbyterian alike were usurpations upon the role of the civil magistrate.[49] Indeed, if Prynne remained consistent about anything during his long career it was probably his anti-clericalism and his general distaste for the theocracy of both prelacy and presbyter.

The proposition that all political power was derived from God and held, in some sense, by divine right was relatively unproblematic in the first half of the seventeenth century. However, the questions of to whom political power first descended and who had prior claims on it were less tractable. Johann P. Sommerville has noted that people in early Stuart England "did distinguish between the thesis that kings (and husbands and clerics) draw their powers immediately from God and the suggestion that they derive them only indirectly from the Almighty but directly from some human person or group."[50] The regicides in their public pronouncements claimed that the

[47] See my critique of Sanderson in chapter 4, above; John B. Sanderson, *"But the People's Creatures" : The Philosophical Basis of the English Civil War* (Manchester, 1989).

[48] Conrad Russell, "Divine Rights in the Early Seventeenth Century," in John Morrill, Paul Slack, and Daniel Woolf, eds., *Public Duty and Private Conscience in Seventeenth-Century England: Essays Presented to G. E. Aylmer* (Oxford, 1993), p. 104.

[49] Glenn Burgess, "The Divine Right of Kings Reconsidered," *EHR* 107 (1992): 837–861; and Glenn Burgess, *Absolute Monarchy and the Stuart Constitution* (New Haven, 1996), ch. 4; Russell, "Divine Rights," *passim*.

[50] Johann P. Sommerville, "English and European Political Ideas in the Early Seventeenth Century: Revisionism and the Case of Absolutism," *JBS* 35 (1996): 187–188.

people were immediately under God, that kingly power was merely magisterial and derivative, and that they enjoyed a divine mandate for their actions in trying and executing the king. John Cook, the king's prosecutor, asserted in his published argument that the High Court of Justice held its mandate *immediately* from God proclaiming

> ... that the glory of this administration may be wholly given to God, I desire observe to the praise of his great name, the work of God upon my own spirit in his gracious assistance and presence with me, as a return of prayer and fruit of Faith, beleeving that God never calls to the acting of any thing, so pleasing to him, as this most excellent Court of Justice is, but he is present with the Honorable Judges, and those that wait upon them ..."[51]

More infamously, he remarked that he went about his business as prosecutor "as cheerfully as to a Wedding."[52] This was, without doubt, an immediate and not a mediate claim to a divine mandate. The claim to a divine mandate for political action did indeed cover a multitude of sins – including regicide.

In direct contrast, John Gauden, later reputed to be the author of the *Eikon Basilike*, framed his objections to the regicide in terms of a rejection of the High Court's claim to a divine mandate:

> ... whatever His [the king's] sin may be, yet I thinke Him not criminall or obnoxious to any Tribunall but that of God, whose Deputation, Authority, or Commission they can in no sort (that I see) produce to any satisfaction of religious minds, who at present undertake to be His Tryers, Judges, Condemners, and Destroyers, onely because the KING is in their power.[53]

Gauden did not question the principle that a divine mandate could theoretically provide such a commission but stated that such a commission "ought to have not onely the stamp and image of prevalent power," but should also have "the superscription of his [God's] word, and the expresse signatures of his will, in the municipall Lawes on the other side, by all which, power is derived, limited and warranted to act with moderation and righteousnesse."[54] A divine mandate was derivable from biblical injunction and in "those setled Lawes of humane societies" by which God's will had become evident.[55] This position necessitated an interpretation of the history of the English law as being "cleerly brought forth" by God's providence.[56] Gauden's argument was based not only on the denial of any scriptural basis for regicide but

[51] John Cook, *King Charls his Case: or an Appeal To all Rational Men, Concerning His Tryal at the High Court of Iustice* (London, 1649), sig. E4r, p. 39.

[52] Cook, *King Charls his Case*, sig. E4r, p. 39.

[53] John Gauden, *The Religious and Loyal Protestation of John Gauden Dr. in Divinity; Against the present Declared Purposes and Proceedings of the Army and others; About the trying and destroying our Soveraign Lord the King* (London, 1649), sig. A2v.

[54] Gauden, *Protestation*, sig. A2v. [55] Gauden, *Protestation*, sig. A3v, p. 2.

[56] Gauden, *Protestation*, sig. A3v, p. 2.

on the contention that the laws of England gave "no subjects, in any Case, Judiciall power over the life of their King, or his Soveraigntie."[57]

Unlike the previous cases discussed here, there can be absolutely no doubt that the actions of the regicides were, by the established law of the land, illegal and unprecedented with regard to both substantive and procedural law. The only possible precedent was that of Richard II, who had renounced his crown under pressure from the leading nobles rather than face public trial and execution.[58] Furthermore, the end of his reign did not mark the transition to a republic but the succession of another claimant to the throne, his cousin Henry Bolingbroke. Furthermore, Henry IV's claim to the crown was based not only on the support of powerful feudal magnates but a close proximity in blood to the deposed king. William Prynne, secluded by the army's purge of the Long Parliament in early December, warned would-be regicides of the illegality of their actions in a tract published early in January 1649:

> ...I shall minde you, that by the Common Law of the Realme the *Statute* of 25 *Edward* III and all other Acts concerning *Treason*, it is no less than High Treason, by overt act, to compasse or imagine the deposition, or death of the King, or of his eldest Son and Heire, though it be never executed; much more if Actually accomplished.[59]

It is beyond question that the regicides not only compassed the death and deposition of the king but brought it to pass by an overt act.

The manner of proceeding against the king was also open to question. The act erecting a High Court of Justice did not specify trial by jury at common law, as was customary, but instead established a judicial body of 135 men named in the act as commissioners of the court to sit in judgment of the king.[60] James Duke of Hamilton, the Earls of Norwich and Holland, Arthur Lord Capel, and Sir John Owen were tried by similar procedures during the weeks following the king's trial.[61] The Leveller tract, *Englands New Chains Discovered*, appearing in late February 1649 objected against the Rump's erection of the High Court because its proceedings infringed on "that great and strong hold of our preservation, the way of tryal by 12 sworn men of the Neighbourhood."[62] Leveller objections to the king's trial were possibly conditioned by fears that they would be next in line for similar treatment.

[57] Gauden, *Protestation*, sig. A4r, p. 3. [58] *State Trials* I: 136–140.

[59] William Prynne, *A Briefe Memento To the Present Unparliamentary Iunto Touching their present Intentions and Proceedings to Depose and Execute, Charles Steward, their lawfull King* (London, 1649), sig. A1r–v, pp. 3–4.

[60] Firth and Rait, *Acts and Ordinances* I, pp. 1253–1255.

[61] The procedures of the High Court of Justice remain largely a mystery. It was an institution that was periodically reestablished throughout the Commonwealth and Protectorate periods and there exists no detailed institutional study of its procedures, leaving questions open as to its alleged irregularity.

[62] John Lilburne et al., *Englands New Chains Discovered*, in William Haller and Godfrey Davies, eds., *The Leveller Tracts, 1647–1653* (New York, 1944), p. 161.

To this effect the pamphlet asserted further that "we know it to be an usual policy to introduce by such means all usurpations, first against Adversaries, in hope of easier admission; as also, for that the same being so admitted, may at pleasure be exercised against any person or persons whatsoever."[63] There is ample reason to believe that the Levellers did wish to see the king brought to justice but not in a manner that would set a dangerous precedent for the infringement of the subject's right to a jury trial.

The language of the act erecting the High Court echoed many of the allegations against Strafford and Laud charging

> ... That Charles Stuart, the now King of England, not content with those many Encroachments which his Predecessors had made upon the People in their Rights and Freedoms, hath had a wicked Design totally to Subvert the Ancient and Fundamental Laws and Liberties of this Nation, and in their place to introduce an Arbitrary and Tyrannical Government, and that besides all other evil ways and means to bring this Design to pass, he hath prosecuted it with Fire and Sword, Levied and maintained a cruel War in the Land, against the Parliament and Kingdom, whereby the Country hath been miserably wasted, the Publick Treasure Exhausted, Trade decayed, thousands of People murdered, and infinite other mischiefs committed ...[64]

The theme of the subversion of the fundamental law of the land was a familiar one. However, while in Strafford's trial the law was presumed to be the king's law and the king was presumed to be the fountain of the law and of justice, here the ancient and fundamental law of the land was presumed to be *separate* from the king's person. The king was merely the "Chief Officer or Magistrate" charged with maintenance of law and justice and not its original.[65] Indeed for Henry Parker writing as early as 1642 the law could "be nothing else amongst Christians but the Pactions and agreements of such and such politique corporations."[66] Furthermore, the act conceptualized Charles's treason of levying war as a crime against the "Parliament and Kingdom." Treason remained a crime against the sovereign power and, in order to try the king for treason, the locus of sovereignty had to be moved to the people as a perpetual, popular corporation. The legal constitutional order needed uncoupling from the person of the king.

Essential to the regicide and the subsequent establishment of a republic was the severing of the law and the state established by it from the monarch in *all* his capacities, politic and natural. This was a radical departure. As C. V. Wedgwood noted in 1961: "It was an axiom in English law that all justice proceeded from the sovereign."[67] More recently Alan Cromartie has remarked that "'The king' as a legal expression was a part of great swathes

[63] Haller and Davies, *Leveller Tracts*, p. 162.
[64] Firth and Rait, *Acts and Ordinances* I, pp. 1253–1254.
[65] Firth and Rait, *Acts and Ordinances* I, p. 1254.
[66] Parker, *Observations*, p. 1 [167]. [67] Wedgwood, *Trial*, p. 96.

of the law."[68] Writs were issued in the king's name under his seal and it was the king who appointed and dismissed magistrates to sit in his courts and administer the law. In order to govern, both the Rump and the Lord Protector afterwards were forced to behave like a king. Cromartie has argued further that the failure of the English republic lay in the inability of the Commonwealths-men to govern without the common law. The idea of monarchical rule was so inextricably bound up with the common law that "to acknowledge legal values was to damn the new regime."[69] Unsurprisingly, one of the first things the Commonwealths-men did in order to push their claim on the law-giving powers of the state was the passing of a statute on 20 January 1649 replacing the term "king" in legal documents with the term "The Keepers of the Liberties of England."[70] Henceforth justice was to proceed not in the king's name but in the name of this novel yet analogous legal expression. A further statute of 11 February 1649 renamed the Court of King's Bench the "Upper Bench."[71]

That the Rump needed to behave like a king in order to govern is without question. However, as the writings of Kantorowicz and Maitland have revealed, in order for a king to govern a far-flung polity it was necessary for the monarch to behave corporately. He needed to act as a body politic, a corporate juristic person.[72] The king could not be everywhere at once in the realm but his majesty was omnipresent in his realm. The Commonwealths-men needed to act as a king only insofar as the king acted as a corporate entity. To identify corporate conceptions of public authority exclusively with monarchical rule is highly problematic. The example of civic corporations comes readily to mind. Corporate thinking was perfectly amenable to classical republicanism, as were legal values. For example, the common lawyer Sir John Davies did not hesitate to cite Cicero with open approval in the preface to his *Irish Reports* as a leading expositor of the rule of law and a champion of legal values.[73] The appeal to fundamental law and legal values was perfectly compatible with both the values of jurisdictional and territorial

68 Alan Cromartie, *Sir Matthew Hale, 1609–1676: Law, Religion and Natural Philosophy* (Cambridge, 1995), p. 61; I would like to thank Dr. Cromartie for allowing me to read the relevant sections of his manuscript before publication.

69 Cromartie, *Hale*, p. 58.

70 Kenyon, *Stuart Constitution*, p. 296; Cromartie, *Hale*, p. 61; the term as it appears in the statute is in Latin: "Custodes libertatis Angliae authoritate Parlimenti", Firth and Rait, *Acts and Ordinances* I, p. 1262.

71 Kenyon, *Stuart Constitution*, p. 296.

72 Ernst L. Kantorowicz, *The King's Two Bodies: A Study in Medieval Political Theology* (Princeton, 1957); F. W. Maitland, "The Crown as Corporation," *LQR* 17 (1901): 131–146.

73 Sir John Davies, *Le Primer Report des Cases & Matters in Ley resolues & adiudges en les Courts del Roy en Ireland. Collect et digest per Sr. John Dauys Chiualer Atturney Generall del Roy en cest Realme* (Dublin, 1615), fol. 9a.

monarchy and the more juristic strains of classical republicanism exemplified by Cicero and other Roman authors.[74] The failure of the English republic was not ascribable to the survival of common-law values but to the enduring centrality and deep embeddedness of the symbols and trappings of monarchical rule in English political culture.[75]

The regicides needed to redescribe their actions in a way that would legitimate not only their actions in trying and executing the king but also their claims to the lawful exercise of sovereignty. One could not be accomplished without the other. It is a truism of the early Stuart period that those attempting to redescribe and legitimate the actions of the state necessarily had to resort to juristic vocabularies and in particular that of the common law. Those seeking patronage at court or ecclesiastical preferment may, of course, have had recourse to different vocabularies – some possibly absolutist in the sense usually attributed to Filmer.[76] Johann Sommerville has recently argued that the common law, a vocabulary perhaps more suited to the king's magistrates, barristers, and, on occasion, parliamentarians and other public figures, was definitely *not* the language of the Stuart court.[77] However, usually barristers acting in a court of law in early Stuart England would be expected to redescribe their actions in terms derived from the common law, its customs, and its disparate written authorities. Unfortunately for the would-be triers of the king the common law and the statutes of the realm provided neither a clear foundation for their actions nor a necessarily legitimate vocabulary for their moral redescription.

When the history of political thought in Stuart Britain considers not only the dissemination of learning within the elite humanist learning cultures of the day but also how practicing magistrates redescribed their actions there is an inevitable emphasis on law-centered ideology and political theory. Men such as Sir John Davies, John Selden, and Sir Matthew Hale were undoubtedly part of the elite humanist learning culture that Richard Tuck has recently emphasized, but they were also public men of subtly differing

74 Norberto de Sousa, "The Idea of a Civil Society and the Roman Tradition of Republicanism," paper prepared for Pick'n'mix meeting 16 May 1994, Jesus College, Cambridge.

75 An important recent discussion is Sean Kelsey, *Inventing a Republic: The Political Culture of the English Commonwealth, 1649–1653* (Stanford, 1997).

76 Linda Levy Peck's recent work on John Cusacke is suggestive of this – an author penning absolutist tracts in order to seek favour and preferment from the king. It is interesting to note, however, that much of Cusacke's writings were not committed to press before the Civil War: Linda Levy Peck, "Kingship, Counsel and Law in Early Stuart Britain," in J. G. A. Pocock, Gordon Schochet, and Lois G. Schwoerer, eds., *Varieties of British Political Thought, 1500–1800* (Cambridge, 1993), 112–113; Glenn Burgess, *Absolute Monarchy and The Stuart Constitution* (New Haven, 1996), p. 37.

77 Johann P. Sommerville, "The Ancient Constitution Reassessed: The Common Law, the Court and the Languages of Politics in Early Modern England," in Malcolm Smuts, ed., *The Stuart Court and Europe: Essays in Politics and Political Culture* (Cambridge, 1996), p. 40.

stripes, whether parliamentarians or officers of the courts.[78] In other words, the leading officers of state had an overlapping membership with many of the kingdom's most exclusive learning circles. Early Stuart political thought and rhetoric must, therefore, be situated not simply within humanist learning cultures of the day but within broader political and institutional contexts – contexts that privileged juristic vocabularies and the canons of legal learning as sources of power and legitimacy.

This section has attempted to situate the trial of the king in such a context. The king's trial was part of a larger effort of the Commonwealths-men – men such as Thomas Challoner, Henry Marten, Thomas Scot, John Cook, and Isaac Dorislaus – to assert their legal title to govern as the people's representatives and their legally appointed magistrates. Whether these men had a coherently thought-out republican vision of England or not remains subject to scholarly debate. It is likely that, at least on an individual level, some of them did. The regicide and the erection of the Commonwealth, however, created greater ideological demands necessitating a more thorough appropriation of classical republican ideas and their marriage to English circumstances. The Commonwealths-men linked classical republicanism to radical constitutionalism in an attempt to redescribe and legitimate their actions. The regicides constructed their political thinking, of necessity, from the materials at hand and drew on existing traditions. The actions of the regicides may have been unprecedented but they did not act in an ideological vacuum. The imperative of early 1649 was simply to seize the organs of government and exercise practical sovereignty while taking legislative steps, initially on 30 January against the return of the hereditary Stuart monarchy and later, with the act abolishing the kingly office, against any form of monarchical rule. Trying the king not only repudiated the king's claim to be the fountain of justice and the supreme law-giver but also served to advance the claims of the Commonwealths-men to state power.

III

The High Court of Justice erected for the trying of Charles Stuart, King of England was to consist of 135 commissioners named in the body of the act. Of these, forty-seven never sat while eight, including Thomas Fairfax and Algernon Sidney, withdrew from the proceedings before the trial. Of the remaining eighty, twenty-one attended the trial at least in part and only the remaining fifty-nine actually set their hands to the king's death warrant. C. V. Wedgwood has speculated that, although some of the regicides were

[78] Richard Tuck, *Philosophy and Government, 1572–1651* (Cambridge, 1993), ch. 1.

no better than the self-seeking scoundrels that royalists portrayed them to be, most of them "acted from a sincere conviction that no other course was open to them as God-fearing Christians and lovers of their country."[79] It is as impossible to travel through time as it is to read minds and, in the absence of deeply private journals and correspondence, the motivations of many regicides, including the ever-inscrutable Oliver Cromwell, will remain subject to endless speculation.[80]

However, it is possible to capture a sense of how the Commonwealthsmen sought publicly to redescribe and legitimate their actions and how the king sought to counter their attempts at moral redescription. The trial of the king was a very public political event. The act erecting the High Court of Justice did not go quietly into the statute books – the court's proceedings were published by the official censor Gilbert Mabbot and the proclamation ordering the king's trial was read aloud first in Westminster Hall on the morning of 9 January and then on the Commons' order at the Old Exchange, Cheapside and at St. Paul's as was customary.[81] This account will not attempt to analyze the motives of the regicides by examining their allegiances on a number of different competing issues such as ecclesiastical government, the legality of the army's December purge, tithes or law reform. The work of Blair Worden and David Underdown has shown, if anything, that a republican does not a regicide make, nor a regicide a republican. The Rump was no monolith but remained divided over a number of issues – divisions that eventually paralyzed and destroyed it.[82] Instead, the emphasis here will be on how those individuals who claimed to be acting for the state, the sole legitimate, legal sovereign authority, attempted to justify their actions in trying and executing the king and in laying claim to the sovereign power.

With the regicide the familiar cast of characters that fought out the major state trials of the early and mid-1640s changed dramatically. Sir John Maynard had been one of the eleven members secluded by the army in 1647 and had moved towards a conciliatory position with the king. William Prynne had been secluded from the Long Parliament by the army's purge in December and had since become an outspoken critic of the proposed course of regicide.[83] The more prominent barristers who had waged state treason

[79] Wedgwood, *Trial*, p. 102.

[80] Some light has recently been shed on the subject by John Morrill and Philip Baker, "Oliver Cromwell, the Regicide and the Sons of Zeruiah," in Jason Peacey, ed., *The Regicides and the Execution of Charles I* (Basingstoke, 2001), pp. 14–35.

[81] PRO SP 16/517/4; Yale Osborn MS fb 146, 9 January 1649.

[82] The two most thorough and compelling studies of the Rump, its politics, and its membership are without doubt Blair Worden's *The Rump Parliament 1648–1653* (Cambridge, 1974) and David Underdown's, *Pride's Purge: Politics in the Puritan Revolution* (Oxford, 1971).

[83] Prynne, *A Briefe Memento*, *passim*; and above.

trials on the Long Parliament's behalf – Henry Rolle, Oliver St. John, and John Wilde – all refused to serve. Sir Matthew Hale, a stalwart in the lost causes of Laud and Maguire, was also absent. St. John, Rolle, and Wilde had been created by parliamentary appointment the Chief Justices of the Common Pleas, King's/Upper Bench, and Chief Baron respectively and their defections were especially damning.[84]

Initially on 6 January the court appointed two clerks, John Phelps and one Mr. Greaves. At the same time counsels were also appointed for the pressing of the case against the king. In the absence of the usual cast of Prynne, Rolle, Maynard, et al. the court appointed John Cook, Isaac Dorislaus, John Aske, and Anthony Steele.[85] The Dutch civil lawyer Dorislaus had once been professor of ancient history at Cambridge and brought an impressive repertoire of classical learning to the prosecution. In December 1627 he had delivered a series of controversial lectures on Tacitus dealing with "different types of monarchies" and arguing "that in some cases a tyrant could be legitimately resisted." These had resulted in an order from the king silencing him.[86] Since the outbreak of the Civil War he had placed his not inconsiderable classical and legal learning in the service of the king's enemies.[87]

On 10 January John Bradshaw was chosen as president of the court.[88] Bradshaw was a judge of the sheriff's court in London who had assisted Prynne in his prosecution of Maguire and had also participated in the abortive proceedings against the Welsh royalist judge David Jenkins.[89] Bradshaw was not in attendance at his appointment and William Say temporarily replaced him. The court ordered Bradshaw to attend them, which he finally did on 12 January at which time he begged to be excused. His request was refused and he "tooke [his] place accordingly" with the court ordering further that he be called by the title "Lord President."[90] Greaves was more successful in evading service. He managed to convince the court on 18 January that he had "greate and important imployment... in the behalfe of the Commonwealth, from w[hi]ch he cannot be spared w[it]hout preiudice to the Publique" and was accordingly excused. He was replaced by Andrew Broughton.[91] Steele played no part in the trial, having been reported by Colonel Robert Tichbourne to be "in his bed very sicke" on 18 January.[92] This left the bulk of the prosecution to Cook, who undertook his task with considerable zeal.

The reasons offered for their absence by Greaves and Steele suggested a view of magistracy in line with classical republican values and a mode of

[84] Wedgwood, *Trial*, p. 95. [85] PRO SP 16/517/4; Wedgwood, *Trial*, p. 104.
[86] Peltonen, *Classical Humanism*, p. 275; see also Kevin Sharpe, *Politics and Ideas in Early Stuart England: Essays and Studies* (London, 1989), pp. 220–223.
[87] Wedgwood, *Trial*, p. 104. [88] PRO SP 16/517/5; Nalson, *True Copy*, sig. C2v, p. 8.
[89] *DNB* II; p. 1085. [90] PRO SP 16/517/5–6. [91] PRO SP 16/517/5.
[92] PRO SP 16/517/11; Nalson, *True Copy*, sig. G1r, p. 21.

civic consciousness consistent with civic humanism. Participation in civil magistracy, public service, was valued because it enabled the citizen to exercise their virtue to the fullest. To be asked to serve was an honor and participation in the enterprise of governance was not to be shunned. The court only excused Greaves because of a more pressing commitment to the service of the Commonwealth. One public duty took precedence over another. Similarly, Colonel Edmond Harvey sought to assure the court on 22 January that his absence was, "not from any dissatisfaction to the proceedings . . . but in regard of other speciall imployment that hee hath in the service of the State."[93] Colonel Tichbourne, speaking for the allegedly ill Steele,[94] was at pains to assert "that hee the said Mr. Steel noe way declineth the service of the said Court out of any disaffection to it but p[ro]fessed himselfe to bee so clere in the businesse that if it should please god to restore him he should manifest his good affections to the said Cause . . ."[95] All of these men may in fact have had serious qualms about the proceedings against the king. However, this was not as significant as the reasons they gave for their absence and the apologies they offered. None wished to be seen as avoiding the service of the state.

On 15 January the counsels for the prosecution presented a draft of the charge to the court, most likely the work of Dorislaus and Cook. At this time a committee was appointed "to whom the Councell might resort for theire further advice concerning any thing of difficulty in relacon to the Charge against the King . . ."[96] This committee consisted of Henry Ireton, Gilbert Millington, Henry Marten, Edmond Harvey,[97] Thomas Challoner,[98] Thomas Harrison, Miles Corbet, Thomas Scot, Nicholas Love, John Lisle, and William Say or any three of them. A second draft was presented to the court on the afternoon of 17 January and sent to committee.[99] On 19 January the charge was brought in once more, read three times and sent back to committee for minor changes.[100] On 20 January the prisoner appeared at the bar to hear the charge and, presumably, to enter a plea.

The procedures of the High Court of Justice remain something of a mystery. It was clear, however, that the procedures were inquisitorial rather than

93 PRO SP 16/517/18.

94 Wedgwood questioned the veracity of Steele's condition suggesting that he had simply lost his nerve but offered no clear grounds for the contention that he was suffering from anything less than a genuine affliction: Wedgwood, *Trial*, p. 108.

95 PRO SP 16/517/11; quotation is from the PRO document, but see also Nalson, *True Copy*, sig. G1r, p. 21 (only spellings differ).

96 PRO SP 16/517/8.

97 I assume that this is the recalcitrant Colonel Edmond Harvey: PRO SP 16/517/7–8; Nalson, *True Copy*, sig. Ff2v, p. 110.

98 I presume that the "Mr. Challoner" mentioned is the eventual regicide Thomas and not James.

99 PRO SP 16/517/10.

100 PRO SP 16/517/11; Nalson, *True Copy*, sig. G2r, p. 23.

adversarial and intended to minimize the number of speaking participants, limiting these roles to the counsels, the Lord President, and the accused. Extant transcripts of the proceedings read like a dialogue between Bradshaw and the king. Commissioners were not forbidden from questioning witnesses but were expected first to move the Lord President to ask the question on their behalf.[101] The regularity of the proceedings against the king is difficult to assess, largely because of Charles's refusal to cooperate and recognize the High Court's jurisdiction. It is worthy of note, however, that in contrast to Star Chamber the High Court appears to have respected an individual's right against self-incrimination. The court excused one witness against the king, a Mr. Holder, because he was already a prisoner and the commissioners deemed that the intended questions of the court tended to make him a self-accuser.[102] Nor was the king required to take an *ex-officio* oath.

The charge against the king, read aloud to the court by John Cook on 20 January, restated the themes of radical constitutionalism and classical republicanism. The charge conceived England as a popular state in which Charles had been entrusted with the powers of chief magistrate provided that he continue to act for the good of the people. This was evident from the preamble, which charged

> That the said Charles Stuart, being admitted King of England, and therein trusted with a limited power to govern by and according to the laws of the land, and not otherwise; and by his trust, oath, and office, being obliged to use the power committed to him for the good and benefit of the people, and for the preservation of their rights and liberties; yet, nevertheless, out of a wicked design to erect and uphold in himself an unlimited and tyrannical power to rule according to his will, and to overthrow the rights and liberties of the people, yea, to take away and make void the foundations thereof, and of all redress and remedy of misgovernment, which by the fundamental constitutions of this kingdom were reserved on the people's behalf in the right and power of frequent and successive Parliaments, or national meetings in Council; he the said Charles Stuart, for accomplishment of such his designs, and for the protecting of himself and his adherents in his and their wicked practices, to the same ends has traitorously and maliciously levied war against the present Parliament and the people therein represented . . .[103]

The king was simply a magistrate who had committed treason against the parliament and people by raising an unlawful and unnatural war in the land to the destruction of the commonwealth.

The charge went on to enumerate Charles's treasonable actions including, most notably, his setting up of his standard of war at Nottingham in August 1642, the engagements at Edgehill and Brentford later that year, at

[101] PRO SP 16/517/6. [102] PRO SP 16/517/26; Nalson, *True Copy*, sig. R2r, p. 63.

[103] Gardiner, *Constitutional Documents*, pp. 371–372; for other copies see Nalson, *True Copy*, sigs. I1r–I2v, pp. 29–32; PRO SP 16/517/14–16; Yale Osborn MS fb 146, 20 January 1649; the latter two copies are subscribed John Cook.

Caversham Bridge, the city of Gloucester, and Newbury the following year, at Cropredy Bridge, Bodmin, and Newbury (again) in 1644, and at the sack of Leicester and the battle of Naseby in 1645.[104] The charge went on to blame Charles for the renewal of the war in 1648, alleging that Charles had levied "cruel and unnatural wars" by which, "much innocent blood of the free people of this nation hath been spilt, many families have been undone, the public treasure wasted and exhausted, trade obstructed and miserably decayed, vast expense and damage to the nation incurred, and many parts of this land spoiled, some of them even to desolation." Charles also stood accused of continuing to issue commissions to his son Charles, Prince of Wales, "and other rebels and revolters," most notably the Earl of Ormonde, and "Irish Rebels" to press forward the armed struggle against people and parliament.[105] In conclusion the charge asserted that the king had carried forward his "wicked designs, wars, and evil practices" in order to advance and uphold "a personal interest of will, power, and pretended prerogative to himself and his family against the public interest, common right, liberty, justice and peace of the people of this nation, by and from whom he was entrusted aforesaid."[106]

It is clear that Charles's principal sin was the levying of war. The other allegations of murder, rape, and the destruction of property were ancillary to this. Strafford and Laud were tried for their roles in the personal rule of the 1630s. Maguire was tried for his role in the Irish Revolt of 1641. Charles in turn was tried largely for bringing war and its attendant destruction on the land. The majority of the depositions given before the court on 24 and 25 January bore this out. For example, one John Bennett, a soldier in the royalist army at the outbreak of the war, testified to the king raising his standard of war above Nottingham Castle in August 1642 and the king's presenting of his regiment and others with their colors.[107] Another deponent, Samuel Morgan, testified that in the autumn of 1642 "upon a Sunday morning in kenton feild [he] sawe the kinge upon Edge Hill in the heade of the Army some two hours before the fight . . ." The same deponent claimed to have seen the king in 1644 dismount his horse in the vicinity of Cropredy Bridge "and drawe upp the body of his Army in p[e]rsone himselfe."[108] The depositions described a number of other events from the war listed in the charge including the siege of Gloucester, the very gruesome royalist sack of Leicester, and the Battle of Naseby.[109] The bulk of the charges emphasized the king, sometimes in armour, standing or riding at the head of his army and taking command

[104] Gardiner, *Constitutional Documents*, p. 372.
[105] Gardiner, *Constitutional Documents*, p. 373.
[106] Gardiner, *Constitutional Documents*, pp. 373–374.
[107] PRO SP 16/517/27–28. [108] PRO SP 16/517/29.
[109] Mabbot in his *A perfect Narrative* did not chose to print the depositions but they are available in detail in both Bradshaw's Journal (PRO SP 16/517/27–32) and in Nalson, *True Copy*, sigs. R2r–X2r, pp. 63–79.

of his forces against those of parliament. All of these depositions were in keeping with accepted medieval definitions of war – in particular the raising of his standard, the wearing of "cote armure" and war harness, and the direction of one's army in the field.[110]

Levying war was a mark of sovereignty and, in the kind of popular state the regicides envisioned, power of war and peace lay not with the king but with the people and their representatives assembled in parliament. However, Charles's actions were not simply usurpation but unnatural. After all, what sovereign people could rationally give their chief magistrate a commission to levy war on them? Such actions were not only irrational but were deemed contrary to the public interest. This interest was defined in the charge as an economic interest as much as simply the peace, physical security, and wellbeing of the king's subjects. War, of course, was then and remains today notoriously bad for business, especially when waged on one's doorstep. The civil wars were both expensive and destructive and the decay of trade and the exhaustion of public finance was inimical to the public interest.

The events of the trial on 20, 22, and 23 January highlighted the conflicting claims to sovereign jurisdiction of the High Court and the king. When asked to give answer to the charge on 20 January Charles refused. Instead he demanded to know by what lawful authority he had been called hither from the Isle of Wight, where he had been engaged in negotiations with the parliamentary commissioners prior to the army's purge of the Long Parliament early in December.[111] He emphasized the term "lawful" because, he acknowledged, "there are many unlawfull authorities in the world," citing the example of highwaymen as robbers stealing men's purses by unlawful means.[112] To enter a plea without first being satisfied as to the authority of the court, Charles affirmed, would be to betray the trust committed to him "by God [and] by ould and lawfull discent . . ."[113] To betray this trust, the king further asserted, was to betray also the liberties of his people.[114] Charles made allusion to the divine right of kings and a descending conception of political power in questioning the court's jurisdiction.

Bradshaw made use of both an ascending and descending conception of power in his response. The two were, of course, not mutually exclusive – a king might hold his power from God yet still be constituted as king by

[110] J. G. Bellamy, *The Law of Treason in England in the Later Middle Ages* (Cambridge, 1970), p. 62.

[111] PRO SP 16/517/16; Nalson, *True Copy*, sig. I2v, p. 33; Mabbot, *A perfect Narrative*, sig. A3r, p. 5.

[112] PRO SP 16/517/16.

[113] PRO SP 16/517/16; see also Nalson, *True Copy*, sig. K1v, K2r, pp. 33, 35; Mabbot, *A perfect Narrative*, sig. A3v, p. 6.

[114] PRO SP 16/517/17.

the people.[115] Furthermore, a magistrate's election by his people might be taken as a sign of divine sanction. The Lord President answered Charles that he was summoned before the court "by the authority of the Com[m]ons of England assembled in Parlia[me]nt in the behalfe of the people of England by w[hic]h people you are elected kinge w[hic]h authority requires you in the name of the People of England to answer them."[116] Bradshaw's response was in keeping with both the values of classical republicanism and radical constitutionalism. Kingship was at best an elected office held in trust not directly from God but from the people immediately under God and subject to resumption by the people should the king misrule. Charles, unsurprisingly, vigorously denied that the kingship of England was ever an elective office but an hereditary one for some thousands of years.[117] He demanded further to know by what scriptural authority and by what "antient lawes and Constitutions of this Realme" he had been called.

Over the course of a heated exchange with Bradshaw he argued that to submit to a usurped authority was to betray both the trust that God had committed to him and the liberties of the people. He warned the court further that if indeed they did act by a usurped authority, that "God in heaven" would call them to account for their actions.[118] Bradshaw, perhaps finally losing his cool, countered the king's claim to divine right by an appeal to divine providence, asserting the court's claim to a divine mandate. He told the king bluntly, "Wee are upon Gods and the kingdomes errand . . ."[119] The conflict was not simply one between ascending and descending conceptions of political power but between rival claims to divine sanction, one flowing from king's divine right to his office and the other, providential in nature, flowing from the court's assertion of a divine mandate. The claim to divine sanction, if not explicitly divine right, formed the common stock from which both parties sought to legitimate their actions.

The following Monday, 22 January, the court met privately in the Painted Chamber of Westminster Hall to consider the king's challenge to their jurisdiction. Bradshaw received the court's approbation for his handling of the king's challenges the previous Saturday and it was resolved on the matter

115 Conrad Russell, *The Causes of the English Civil War* (Oxford, 1990), p. 147; John Guy, "The King's Council and Political Participation," in Alistair Fox and John Guy, eds., *Reassessing the Henrician Age: Humanism, Politics and Reform 1500–1550* (Oxford, 1986), p. 124.

116 PRO SP 16/517/17; see also Nalson, *True Copy*, sig. K2r, p. 35; Mabbot *A perfect Narrative*, sig. A3v, p. 6.

117 PRO SP 16/517/17: Mabbot, *A perfect Narrative*, sigs. A3v–A4r, pp. 6–7.

118 PRO SP 16/517/17; Nalson, *True Copy*, sig. K2v, p. 36.

119 PRO SP 16/517/17; Yale, Osborn MS fb 146, 20 January 1649; Mabbot's account differs slightly, with Bradshaw answering "upon Gods Authority and the Kingdomes": Mabbot, *A perfect Narrative*, sig. A4v, p.8.

"that the king should not be suffered to Argue the Courts Iurisdiccon or that w[hic]h constituted them a court of w[hic]h debate they had not proper Cognisance nor could they being a derivative iudge of that Supreame Court w[hic]h made them Iudges and from which there was noe appeale . . ."[120] Not only was the king forbidden to dispute the authority of the court; the court itself denied its own competence to determine such a question. The court's own authority was merely derivative from the supreme power of the people's representatives, the Commons of England assembled in parliament, from whose judgment there was no appeal. Essentially, the court claimed control over a mark of sovereignty, the right of final appeal, on behalf of the Rump.

At the beginning of proceedings on the afternoon of 22 January John Cook moved that if the king continued in his obstructionist ways he should be "taken pro Confeso," at which time the court would "proceede according to Iustice."[121] Like the Irish rebel Brian O'Rourke over half a century before the king would stand mute and be sentenced. The king continued in his previous course, pleading "the freedome and Libertie of the People of England" and arguing that if an unlawful power "may make Lawe, may alter the fundamental Lawes of the Kingdome, I doe not knowe what subiect hee is in England can bee assured of his life, or any thinge hee can call his owne."[122] The act erecting the High Court and the charge against the king had accused Charles of subverting the fundamental laws of the land through his assumption of a tyrannical power and the bringing of war upon the land. Two could play that game. Strafford and Laud had stood accused of subverting the law through the pursuit of legal proceedings that fell outside their respective jurisdictions. Faced with a novel, extraordinary tribunal claiming a divinely derived jurisdiction over his fate, the king developed a similar argument, reappropriating the rhetoric of fundamental law in his defense. The subversion of the law was, after all, the subversion of the ordinary course of justice.

The king also made appeal to law and reason protesting that, although he was no lawyer, he did "knowe as much Lawe as most Gent[lemen] in England" and that should he "impose a beleefe vpon any man w[it]hout reasons given for it, It were vnreasonable . . ."[123] Glenn Burgess has argued for a model of common-law discourse in which the rationality of the common law took precedence over its immemorality. Coke, he has argued, was atypical in his stress on the immemorality of the common law and the majority of common lawyers, men such as Davies and Selden, saw the binding

120 PRO SP 16/517/19; see also Nalson, *True Copy*, sig. L1v, p. 38.
121 PRO SP 16/517/20; Nalson, *True Copy*, sig. M1r–v, pp. 41–42.
122 PRO SP 16/517/20; Mabbot, *A perfect Narrative*, sig. B2r, p. 11.
123 PRO SP 16/517/20–21; Mabbot, *A perfect Narrative*, sig. B2v, p. 12.

force of the customary law of the land coming from the presumption that it was the embodiment of reason: "No custom could make a law valid when it was in conflict with reason; custom was a means of discovering rational principles, or axioms, not an alternative to them."[124] The appeal to reason, however, was filtered through practice. There was a presumption that, customary law of the land having developed through past usage, a practice was "tried reason" and that the common law was the distilled essence of practical reason.[125]

Bradshaw's response was a direct appeal to the rationality of the polity and embodied a position suggestive of legal positivism and markedly different from the presumptive rationality of the common law. He asserted that, "The Voate of the Com[m]ons of England in Parliam[en]t... is the Reason of the Kingdom: It is the Law of the kingdome and they are those that have given you that Lawe, according to w[hic]h you should have Ruled and Raigned."[126] Legal positivism is a term applied to a command-based rather than community-based conception of legalism. According to Dworkin, this holds that within every polity there is a sovereign body or individual "whose commands are habitually obeyed and who is not in the habit of obeying anyone else."[127] A proposition in law had force if it accurately reported the past commands of the sovereign.[128] The prescription of the sovereign's command, not the prescription of tried usage or inherited custom, took precedence. Early modern jurists and politicians no doubt had a sense of law *both* as enacted through king in parliament as statute and as customary, with some such as Coke emphasizing the latter and others such as Lord Chancellor Ellesmere and, at certain points in his career, William Prynne emphasizing the former. The High Court's claim to a right of judgment was founded upon a commission derived from a statute enacted by the claimants of the sovereign law-giving authority – the representatives of the Commons of England assembled in parliament.

The regicides, lacking any clearly defined municipal custom of king-killing, were compelled to make a direct, unmediated appeal to the rationality of the polity. Bradshaw's description of the vote of the Commons of England as the "Reason of the Kingdom" alluded strongly to this. John Cook in his published argument asserted that it was "out of the sphaere of all earthly Law-givers to comprehend and express all particular cases that may possibly

124 Glenn Burgess, *The Politics of the Ancient Constitution: An Introduction to English Political Thought, 1603–1642* (London, 1992), p. 53.
125 Burgess, *Politics*, ch. 2.
126 PRO SP 16/517/21; Nalson, *True Copy*, sig. M2v, p. 44; Mabbott, *A perfect Narrative*, sigs. B2v–B3r, pp. 12–13.
127 Ronald Dworkin, *Law's Empire* (London, 1986), p. 33.
128 Dworkin, *Law's Empire*, p. 33.

happen ..." Accordingly, it was necessary that, "as particulars occur, rational men ... reduce them to general reasons of State, so as every thing may be adjudged for the good of the Community."[129] When custom and precedent fell silent, a direct appeal to reason of state was necessary. Charles's actions in levying war against his people and parliament were unnatural, unprecedented, and destructive to the state itself. Accordingly, extraordinary measures were justified for the preservation of the common good. The appeal to reason was the common ground on which both parties attempted to legitimate their jurisdictional claims. They did so, however, from subtly differing jurisprudential positions. The regicides appealed directly to reason *and* to fundamental law, while the king resorted to the presumptive reason of the ancient law of the land.

On the afternoon of 23 January the king once again appeared at the bar. John Cook opened proceedings, accusing Charles of violating his coronation oath which he had taken "to maintaine the lawe and to keepe the Peace of the Kingdome" and alleging that the king had set up his standard of war at Nottingham "out of a wicked designe to subverte and destroy the ... Lawe, and to introduce an Arbitrary and Tirannicall Government in defiance of Parliamentary authority ..."[130] He moved once again that if the king continue in his conduct he should be found *pro confesso* and the court would proceed to sentencing.[131] Bradshaw reaffirmed the court's jurisdiction derived from "the Supreame and highest Authority of England ... from w[hic]h there is no appeale" and once again demanded that the king enter a plea.[132] Charles, however, stubbornly persisted, continuing to identify his cause with the liberties of the people and asserting his obligation to maintain these liberties and "to defende ... the ancient Lawes of the Kingdom ..." As for the charge itself, he was dismissive: "I value it not a Rush ..."[133] Both sides in the trial identified legality with legitimacy and rationality with law. The officers of the court portrayed the king as the destroyer and subverter of the law and the king in response pointed out the irregularity of the proceedings against him and sought to present himself as a champion of the ancient constitution and the liberty of the subject.

The court was unsympathetic and proceeded on 24 and 25 January to the examination of witnesses and the taking of depositions. The majority of these, as previously noted, dealt with the king's conduct during the war and involved the king being seen at the head of his army, raising his standard

[129] Cook, *King Charls his Case*, sig. D2r, p. 27.
[130] PRO SP 16/517/23; see also Mabbott, *A perfect Narrative*, sig. B4v, p. 16.
[131] PRO SP 16/517/23; Nalson, *True Copy*, sig. P2v, p. 56; Mabbott, *A perfect Narrative*, sig. C1r, p. 17.
[132] PRO SP 16/517/24.
[133] PRO SP 16/517/24; see also Nalson, *True Copy*, sig. Q1r–v, pp. 57–58.

and wearing "cote armure" in warlike fashion. The depositions, however, also included a report of treasonable words attributed to the king given as evidence of the king's treasonable intentions to renew the struggle and his lack of good faith in dealing with the parliamentary commissioners the previous autumn on the Isle of Wight. Henry Gooch, a barrister of Gray's Inn, reported that he, having access to a discourse between the king, the Marquess of Hertford, and Commissary Morgan, heard the king remark that although "for the p[re]sent hee was contented to giue the Parliam[en]t leave to call theire owne warr what they pleased ... hee neither did at that tyme, nor ever should decline the Iustice of his owne Cause."[134] The king then allegedly told the deponent that he, being upon a treaty, would not dishonor himself by the issuing of commissions for the continuing of the conflict. However, the king said also that, should the deponent or any of his allies "goe over to the Prince his sonne (who had his full authority from him) hee ... should receive whatever commissions should bee desired ..."[135] Gooch's testimony was, like the previous depositions, closely harmonized with the charge. Consistent with the words of the charge, the king had not only brought a destructive war on the land but also conspired its renewal with his son Charles and others. Treasonable words were given as evidence to the king's treasonable intentions.

The prosecution also returned to the familiar charge that the king had conspired to bring an Irish army into England during the first Civil War. The basis of this charge was the single testimony of Richard Price of London, a scrivener, who claimed to have visited the king at Oxford in 1643 on a safe conduct as part of the king's bid to turn the London Independents to his cause. The king had purportedly promised, "in the word of a kinge that if the Independents would turne to him and bee active for him against the Parliam[en]t as they had bin for them against him[,] Then hee would graunt them whatsoever freedome they would desire."[136] The king allegedly offered religious toleration in exchange for support. Price deponed further that the king had then referred him to the Earl of Bristol for further discussions. Bristol had purportedly remarked that the king's "Irish Subiects had given the Rebells ... a greate defeate" and that Lord Byron's forces massing before Nantwich "would be strengthened w[it]h more Souldiers out of Ireland w[hic]h were come and expected dayly."[137] As with the trial of Strafford the prosecution played the anti-Irish, anti-popery card. Not only did the king unnaturally levy war on his own people, he conspired with

[134] PRO SP 16/517/32; Nalson, *True Copy*, sig. X1r, p. 78 (only spellings differ).

[135] PRO SP 16/517/32; Nalson, *True Copy*, sig. X1r, p. 78; it should be noted that the veracity of Price's testimony is highly questionable.

[136] PRO SP 16/517/33; Nalson, *True Copy*, sig. X2v, p. 80.

[137] PRO SP 16/517/33; Nalson, *True Copy*, sig. X2v, p. 80.

rebels and papists from outside the realm of England in the levying of that war.

On 25 January, following the depositions, the court resolved "to p[ro]ceede to Sentence of Condempnacon against Charles Stuart Kinge of England," and that this condemnation "shall bee for a Tyrrant Traytor and Murtherer."[138] It was resolved further that the king would be condemned also "for being a Publique Enemy to the Common Wealth of England [and] That this . . . shall extend to death."[139] A committee consisting of Thomas Scot, Henry Marten, Thomas Harrison, John Lisle, William Say, Henry Ireton, and Nicholas Love or any three of them was appointed to draw up a sentence which was presented to the court in draft on 26 January in the Painted Chamber.[140] The king would appear for sentencing the following day.

The events of 20 to 25 January revealed that Charles's crime was clearly a treason against the state. The prosecution's actions and their choice of vocabulary were informed by strong conceptions of the common good, whether that was conceived of as the public interest, the public good, or, more traditionally, the commonwealth. These terms were analagous to an impersonal or corporate state. The fiction that the king could do no wrong was utterly abandoned. There was no appeal to the "evil counsellors" argument that had informed the impeachments of the early Long Parliament. In the eyes of the prosecution the king was, in keeping with classical republican values, merely an elected magistrate, no more infallible than the Pope, who had done tangible wrong in bringing war, both destructive to property and costly in blood, on the land. The king had violated the trust reposed in him by the people to administer his office for the public good. He had appropriated a mark of sovereignty, the right of war and peace, for the advancement of his private interest and that of his family over and above that of the public.

The king in his defense appealed to a number of arguments which, to a modern commentator, might seem incompatible. These included an appeal to the fundamental and ancient laws of the land, the liberty of the subject, *and* the divine right of kings. He did so without any apparent contradiction. The court in turn opposed the king with their own appeal to fundamental law as well as a direct appeal to the rationality of the polity. They also advanced not only an assertion of the popular origins of magistracy but their own rival claim to a divine sanction for their actions, if not an explicit claim to hold their places of magistracy by divine right. The picture that emerged from the trial on 20, 21, and 23 January is of hostile interests drawing on

[138] PRO SP 16/517/33; Nalson, *True Copy*, sig. Y1r, p. 81; Mabbot did not provide a narrative of the proceedings of 24 and 25 January.

[139] PRO SP 16/517/33; Nalson, *True Copy*, sig. Y1r, p. 81.

[140] PRO SP 16/517/33–34.

both imperfectly shared and competing ideological resources. All appealed to law and to reason and to a divine sanction because these were the common currency with which political actors in early Stuart England redescribed and legitimized courses of political action.

IV

The king appeared for sentencing on the afternoon of 27 January 1649. Charles remained defiant, refusing to submit to the jurisdiction of the court and asking that before sentencing he "be heard in the Painted Chamber before the Lords and Com[m]ons . . ."[141] He pleaded both the "peace" and "welfare" of the kingdom as well as the "liberty of the subject."[142] Bradshaw accused him, once again, of declining the jurisdiction of the court. The king replied that the court was mistaken to see his actions as a declining of their jurisdiction yet he continued to affirm that he could not acknowledge it.[143] Bradshaw told the king plainly that, "This Court is founded vpon the Authority of the Com[m]ons of England in whom rests the Supreme Iurisdiccon"[144] and that which the king proposed was the erection of a co-ordinate jurisdiction in derogation of the supreme authority of the Commons of England assembled in parliament.[145] Essentially, the king refused to acknowledge the legality of the Rump's claims to be the supreme law-giver in the state.

After this sharp exchange the Lord President launched into "some Discourse . . . for vindicating the Parliaments Justice, explaining the Nature of the Crimes of which the Prisoner stood charged, and for which he was to be condemned."[146] Bradshaw's speech to the High Court of Justice, probably the composition of Dorislaus, was printed by the official censor Gilbert Mabbott in his account of the trial. The speech constituted a reinterpretation of the origins of the English polity as a popular state and a redefinition of kingship as a popularly elected magistracy limited by a particular commission. This was consistent both with radical constitutionalism and with at least some of the values of classical republicanism concerning the desirability of elected magistracy over hereditary. In this narrow sense it was one of the first halting, guarded, and limited attempts at the restatement of the terms in

141 PRO SP 16/517/36.
142 PRO SP 16/517/36–37; Mabbot, *A perfect Narrative*, sig. D1r–v, pp. 25–26.
143 PRO SP 16/517/37. 144 PRO SP 16/517/37.
145 PRO SP 16/517/36–37; Nalson, *True Copy*, sig. Z2v, p. 88; Mabbot, *A perfect narrative*, sig. D2r, p. 27.
146 Nalson, *True Copy*, sig. Aa1r, p. 89, Yale Osborn MS fb 146, 27 January 1649: neither the Yale manuscript nor Nalson reproduces the text of Bradshaw's speech, although Mabbot and PRO SP 16/517/38–43 reproduce it in full.

which Englishmen lived as civic beings in terms of republicanism. However, the speech was, as Scott and Worden have maintained, limited and defensive, seeking only to justify a particular set of actions. It reflected a radical monarchical republicanism at best: monarchy was not the target but hereditary monarchy, and in particular that of the Stuarts. Although it did reveal at times an awareness of civic humanist values, its primary task was not the systematic restatement of the conditions in which Englishmen lived as civic beings.

Bradshaw moved quickly to the key issue of who was the sovereign lawgiver in the state. He pointed out that the king's claim to have "endeavoured and studdied the Peace of the Kingdom" was belied by his actions and that if "Actions must expound Intentions" his actions had been contrary.[147] Bradshaw told the king that he had held himself "and let fall such language" as though the law had been his superior and maintained the pretense that he had ruled according to the law.[148] The key issue Bradshaw identified was the question of who held the law-giving power. He told the king that "... the difference has bin who shall bee Exposite[r]s of this Lawe, Whether you and yo[ur] p[ar]tie out of the Courts of Iustice shall take upon them to expound the Law, or the Courts of Iustice, that are the Expounders, Nay the Soveraign and the highest Court of Iustice the Parliament of England, that is not only the highest Expounder but the sole maker of the Lawe."[149] The king and his party had set themselves "against the Resolucon of the Highest Co[ur]t of Iustice," the Commons of England assembled in parliament. Consequently he and his party had set themselves above that which was itself "superior to the lawe" as "the parent and the author of the Law... the People of England."[150] Once again, this was a position more in keeping with a command theory of sovereignty roughly analogous to legal positivism than the Cokean appeal to immemorial custom.

This was essentially a Roman-law conception of treason applied to a popular state. Only the people were sovereign and for any magistrate or pretended magistrate to attempt the giving or making of law without their consent, or beyond the boundaries of their particular commission, was high treason. The absolutist John Cusacke may have been a minority voice in the 1630s but he was simply restating the Roman law of treason when he asserted that "the king makes the laws of England and to admit any other lawmaker in England is high treason ..."[151] While relocating the locus of legal

[147] PRO SP 16/517/38; Mabbot, *A perfect Narrative*, sig. D4r, p. 31.
[148] PRO SP 16/517/38; Mabbot, *A perfect Narrative*, sig. D4r, p. 31.
[149] PRO SP 16/517/38; Mabbot, *A perfect Narrative*, sig. D4r, p. 31.
[150] PRO SP 16/517/38; Mabbot, *A perfect Narrative*, sig. D4v, p. 32.
[151] Quoted in Peck, "Kingship, Counsel and Law," p. 113.

sovereignty in the people, Bradshaw was in fundamental agreement with this statement. Treason remained essentially the unlawful seizure or appropriation of sovereign power and that power received practical definition in the marks and rights of sovereignty.

Bradshaw then embarked on a lengthy redescription of both the English monarchy and kingship in general as a form of elected magistracy. He did so by appealing to a popular conception of the origins of government. He argued that the people of England, "at the first, as other Countries have done, did chuse to themselves this forme of Government..."[152] For the proper administration of justice and the preservation of the peace the people gave their governors laws "according to w[hi]ch they should govern..."[153] However, should the laws "prove inconvenient or p[re]iudiciall to the publique, they had a power in them, A Power reserved and innate to alter them as they should see cause..."[154] Bradshaw affirmed with the royalists that it was true that, in some sense, the king had no peer in his realm.[155] However, he also invoked a maxim popularized by conciliarist thinkers such as Gerson, telling the king that although he was peerless in the sense of being "Maior Singulis" he was still "Minor Vniversis" and that he had his superior in god and in law.[156] Consistent with the principles of radical constitutional thinking the status of the king was reduced from that of sovereign to that of magistrate in a popular state. Bradshaw asserted that the king "must vnderstand that hee is but an Officer in trust, and hee ought to discharge that trust for the People, and if hee doe not they are to take order for the Animadversion and Punishment of such an offending Governor."[157] This law was not a new law, argued Bradshaw, but was "Lawe of ould."[158]

Bradshaw then launched into a veritable paean on the virtues of parliaments, praising them in their capacity for redressing the people's grievances. He accused Charles of attempting to do away with them forever, arguing that they were kept anciently twice a year so "that the subiect vpon any occasion might have a ready remedy and redresse for his Grievance" and that later, under Edward III, it was decreed by statute that parliaments were to be held annually.[159] He referred to the "sadd consequence" of the personal rule of 1629–40, a period in which the realm was governed by an "high and Arbitrary hande."[160] He told the king that the Long Parliament had been called "when god by his p[ro]vidence... brought it about that you could no longer decline the Calling of a Parliam[en]t..."[161] In attempting

[152] PRO SP 16/517/38. [153] PRO SP 16/517/38. [154] PRO SP 16/517/38.
[155] "Rex non habet parem in Regno suo": PRO SP 16/517/538.
[156] PRO SP 16/517/38–39. [157] PRO SP 16/517/39. [158] PRO SP 16/517/39.
[159] PRO SP 16/517/39. [160] PRO SP 16/517/39. [161] PRO SP 16/517/39.

to dispense with parliaments Charles's intent to subvert the fundamental law of the land was manifest, "for the greate Bulwarke of the Liberties of the People is the Parliam[en]t of England, and by subverting and Rooting vpp that . . . at one . . . blow confounded the Liberties and the Propriety of England . . ."[162]

Bradshaw also made use of examples drawn from classical antiquity, suggesting an active appropriation of classical republicanism. He likened the parliament to the tribunes of ancient Rome and the ephori of Lacedemonia, arguing that, although Rome lost its liberty under the emperors, there were still some "famous acts of Iustice" to be found under the Empire such as the condemnation of the tyrant Nero by the Senate. The loss of republican virtue did not, of course, preclude the possibility of acting virtuously. Just actions could still occur within an institutional framework such as imperial Rome that was inimical to virtue. The Lord President also accused Charles of emulating the Roman tyrant Caligula, who had reputedly expressed the wish that the people of Rome possessed a single neck so, "That at one blowe hee might haue cutt it off."[163] He argued that in England "the Body of the People . . . hath bin no where els rep[re]sented but in the Parliam[en]t" and that, if the king had been able to confound it, he would have "at one blowe cutt off the Necke of England . . ."[164] The notion of a body politic remained but it was reconstrued in terms of a popular state in which magistrates exercised their offices like the tribunes of ancient Rome for the preservation of the common good. The likening of parliament to the tribunes of ancient Rome was also highly significant in that it suggested a well-developed appropriation of Roman law. Originally the term *maiestas* or treason in Roman law was identified with the plebes and with the powers and dignities of their representatives the tribunes, and treason was a crime in derogation of these powers. Only later under the early Augustan Principate did *maiestas* become identified with the office and dignity of the emperor.[165]

Bradshaw then presented a plethora of examples drawn from both English and European history and from classical antiquity intended to illustrate the elective and magisterial character of kingly government in all states. Aside from the aforementioned example of the emperor Nero, he also drew on the history of the Scottish monarchy, arguing that in ancient times Scottish kings were elected and that the Scots had on many occasions deposed and punished

[162] I have removed from the quotation only the second-person pronouns and possessives as these remarks were addressed directly to the king: PRO SP 16/517/39.

[163] PRO SP 16/517/40. [164] PRO SP 16/517/40.

[165] This transition from popular to imperial majesty is discussed in Richard A. Bauman, *Crimen Maiestatis in the Roman Republic and Augustan Principate* (Johannesburg, 1967).

"theire offending and transgressing kings."[166] More provocatively, he cited the example of Charles's grandmother set aside in favor of his infant father, James VI, in the 1560s, asserting that "the State did it . . ."[167] In the case of England his cause was undoubtedly helped by the fact that the hereditary principle of succession was often more preached than practiced. Bradshaw cited the depositions of Edward II and Richard II as obvious examples, arguing that of the twenty-four kings of England who had reigned since the Norman conquest "more then one halfe of them came in by the State and not meerly vpon the poynt of Descent . . ."[168]

Bradshaw's use of the term "state" in this context was highly significant. The king was not God's anointed, holding his crown by hereditary right, but a magistrate who had gained his place of office by the consent of "the state" and was entrusted for the protection of the people and the promotion and preservation of the common good. He used explicitly contractarian language, arguing that "there is a Contract and Bargaine made betwixt the Kinge and his People" sealed by the coronation oath. In a possible allusion to James VI and I's *The Trew Law of Free Monarchies*,[169] he spoke of the dual nature of allegiance. The bonds of allegiance were reciprocal, with the king acting as the people's protector in return for their allegiance. If this bond were broken, then "farewell Soveraignty." Charles, rather than acting as "the Protector of England," had instead become "the destroyer of England," and it was left for "all England and all the world" to judge.[170] Bradshaw's rhetoric revealed an understanding of the state that was impersonal in the sense that the king was inferior to the state. The monarch was granted his authority as chief public officer by the contracted consent of the governed to maintain their state. The state was not *his*, and nor was the law, but the duties of his office demanded that he maintain both.

Bradshaw ended by accusing the king of being "a Tyrrant, Traytor, a Murtherer, and a Publique Enemy to the Comon Wealth of England." To all this the king responded with a single perfunctory "Hagh." Bradshaw in response became more colorful and abusive, launching into a lengthy admonishment of Charles. While the king's disorderly conduct had preoccupied the court on 20, 22, and 23 January, the contents of the charge and the depositions had been relatively restrained, sticking to the particulars of raising war in the realm and coldly enumerating examples of where Charles had

166 PRO SP 16/517/40. 167 PRO SP 16/517/40. 168 PRO SP 16/517/40.

169 James VI and I, *The Trew Law of Free Monarchies: or The Reciprock and Mvtvall Dvtie Betwixt A Free King, And His naturall Subiects*, in Johann P. Sommerville ed., *King James VI and I, Political Writings* (Cambridge, 1994), pp. 62–84.

170 PRO SP 16/517/41.

transgressed. Now the gloves were off, with the Lord President accusing the king of mass murder, shedding blood in violation not only of the law of the land, of nations, and of nature but of God's law as expressed in scripture.[171] Bradshaw also made more explicit appeal to a divine mandate for the court's actions. He claimed that the court had been called to their present employment out of a consciousness of their duty owed "both vnto God and vnto the Kingdom" and that the court wished that God give the king a sense of his sins so that he might repent.[172] Charles interrupted, asking again that he might be heard. After another sharp exchange with the Lord President he was led away.

As an attempt to restate the terms on which Englishmen lived as civic beings, Bradshaw's speech was very limited. Bradshaw may have seen the High Court as performing an important public duty that was crucial to the public interest and was, to some extent, undoubtedly, informed by an ideology of civic humanism that valued service to the state and the *vita activa*. However, he did not systematically unpack an ideology of civic activism. His speech's primary aim was to redefine the nature of kingship, both in England and elsewhere, as an elected magistracy, limited by law, and entrusted to Charles for the promotion of the common good. This was consistent with classical republican values, at least in the restricted sense that elected magistracy was to be preferred over hereditary, but it was not a call for a mixed constitution, nor even for an end of monarchy *per se*. Elected magistracy was more conducive to the common good because it better provided that those most capable of virtue were placed in positions of public trust and those less virtuous were excluded.

The concept of treason standing behind Bradshaw's argument was consistent with Roman law, albeit in the context of a popular republican state. The Lord President's allusions to republican Rome and in particular his identification of parliament with the tribunate – the representatives of the plebes and the bearers of republican *maiestas* – made this manifest. Charles had attempted to rule and give law by his own will independent of the people and their representatives assembled in parliament and in pursuit of this goal had sought to put an end to parliaments for good. Charles's actions of the personal rule as well as the Civil War were held against him. As the people and their representatives were sovereign in this popular state, the king, as a mere magistrate, limited by his particular commission, had overstepped the boundaries of his office and encroached on the sovereign power. He had effected this both in seeking to rule without parliament and in levying war on the parliament and people.

[171] Genesis 9: 35; PRO SP 16/517/41–42. [172] PRO SP 16/517/42.

V

On 27 January 1649 Charles Stuart, King of England, was sentenced by the High Court of Justice sitting in Westminster Hall.[173] The contents of the sentence were familiar fare, reiterating much of the charge against the king: Charles had been "admitted King of England and therein trusted with a limited power to govern by, and according to the law of the land" and, according to his coronation oath, he was "obliged to use the power committed to him for the good and the benefit of the people, and the preservation of their rights and liberties . . ."[174] Instead, Charles had tried to assume to himself "an arbitrary and tyrannical power" and rule according to his will alone without parliaments, placing his own "personal interest of will and power" and that of his family ahead of "public interest, common right, liberty, justice, and peace of the people of this nation."[175] To this end he had raised a bloody, destructive, and unnatural war against parliament and people and, when defeated twice, had conspired still to renew the conflict.[176] In short, all of the kingdom's ills of the last two decades were placed at Charles's feet.

What is striking about Charles's trial is the continuities. The corporate character of the state remained – it was still a political body, rendered as such by the fundamental law of the land. However, it was no longer the king's political body, nor was it his state to hold and to maintain. Neither was the law the king's law. The king was merely an elected magistrate entrusted with a commission for the maintenance of the law, the peace of the kingdom and the promotion of the common good. The regicides attempted to reduce kingship from sovereignty to magistracy – a task that was consistent both with the values of classical republicanism and radical constitutionalism. The positive powers of the state constituted in the marks and right of sovereignty – power to give law, power to levy war, power to appoint magistrates – remained largely unchanged in their basic definitions and it was still high treason to assume them unlawfully. They were, however, no longer exclusively identified with a hereditary monarchy. The regicides attempted to legitimate their actions by redescribing England as a popular state in which the people were sovereign. This rendered a conception of the state that was impersonal and corporate in character, if not fully abstract.

173 For copies of the sentence see PRO SP 16/517/43–44; Nalson *True Copy*, sig. Aa1r–2v, pp. 89–92; Gardiner, *Constitutional Documents*, pp. 377–380.

174 Gardiner, *Constitutional Documents*, p. 377.

175 Gardiner, *Constitutional Documents*, pp. 377–378.

176 Gardiner, *Constitutional Documents*, pp. 377–379.

Conclusion

This study has not been an attempt at comprehensively retelling the story of the English law of treason during the Civil War. Rather, it has endeavored to show how on four important occasions of state political ideas were deployed for the purpose of redescribing and legitimating particular courses of political action. In this way imperfectly shared political ideas and vocabularies came to play a concrete role in the shaping of political life. Without needlessly resurrecting Whig narratives of the rise of absolutism versus the triumph of parliamentary liberty, it is still credible to characterize the English Civil War as a struggle for sovereignty. It was a struggle for the control and ultimately the very definition of the positive powers of the state – powers with which Charles I was no longer trusted after a decade of personal rule that had seen ship money, a disastrous Scottish war, a complete cessation of parliaments, and, most disturbingly, "Popish innovations" in the Church of England.

These positive powers were, generally speaking, law-giving (whether judicial or legislative), war and peace, coinage, taxation, the appointment of ministers and magistrates, and, especially, power to determine the doctrine and discipline of the established church. Legal-constitutional and religious perceptions of misgovernment in the first two years of the Long Parliament were closely intertwined. The religious and the legal-constitutional were hardly, as John Morrill has suggested, "quite separable and distinct perceptions of misgovernment" for William Prynne, Oliver St. John, Samuel Browne, John Hampden, or the subsequent royalist, Edward Bagshawe.[1] The dichotomy is misleading in that it fails to capture the full extent of Erastian discontent with an increasingly bold and autonomous clerical estate. The spiritual well-being of the kingdom was not a concern that could be easily shunted aside and there can be no doubt that religion took precedence. However, it did so by virtue of being perceived as the most crucial and pressing issue within a

[1] J. S. Morrill, "The Religious Context of the English Civil War," in Richard Cust and Ann Hughes, eds., *The English Civil War* (London, 1997), p. 161.

broader legal-constitutional framework. Power over the established church was as much a mark of sovereignty as power over taxation and, if Bodin had hesitated to say so, Haywarde and the Erastians of the early 1640s did not. These individuals saw treason in terms similar to Roman law as the unlawful assumption of any or all of these powers. The central issue was not so much the subject's right to resist as the question of *who* was to govern and in *whose name* they governed, both in church and in state. Practical issues of governance stood behind the impending struggle for sovereignty.

The nature of this struggle was necessarily ideological. However, the ideological positions from which this struggle proceeded at the calling of the Long Parliament were far from clearly defined. This was not a conflict driven, in the words of Justin A. I. Champion, by "rival accounts of the legitimate location of legal sovereignty," as J. H. Hexter and Johann Sommerville have argued.[2] In 1640 it was a relatively uncontentious proposition that the king acting in his regal and legal capacity declared and made law, but what this meant in practice was far from clear. The conflicts of the mid-seventeenth century reflected a struggle for the constitutional definition of sovereignty. The status of executive legislative orders such as proclamations was not clear and the jurisdictions of the Privy Council and the prerogative courts lacked clear delineation. What was clear was that neither Thomas Wentworth nor William Laud were lawful kings of England and that, if they had acted in derogation of the sovereign power, they were traitors.

The struggle for sovereignty thus proceeded not from pre-formed, antithetical ideological foundations but was carried out in an improvised, haphazard fashion with whatever ideological resources were available. Political arguments were derived from history, custom, common law, natural law, civil law, divine law, or the appeal to necessity. They were supported by authorities as diverse as Jean Bodin, Sir John Fortescue, Sir Edward Coke, Cicero, and the Bible, to name a handful. These resources were sometimes shared and sometimes competing. A succession of changing parliamentarian juntos, beginning with Pym and St. John in 1641 and ending finally with Cromwell, Ireton, Scott, and Challoner in 1649, conducted this struggle first against the king's evil counselors in the name of his regal authority and then finally against the king himself in the name of the keepers of the liberty of England. Glenn Burgess and Paul Christianson have argued that the hegemony of the common law as a master language provided early Stuart political life with established conventions of political argument, determining the proper roles and places of potentially rival vocabularies such as the civil law, the law of

[2] Justin A. I. Champion, "Philosophy, State and Religion: Languages of Political Theory in Early Modern England," *Parliamentary History* 14 (1995): 189; J. H. Hexter, "The Early Stuarts and Parliament: Old Hat and the *Nouvelle Vague*," *Parliamentary History* 1 (1982): 207.

nations, natural law, divine right, and absolutism.[3] However, the outbreak of hostilities in 1642 created an ideological free-for-all, with ideas and the textual authorities behind them being freely appropriated in a confusing tangle of polemics. Divisions on substantive issues unquestionably existed during the years leading up to the Civil War but only gradually did they resolve themselves into the deeper ideological polarities of the second half of the century. Both the personal rule of the 1630s and the civil wars of the 1640s were catalysts in the fostering of deepening ideological divisions – not, as some have claimed, the product of them.[4]

The central theme of this study has been the shift from a mixed corporate and personal conception of public authority or the "state" to an impersonal or "abstract" conception of the state. Both conceptions of public authority were available to English jurists and public men on the eve of the English Civil War. The former manifested itself in what Kantorowicz characterized as the theory of the king's two bodies. This held that the monarch possessed two capacities, one natural and one politic, and that when the monarch acted in his or her legal and regal capacity, he or she acted as a corporation, an abstract juristic person. While the king's natural body could only be in one place at one time, his majesty and the protection of his law extended throughout his dominions, meaning that crimes such as treason could be committed in any corner of his realms. Because the king's public authority was *inseparable* from his natural person and that of his bodily heirs, a treason against the king's political body was also a crime against his natural body. Thus, for example, the subversion or destruction of the king's law or alternately his people was conceivably a constructive compassing of the king's death and treason under the first head of 25 Edward III. To modern eyes this may have been a rather strained construction; however, it did provide the necessary bridge between the idea of treason as a crime against the king's person and the notion of treason as a crime against the state. Furthermore, this notion of public authority was a commonplace well before the calling of the Long Parliament.

In public-law terms the early modern state was, essentially, a corporation, a body politic – corporate rather than purely abstract. This was also a relatively unproblematic statement in 1641. However, in the context of the early Stuart plural monarchy there were difficulties. Britain was not a single body

[3] Glenn Burgess, *The Politics of the Ancient Constitution: An Introduction to English Political Thought, 1603–1642* (London, 1992); Paul Christianson, "Royal and Parliamentary Voices on the Ancient Constitution," in Linda Levy Peck, ed., *The Mental World of The Jacobean Court* (Cambridge, 1991), pp. 71–95.

[4] Johann P. Sommerville, *Politics and Ideology in England, 1603–1640* (London, 1986); John B. Sanderson, *"But the People's Creatures": The Philosophical Basis of the English Civil War* (Manchester, 1989).

politic but several united by a single personal allegiance. The status of Ireland within this multiple kingdom was especially problematic. Was it a conquered nation? And if it was, how was it to be governed? The overwhelming consensus of those involved in the trials of Strafford and Maguire was that, whether a conquered nation or not, Ireland was to be governed by the common law, the statutes of that realm, those statutes of England in which Ireland was named and those statutes of England that Poynings' legislation brought into force there.[5] However, what this meant in practice was subject to some dispute with both the apologists of the Straffordian rule in Ireland and the prosecutors of Maguire arguing for substantial divergence and *exception* from English practice in that realm on the basis of "necessity." Strafford's alleged abuse of conciliar justice and martial law contrary to Magna Carta could thus be justified, as could Maguire's outing of his trial by peers of Ireland. It may have been the same policy of law as England that rendered Ireland a political body, that of the common law, but it remained unresolved what in practice this entailed.

The king's authority needed to be conceived of corporately in order for him to govern his disparate possessions. For example, only by acting as a body politic through inferior magistrates could he govern Ireland – a possession no English king actually visited from the time of Richard II to 1689. The same might also be said for outlying regions of the English polity. The regicides redefined kingship as an inferior magistracy in a popular state but the political body of the whole state remained a perpetual corporation. This was not full-blown republicanism but a rather extreme version of what Patrick Collinson has called "monarchical republicanism," or what Richard Tuck has called aristocratic republicanism – "a constitution not necessarily without a prince (though such a thing could be contemplated), but if there were to be a prince, one with him treated as *primus inter pares*, 'choicest of the chosen' – a kind of president in other words."[6] While many regicides such as Challoner, Scot, and Marten may have wanted a more thorough appropriation of classical republican models, the High Court of Justice stopped short of a comprehensive restatement of the terms in which Englishmen lived as civic beings in the vocabulary of classical republicanism and civic humanism. The actions of the court attacked not the institution of monarchy *per se* but that of *hereditary* monarchy in particular. This may have reflected classical republican values concerning the superiority of elected magistracy to hereditary office-holding, but it was far from the thoroughgoing rejection of monarchical rule in any form that would come in the months following

[5] Whether Ireland had to be named generally or particularly remained subject to dispute: see chapter 5, above.

[6] Richard Tuck, *Philosophy and Government, 1572–1651* (Cambridge, 1993), p. 238.

the abolition of the kingly office. If the regicide was an act of civic humanism, it was a very guarded one.

The history of political thought usually traces innovation and change to the appearance of key texts that radically redefined the nature of political authority and political obligation. Thomas Hobbes's *Leviathan* and John Locke's *Two Treatises of Government* were two such texts and the continuing lively scholarly debate on their meaning and origins reflects the lasting power of their arguments. However, rather than attempting to locate published texts in their historical contexts this study has pursued an alternate strategy in bridging what Quentin Skinner has decried as the false dichotomy between political thought and action. The objective here has been to show how political innovation sprang from simply the redeployment of pre-existing, commonplace political ideas. Major state treason trials were public, political events – ideological events – in which political thought and action were indistinguishable. However, the commonplace familiarity of many Civil War political ideas does not mean that the events of the 1640s were not in some sense "revolutionary." On the contrary, it means merely that it was a revolution that received its justification, of necessity, within pre-existing conceptual horizons.

BIBLIOGRAPHY

MANUSCRIPT SOURCES

HELD IN THE UNITED KINGDOM

Bodleian Library, Oxford

Tanner MS 418 Irish Cases.

British Library, London

Harleian MSS 162–164, Parliamentary Journal of Sir Simonds D'Ewes. Sloane MS 3828, fols.64r–74r, A Report on the Triall of the Lord McGuire – accused and hanged in England for Treason in Ireland. Drawn by Heneage Finch Esq. since Lord Chancellor of England.

House of Lords Record Office, London

House of Lords, Manuscript Minutes

Inner Temple Library, London

Petyt MS. 511 vol. 23, A Collection of Cases, Arguments and Notes by William Prynne 1634–1666, The Case of Cornelius Magwire, Baron of Enniskillen in the Realme of Ireland, fols. 120v–115v (this section of the volume is bound upside down so that the foliation marks are backwards).

Public Record Office, London

SP 16/517/1–48, A Journall of the Proceedings of the High Court of Iustice erected by Act of the Commons of England.

Worcester College, Oxford

Clarke MS LXXI.

HELD IN THE UNITED STATES

Harvard Law School, Cambridge Mass.

HLS MS 113, Reports in King's Bench 1639–1646, by Sir Arthur Turnour (d. 1651), Report of Maguire's trial, fols. 186–222.

Yale University, Beinecke Rare Books Library, New Haven, Conn.

Osborn MS fb 146, High Court of Justice for the trying and judging of Charles Stuart, King of England. ca. 1650.

PRINTED PRIMARY SOURCES

SIXTEENTH AND SEVENTEENTH-CENTURY SOURCES PUBLISHED BEFORE 1700

Bagshawe, Edward, *Two Arguments in Parliament, the First Concerning the Cannons, the Second Concerning the Paemvnire vpon those Cannons*. London, 1641.

Coke, Sir Edward. *The First Part of the Institutes of The Lawes of England. Or A Commentarie vpon Littleton, not the name of a Lawyer onely, but of the Law it selfe*. London, 1628.

The Second Part of the Institutes of the Lawes of England. London, 1642.

The Third Part of the Institutes of the Laws of England concerning High Treason, and other Pleas of the Crown, and Criminall causes. London, 1644.

The Fourth Part of the Institutes of the Laws of England Concerning The Jvrisdiction of Courts. London, 1644.

Constitutions and Canons Ecclesiasticall; Treated upon by the Archbishops of Canterbury and York, Presidents of the Convocations for the respective Provinces of Canterbury and York, and the rest of the Bishops and Clergie of those Provinces; And agreed upon with the Kings Majesties Licence in their severall Synods begun at London and York 1640. London, 1640.

Cook, John. *King Charls his Case: or an Appeal To all Rational Men, Concerning His Tryal at the High Court of Iustice*. London, 1649.

Cowell, John. *The Interpreter: or Booke Containing the Signification of Words*. Cambridge 1607.

Croke, Sir George. *The Reports of Sir George Croke*, ed. and trans. Harbottle Grimstone. London, 1657.

Crompton, Richard. *L'Avthoritie et Ivrisdiction des Covrt de la Maiestie de la Roygne: Nouelmant collect & compose, per R. Crompton del milieu Temple Esquire, Apprentice del Ley*. London, 1594; reprinted London, 1637.

Dalton, Michael. *The Countrey Iustice*. London, 1618.

Davies, Sir John. *Le Primer Report des Cases & Matters in Ley resolues & adiudges en les Courts del Roy en Ireland. Collect et digest per Sr. John Dauys Chiualer Atturney Generall del Roy en cest Realme*. Dublin, 1615.

Fulbecke, William. *A Parallele or Conference of The Civil Law, the Canon Law and the Common Law of this Realme of England. Wherin the agreement and disagreement of these three Lawes, and the causes and reasons of the said disagreement, are opened and discussed*. London, 1602; reprinted London, 1618.

Fuller, Nicholas. *The Argument of Nicholas Fuller of Grayes Inne Esquire, in the Case of Thomas Lad, and Richard Mansell his Clients*. London, 1607; reprinted London, 1641.

Gauden, John. *The Religious and Loyal Protestation of John Gauden Dr. in Divinity; Against the present Declared Purposes and Proceedings of the Army and others; About the trying and destroying our Soveraign Lord the King*. London, 1649.

[Haywarde, John]. *A Reporte of a Discourse Concerning Svpreme power in Affaires of Religion*. London, 1606.

Hunton, Philip. *A Treatise of Monarchie, Containing two Parts: 1. Concerning Monarchy in generall 2. Concerning this particular Monarchy*. London, 1643.

Jenkins, David. *The Works of That Grave and Learned Lawyer Iudge Ienkins, Prisoner in Newgate upon Divers Statutes Concerning the Liberty and Freedome of the Subiect*. London, 1648.

Lilburne, John. *The Free-mans Freedome vindicated*. London, 1646.

Mabbot, Gilbert. *King Charls his Tryal or A perfect Narrative of the whole proceedings of the High Court of Iustice*. London, 1649.

Marsh, John. *An Argument or, Debate in Law: of the Great Question concerning the Militia; As it is now settled by Ordinance of both the Houses of Parliament*. London, 1642.

Maynard, Sir John. *Mr. Maynards Speech Before Both Houses in Parliament, upon Wednesday the xxiiiij. of March, in reply upon the Earle of Straffords Answer to his Articles at the Barre*. London, 1641.

Nalson, John. *A True Copy of The Journal of The High Court of Justice for the Tryal of King Charles I as it was Read in the House of Commons, and Attested under the hand of Phelps, Clerk to that Infamous Court*. London, 1684.

Prynne, William. *Sovereign Power of Parliaments and Kingdomes: Divided into Fovr Parts Together with an Appendix*. London, 1643.

Canterburies Doome. Or, The First Part of a Compleat History of The Commitment, Charge, Tryall, Condemnation, Execution of William Lavd Late Archbishop of Canterbury. London, 1646.

A Briefe Memento To the Present Unparliamentary Iunto Touching their present Intentions and Proceedings to Depose and Execute, Charles Steward, their lawfull King. London, 1649.

The Subjection of all Traytors, Rebels, as well Peers, as Commoners in Ireland, to the Laws, Statutes, and Trials by Juries of good, and lawfull men of England, in the Kings Bench at Westminster, for Treasons perpetrated by them in Ireland, or any foreign Country out of the Realm of England. Being An Argument at Law made in the case of Connor Magwire, an Irish Baron. London, 1658.

Prynne, William et al. *The Whole Triall of Connor Lord Macguire, with The perfect copies of the Indictment, and all the evidences against him*. London, 1645.

Pym, John. *The Speech or Declaration of John Pym, Esquire: After the Recapitulation or summing up of the Charge of High Treason against, Thomas Earle of Strafford, 12 April. 1641*. London, 1641.

Rushworth, John. *The Tryal of Thomas Earl of Strafford upon an impeachment of high treason*. London, 1680; 2nd edn. London, 1700.

Historical Collections, vol. III. London, 1692.

St. John, Oliver. *An Argument of Law concerning the Bill of Attainder of High Treason of Thomas Earle of Strafford: At a Conference in the Committee of both Houses of Parliament*. London, 1641.

Master St. John His Speech in Parliament On Munday January the 17th An. Dom. 1641. Concerning the Charge of treason then exhibited to the Bishops, Formerly accused by the House of Commons. London, 1642.

Stow, John. *The Annales, or Generall Chronicle of England, begun first by maister Iohn Stow and after him continued and augmented with matters forreyn and domestique, auncient and moderne, unto the ende of this present yeare 1614*. London, 1615.

PRIMARY SOURCES PUBLISHED SINCE 1700

Aston, Sir Thomas. *The Short Parliament (1640) Diary of Sir Thomas Aston*, ed. Judith Maltby. Camden 4th Ser., vol. 35. London, 1988.

Baillie, Robert. *Letters and Journals of Robert Baillie*, 2 vols., ed. D. Laing. Edinburgh, 1841–2.

Ball, W., ed. *The Statutes at Large passed in the parliaments held in Ireland*, 20 vols. Dublin, 1784–1801.

Bidwell, William B. and Jansson, Maija, eds., *Proceedings in Parliament 1626*, vol. III: *The House of Commons*. New Haven, 1992.

Bodin, Jean. *Six Bookes of a Commonweale*, trans. Richard Knolles and ed. Kenneth D. McRae. Cambridge, Mass., 1962.

Bodin, On Sovereignty, ed. and trans. Julian H. Franklin. Cambridge, 1992.

Bracton, Henry de. *On the Laws and Customs of England*, 4 vols., ed. and trans. S. E. Thorne. Cambridge, Mass., 1968.

Brutus, Stephanus Junius [Mornay, Philippe? Languet, Hubert?]. *Vindiciae, Contra Tyrannos: or concerning the legitimate power of a prince over the people, and of the people over a prince*, ed. and trans. George Garnett. Cambridge, 1994.

Cicero in twenty-eight volumes X In Catalinam I–IV, Pro Murena, Pro Sulla, Pro Flacco, trans. C. MacDonald. Cambridge, Mass., 1977.

Cobbett W., Howell T. B. et al., eds., *A Complete Collection of State Trials*, 33 vols. London, 1809–26.

Coke, Sir Edward. *The Reports of Sir Edward Coke, knt. In thirteen parts*, ed. John Henry Thomas and John Farquhar Fraser. London, 1826.

Culpeper, Sir Cheney. *The Letters of Sir Cheney Culpeper 1641–1657*. In M. J. Braddick and Mark Greengrass, eds., *Seventeenth-Century Political and Financial Papers*. Camden Society. 5th Ser. 33, London, 1996.

Darcy, Patrick. *An Argument Delivered by Patricke Darcy Esquire; by the Expresse Order of the House of Commons in the Parliament of Ireland, 9. Iunii 1641*. Waterford 1643; reprinted Dublin, 1764.

Davies, Sir John. *A Report of Cases and Matters in Law, Resolved and Adjudged in the King's Courts in Ireland. Collected and Digested by Sir John Davies, Knight, The King's Attorney-General in that Kingdom. Now first translated into English*. Dublin, 1762.

A Discovery of the True Causes Why Ireland Was Never Entirely Subdued [and] Brought Under Obedience of the Crown of England Until the Beginning of His Majesty's Happy Reign, ed. James P. Myers, Jr. Washington, D.C., 1988.

Elton, G. R. *The Tudor Constitution: Documents and Commentary*, 2nd edn. Cambridge, 1982.

Filmer, Sir Robert. *The Freeholder's Grand Inquest*. In Johann P. Sommerville, ed., *Patriarcha and Other Writings*. Cambridge, 1991.

Firth, C. H. and Rait R. S., eds. *Acts and Ordinances of the Interregnum*, 2 vols. London, 1911.

Fortescue, Sir John. *On the Laws and Governance of England*, ed. and trans. Shelley Lockwood. Cambridge, 1997.

Gardiner, S. R., ed. *Constitutional Documents of the Puritan Revolution, 1625–1660*, 3rd edn. Oxford, 1906.

Hall, G. D. G., ed. and trans. *The Treatise on The Laws and Customs of The Realm of England Commonly Called Glanvill*. Oxford, 1993.

Haller, William, ed. *Tracts on Liberty in the Puritan Revolution*, 3 vols. New York, 1933.

Haller, William and Davies, Godfrey, eds. *The Leveller Tracts 1647–1653*. New York, 1944.

HMC House of Lords. *The Manuscripts of The House of Lords, Addenda 1514–1714*, vol. XI, new series, ed. Maurice F. Bond. London, 1962.

Hobbes, Thomas. *De Cive: The English version entitled in the first edition Philosophicall Rudiments concerning Government and Society*, ed. Howard Warrender. Oxford, 1983.

Leviathan, ed. Richard Tuck. Cambridge, 1990.

Holinshed, Raphael. *The Chronicles of Ireland* in *Holinshed's Chronicles: England, Scotland and Ireland with a New Introduction by Vernon F. Snow*, 6 vols. New York, 1965; reprinted New York, 1976.

James VI and I. *Political Writings*, ed. Johann P. Sommerville. Cambridge, 1994.

Jansson, Maija, ed. *Two Diaries of the Long Parliament*. Gloucester, 1984.

Kenyon, J. P. *The Stuart Constitution 1603–1688: Documents and Commentary*, 2nd edn. Cambridge, 1986.

Knafla, Louis, ed. *Law and Politics in Jacobean England: The Tracts of Lord Chancellor Ellesmere*. Cambridge, 1977.

Knowler, William, ed. *The Earl of Strafforde's Letters and Dispatches with an Essay towards his Life by Sir George Radcliffe*, 2 vols. London, 1739.

Lane, Sir Richard. *Lane's Exchequer Reports being a reprint of Reports of Cases in the Court of Exchequer from 1605 to 1612 by the Hon. Richard Lane with Notes and a Life of the Reporter by Charles Francis Morrell*. London, 1884.

Laud, William. *The Works of the most reverend father in God William Laud, D.D. sometime Lord Archbishop of Canterbury*, 7 vols, ed. J. Bliss and W. Scott. Oxford, 1847–60.

Milton, John. *The Prose of John Milton: Selected and Edited from the Original Texts with Introductions, Notes and Translations*, ed. J. Max Patrick. Garden City, N.Y., 1967.

Mommsen, Theodor, Kreuger, Paul, and Watson, Alan, eds. *The Digest of Justinian*, vol. IV, trans. Alan Watson. Philadelphia, 1985.

Notestein, Wallace, ed. *The Journal of Sir Simonds D'Ewes from the beginning of the Long Parliament to the opening of the Trial of the Earl of Strafford*. New Haven, 1923.

Selden, John. *The Table Talk of John Selden, A New Edition with a Biographical Preface*. Chiswick, 1818.

Smith, Sir Thomas. *De Republica Anglorum*, ed. Mary Dewar. Cambridge, 1982.

Statutes at Large, 18 vols. London, 1763–1800.

The Statutes of the Realm, 11 vols. London, 1963.

Thomas, J. A. C., ed. and trans. *The Institutes of Justinian: Text, Translation and Commentary*. Cape Town, Wynberg and Johannesburg, 1975.

Tierney, Brian, ed. *The Middle Ages I: Sources of Medieval History*, 4th edn. New York, 1983.

Verney, Sir Ralph. *Verney's Notes of the Long Parliament*, ed. J. Bruce. Camden Series 31, 1845.

SECONDARY SOURCES

BOOKS AND ARTICLES

Adamson, J. S. A. "The Baronial Context of the English Civil War." *TRHS* 5th Ser. 40 (1990): 93–120.

Alford, Stephen. *The Early Elizabethan Polity: William Cecil and the British Succession Crisis, 1558–1569*. Cambridge, 1998.

Axton, Marie. *The Queen's Two Bodies: Drama and the Elizabethan Succession*. London, 1977.

Baker, J. H. *An Introduction to English Legal History*, 3rd edn. London, 1990.

Baldwin, Geoff. "Revisionism and the Ancient Historicism." *HJ* 40 (1997): 519–525.

Barnes, T. G. *Somerset 1625–40: A County's Government During the "Personal Rule."* London, 1961.

"Review: *Tudor Law of Treason; an Introduction*, by J. G. Bellamy." *AHR* 85 (1980): 1190–1191.

Bauman, Richard A. *Crimen Maiestatis in the Roman Republic and Augustan Principate*. Johannesburg, 1967.

Bellamy, J. G. *The Law of Treason in England in the Later Middle Ages*. Cambridge, 1970.

The Tudor Law of Treason: An Introduction. Toronto, 1979.

Berkowitz, David S. "Reason of State in England and the Petition of Right 1603–1629." In Roman Schnurr, ed., *Staatsrason: Studien zur Geschichte eines politischen Begriffs*. Berlin, 1975, pp. 164–212.

Black, Stephen F. "Coram Protectore: The Judges of Westminster Hall under the Protectorate of Oliver Cromwell." *AJLH* 20 (1976): 32–64.

"The Courts and Judges of Westminster Hall During the Great Rebellion 1640–1660." *JLH* 7 (1986): 23–52.

Burgess, Glenn. "Common Law and Political Theory in Early Stuart England." *Political Science* 40 (1988): 5–17.

The Politics of the Ancient Constitution: An Introduction to English Political Thought, 1603–1642. London, 1992.

"The Divine Right of Kings Reconsidered." *EHR* 107 (1992): 837–861.

Absolute Monarchy and the Stuart Constitution. New Haven, 1996.

"Was the English Civil War a War of Religion? The Evidence of Political Propaganda." *HLQ* 61 (2000): 173–201.

Burke, Peter. "Tacitism." In T. A. Dorey, ed., *Tacitus*. New York, 1969, pp. 149–179.

"Tacitism, Scepticism, and Reason of State." In J. H. Burns and M. Goldie, eds., *The Cambridge History of Political Thought, 1450–1700*. Cambridge, 1991, pp. 479–498.

Burns, J. H. "Fortescue and the Political Theory of Dominium." *HJ* 28 (1985): 777–797.

Lordship, Kingship, and Empire: The Idea of Monarchy 1400–1525. Oxford, 1992.

Carlton, Charles. *Archbishop William Laud*. London, 1987.

Carter, Patrick. "Parliament, Convocation and the Granting of Clerical Supply in Early Modern England," *Parliamentary History* 19 (2000): 14–26.

Champion, Justin A. I. "Philosophy, State and Religion: Languages of Political Theory in Early Modern England," *Parliamentary History* 14 (1995): 187–198.

Chartier, Roger. "Texts, Printing, Readings." In Lynn Hunt, ed., *The New Cultural History*, Berkeley, Calif., 1989, pp. 154–175.

The Order of Books, trans. Lydia G. Cochrane. Cambridge, 1994.

Chrimes, S. B. *English Constitutional Ideas in the Fifteenth Century*. New York, 1966.

Christianson, Paul. "John Selden, the Five Knights Case and Discretionary Imprisonment in Early Stuart England." *Criminal Justice History* 4 (1985): 65–87.

"Royal and Parliamentary Voices on the Ancient Constitution." In Linda Levy Peck, ed., *The Mental World of the Jacobean Court*. Cambridge, 1991, pp. 71–95.

"Politics, Patronage and Conceptions of Governance in Early Stuart England: The Duke of Buckingham and his Supporters in the Parliament of 1628." *HLQ* 60 (1999): 289–302.

Clarke, Aidan. *The Old English in Ireland, 1625–42*. Worcester and London, 1966.

"The History of Poynings' Law, 1615–41." *IHS* 18 (1972): 207–222.

"Patrick Darcy and the Constitutional Relationship between Ireland and Britain." In Jane H. Ohlmeyer, ed., *Political Thought in Seventeenth Century Ireland: Kingdom or Colony?* Cambridge, 2000, pp. 35–55.

Collins, Jeffrey R. "Christian Ecclesiology and the Composition of *Leviathan*: A Newly Discovered Letter to Thomas Hobbes," *HJ* 43 (2000): 217–231.

Collinson, Patrick. "The Monarchical Republic of Queen Elizabeth I." *Bulletin of the John Rylands Library* 69 (1987): 394–424.

Connolly, Willaim E. *The Terms of Political Discourse*, 2nd edn. Princeton, 1983.

Cope, Esther S. "Sir Edward Coke and Proclamations 1610." *AJLH* 15 (1971): 215–221.

"The Short Parliament of 1640 and Convocation." *JEH* 25 (1974): 167–184.

Crawford, Patricia. "'Charles Stuart, That Man of Blood.'" *JBS* 16 (1977): 41–61.

Cressy, David. "Conflict, Consensus, and the Willingness to Wink: The Erosion of Community in Charles I's England." HLQ 61 (2000): 131–149.

Cromartie, Alan. *Sir Matthew Hale, 1609–1676: Law, Religion and Natural Philosophy*. Cambridge, 1995.

"Harringtonian Virtue: Harrington, Machiavelli, and the Method of the Moment." *HJ* 41 (1998): 987–1009.

"The Constitutionalist Revolution: The Transformation of Political Culture in Early Stuart England." *P&P* 163 (1999): 77–120.

Cross, Claire. *The Royal Supremacy in the Elizabethan Church*. London, 1969.

Cuttler, S. H. *The Law of Treason and Treason Trials in Later Medieval France*. Cambridge, 1981.

Davies, Julian. *The Caroline Captivity of the Church: Charles I and the Remoulding of Anglicanism*. Oxford, 1992.

Dickson, William K. "The Scots Law of Treason." *Juridical Review* 10 (1898): 251–254.

Dworkin, Ronald. *Law's Empire*. London, 1986.

Edwards, R. Dudley. "'Magna Carta Hiberniae.'" In John Ryan, ed., *Essays and Studies Presented to Professor Eoin MacNeill on the Occasion of His Seventieth Birthday*. Dublin, 1940, pp. 307–318.

Ellis, Steven G. *Tudor Ireland: Crown Community and the Conflict of Cultures, 1470–1603*. London, 1985.

Elton, G. R. *Policy and Police: The Enforcement of the Reformation in the Age of Thomas Cromwell*. Cambridge, 1972.

Figgis, J. N. *The Divine Right of Kings*, ed. G. R. Elton. New York, 1965 [Cambridge, 1896].

Fitzpatrick, Brendan. *Seventeenth-Century Ireland*. Dublin, 1988.

Fox, Adam. "Custom, Memory and the Authority of Writing." In Paul Griffiths, Adam Fox, and Steve Hindle, eds., *The Experience of Authority in Early Modern England*. London, 1996, pp. 89–116.

Franklin, Julian H. *Jean Bodin and the Rise of Absolutist Theory*. Cambridge, 1973.
Garfinkel, Abraham. *Studies in Ethnomethodology*. Englewood Cliffs, 1967.
Glover, Samuel Dennis. "The Putney Debates: Popular versus Elitist Republicanism." *P&P* 164 (1999): 47–80.
Gough, J. W. *Fundamental Law in English Constitutional History*. Oxford, 1955.
Gray, Charles M. "The Boundaries of the Equitable Function." *AJLH* 20 (1976): 192–226.
Guy, John. "The King's Council and Political Participation." In Alastair Fox and John Guy, eds., *Reassessing the Henrician Age: Humanism, Politics and Reform 1500–1550*. Oxford, 1986, pp. 121–147.
Tudor England. Oxford, 1988.
"The Rhetoric of Counsel in Early Modern England." In Dale Hoak, ed., *Tudor Political Culture*. Cambridge, 1995, pp. 292–310.
Hart, James S. *Justice Upon Petition: The House of Lords and the Reformation of Justice, 1621–1675*. London, 1991.
Hartz, Louis. *The Liberal Tradition in America*. New York, 1955; reprinted New York, 1991.
Hassall, W. O., ed. *A Catalogue of the Library of Sir Edward Coke, with a Preface by S. E. Thorne*. New Haven, 1950.
Hast, Adele. "State Treason Trials during the Puritan Revolution 1640–1660." *HJ* 15 (1972): 37–53.
Helgerson, Richard. *Forms of Nationhood: The Elizabethan Writing of England*. Chicago, 1992.
Helmholz, R. *Roman Canon Law in Reformation England*. Cambridge, 1990.
Hexter, J. H. "The Early Stuarts and Parliament: Old Hat and the *Nouvelle Vague*." *Parliamentary History* 1 (1982): 181–215.
Hill, J. E. Christopher. "The Norman Yoke." In J. E. Christopher Hill, *Puritanism and Revolution*. London, 1958, pp. 50–122.
Hill, L. M. "The Two Witness Rule in English Treason Trials: Some Comments on the Emergence of Procedural Law." *AJLH* 12 (1968): 95–111.
Holdsworth, Sir William. *A History of the English Law*, 16 vols. 6th edn. London, 1903; reprinted London, 1938.
Johns, Adrian. *The Nature of the Book: Print and Knowledge in the Making*. Chicago, 1998.
Jones, David M. "Sir Edward Coke and the Interpretation of Lawful Allegiance in Seventeenth-Century England." *HPT* 7 (1986): 321–340.
Jones, W. J. *Politics and the Bench*. London, 1971.
Kantorowicz, Ernst L. *The King's Two Bodies: A Study in Medieval Political Theology*. Princeton, 1957.
Kearney, Hugh. F. *Strafford in Ireland, 1633–1641: A Study in Absolutism*. Manchester, 1959.
Keeler, Mary Frear. *The Long Parliament, 1640–41: A Biographical Study of its Members*. Philadelphia, 1954.
Kelley, Donald R. "History, English Law and the Renaissance." *P&P* 65 (1974): 24–51.
Kelsey, Sean. *Inventing a Republic: The Political Culture of the English Commonwealth, 1649–1653*. Stanford, 1997.
Koenigsberger, H. G. "Monarchies and Parliaments in Early Modern Europe: Dominium Regale or Dominium Politicum et Regale." *Theory and Society* 5 (1978): 191–217.
Early Modern Europe, 1500–1789. London, 1987.

Kraye, Jill, ed. *The Cambridge Companion to Renaissance Humanism*. Cambridge, 1996.
Kristeller, Paul Oskar, *Renaissance Thought and its Sources*. New York. 1979.
Lamont, William M. *Marginal Prynne, 1600–1669*. Toronto and London, 1963.
Godly Rule: Politics and Religion 1603–1660. London, 1969.
Lander, J. R. "Attainder and Forfeiture, 1453–1509." *HJ* 6 (1961): 119–151.
Langbein, John. *Torture and the Law of Proof: Europe and England in the Ancien Regime*. Chicago, 1977.
Lear, Floyd Seyward. *Treason in Roman and Germanic Law*. Austin, Tex., 1965.
Lehmberg, S. E. "Parliamentary Attainder in the Reign of Henry VIII." *HJ* 18 (1975): 675–702.
Levack, Brian P. *The Civil Lawyers in England, 1603–1641: A Political Study*. Oxford, 1973.
The Formation of the British State: England, Scotland and the Union, 1603–1707. Oxford, 1987.
"Law and Ideology: The Civil Law and Theories of Absolutism in Elizabethan and Jacobean England." In Heather Dubrow and Richard Strier, eds., *The Historical Renaissance: New Essays on Tudor and Stuart Literature and Culture*. Chicago, 1988, pp. 220–241.
Little, Patrick. "The Earl of Cork and the Fall of the Earl of Strafford 1638–41." *HJ* 39 (1996): 619–635.
Macguire, Nancy Klein. "The Theatrical Mask/Masque of Politics: The Case of Charles I." *JBS* 28 (1989): 1–22.
Mackenny, Richard. *Sixteenth-Century Europe, Expansion and Conflict*. New York, 1993.
Maitland, F. W. "The Crown as Corporation." *LQR* 17 (1901): 131–146.
The Constitutional History of England, ed. H. A. L. Fisher. Cambridge, 1908; reprinted Cambridge, 1965.
Malcolm, Joyce Lee. "Doing No Wrong: Law, Liberty, and the Constraint of Kings." *JBS* 38 (1999): 161–186.
McIlwain, C. H. *The High Court of Parliament and its Supremacy: An Historical Essay on the Boundaries Between Legislation and Adjudication in England*. New Haven, 1910.
Mendle, Michael. "Politics and Political Thought, 1640–42." In Conrad Russell, ed., *The Origins of the English Civil War*. London, 1973, pp. 219–245.
"Parliamentary Sovereignty: A Very English Absolutism." In Nicholas Phillipson and Quentin Skinner, eds., *Political Discourse in Early Modern Britain*. Cambridge, 1993, pp. 97–119.
Henry Parker and the English Civil War: the Political Thought of the Public's Privado. Cambridge, 1995.
Miller, Peter N. *Defining the Common Good, Empire, Religion and Philosophy in Eighteenth-Century Britain*. Cambridge, 1994.
Milton, Anthony. "Thomas Wentworth and the Political Thought of the Personal Rule." In J. F. Merritt, ed., *The Political World of Thomas Wentworth, Earl of Strafford, 1621–1641*. Cambridge, 1996, pp. 133–156.
Moretti, Franco. "The Great Eclipse: Tragic Form as the Deconsecration of Sovereignty." In Franco Moretti, *Signs Taken for Wonders: Essays in the Sociology of Literary Forms*, trans. Susan Fischer et al. London, 1983; revised edn. London, 1988, pp. 43–82.
Morgan, Hiram. "Extradition and Treason-trial of a Gaelic Lord: The Case of Brian O'Rourke." *Irish Jurist* 22 (1987): 285–301.

Morrill, J. S. "The Religious Context of the English Civil War." In Richard Cust and Ann Hughes, eds., *The English Civil War*. London 1997, pp. 159–181.
Morrill, John and Baker, Philip. "Oliver Cromwell, the Regicide and the Sons of Zeruiah." In Jason Peacey, ed., *The Regicides and the Execution of Charles I*. Basingstoke, 2001, pp. 14–35.
Mosse, George L. "The Influence of Jean Bodin's *République* on English Political Thought." *Medievalia et Humanistica* 5 (1948): 73–83.
Nenner, Howard. "The Trial of the Regicides: Retribution and Treason in 1660." In Howard Nenner, ed., *Politics and the Political Imagination in Later Stuart Britain*. Rochester, 1997, pp. 21–42.
Oakley, Francis. "'Anxieties of Influence': Skinner, Figgis, Conciliarism and Early Modern Constitutionalism." *P&P* 151 (1996): 60–110.
Orr, D. Alan. "England, Ireland, Magna Carta and the Common Law: The Case of Connor Lord Maguire, Second Baron of Enniskillen." *JBS* 39 (2000): 389–421.
Palmer, William. "Invitation to a Beheading: Factions in Parliament, the Scots and the Execution of Archbishop William Laud in 1645." *Historical Magazine of the Protestant Episcopal Church* 52 (1983): 17–27.
Parker, David. "Law, Society and the State in the Thought of Jean Bodin." *HPT* 2 (1981): 253–285.
Patterson, Annabel. "For Words Only: From Treason Trial to Liberal Legend in Early Modern England." *Yale Journal of Law and the Humanities* 5 (1993): 389–416.
Pawlisch, Hans S. "Sir John Davies, The Ancient Constitution and the Civil Law," *HJ* 23 (1980): 689–702.
Sir John Davies and the Conquest of Ireland: A Study in Legal Imperialism. Cambridge, 1985.
Pearl, Valerie. "Oliver St. John and the 'middle group' in the Long Parliament: August 1643–May 1644." *EHR* 81 (1966): 490–519.
Peck, Linda Levy. "Kingship, Counsel and Law in Early Stuart Britain." In J. G. A. Pocock, Gordon Schochet, and Lois G. Schwoerer, eds., *Varieties of British Political Thought, 1500–1800*. Cambridge, 1993, pp. 80–115.
"Beyond the Pale, John Cusacke and the Language of Absolutism in Early Stuart Britain." *HJ* 41 (1998): 121–149.
Peltonen, Markku. *Classical Humanism and Republicanism in English Political Thought, 1570–1640*. Cambridge, 1995.
Perceval-Maxwell, Michael. "Ireland and the Monarchy in the Early Stuart Multiple Kingdom," *HJ* 34 (1991): 279–295.
The Outbreak of the Irish Rebellion of 1641. Montreal and Kingston, 1994.
Pincus, Steve. "Reconceiving Seventeenth-Century Political Culture." *JBS* 38 (1999): 98–111.
Pocock, J. G. A. *The Machiavellian Moment: Florentine Political Thought and the Atlantic Republican Tradition*. Princeton, 1975.
The Ancient Constitution and the Feudal Law: A Study of English Historical Thought in the Seventeenth Century, 2nd edn. Cambridge, 1987.
Pollock, Sir Frederick, *The Expansion of Common Law*. London, 1904.
Post, Gaines. *Studies in Medieval Legal Thought: Public Law and the State*. Princeton, 1964.
Price, Polly J. "Natural Law and Birthright Citizenship in *Calvin's Case*." *Yale Journal of Law and the Humanities* 9 (1997): 73–145.

Russell, Conrad. "The Theory of Treason in the Trial of Strafford." *EHR* 80 (1965): 30–50.

The Crisis of Parliaments: English History, 1509–1660. Oxford, 1971.

Parliaments and English Politics, 1621–1629. Oxford, 1979.

"The British Problem and the English Civil War." *History* 72 (1987): 395–415.

The Causes of the English Civil War. Oxford, 1990.

"Divine Rights in the Early Seventeenth Century." In John Morrill, Paul Slack, and Daniel Woolf, eds., *Public Duty and Private Conscience in Seventeenth-Century England: Essays Presented to G. E. Aylmer*. Oxford, 1993, pp. 101–120.

The Fall of The British Monarchies, 1637–42. Oxford, 1991; reprinted Oxford, 1995.

"Whose Supremacy? King, Parliament and the Church, 1530–1640." *Lambeth Palace Library Annual Review* (1995): 53–64.

"Parliamentary History in Perspective, 1604–1629." In Richard Cust and Ann Hughes, eds., *The English Civil War*. London, 1997, pp. 32–61.

"Parliament, the Royal Supremacy and the Church." *Parliamentary History* 19 (2000): 27–37.

Salmon, J. H. M. "Cicero and Tacitus in Sixteenth-Century France." *AHR* 85 (1980): 307–331.

"Seneca and Tacitus in Jacobean England." In Linda Levy Peck, ed., *The Mental World of the Jacobean Court*. Cambridge, 1991, pp. 169–188.

Sanderson, John B. *"But the People's Creatures": The Philosophical Basis of the English Civil War*. Manchester, 1989.

Scott, Jonathan. *Algernon Sydney and the Restoration Crisis, 1677–1683*. Cambridge, 1991.

"The English Republican Imagination." In J. S. Morrill, ed., *Revolution and Restoration: England in the 1650s*. London, 1992, pp. 35–54.

Seaberg, R. B. "The Norman Conquest and the Common Law: The Levellers and the Argument from Continuity." *HJ* 24 (1981): 791–806.

Sharpe, Kevin. *Politics and Ideas in Early Stuart England: Essays and Studies*. London, 1989.

The Personal Rule of Charles I. New Haven, 1992.

Sharpe, Kevin and Brooks, Christopher. "Debate: History English Law and the Renaissance." *P&P* 72 (1976): 133–142.

Skinner, Quentin. "History and Ideology in the English Revolution." *HJ* 8 (1965): 151–178.

"Conquest and Consent: Thomas Hobbes and the Engagement Controversy." In G. E. Aylmer, ed., *The Interregnum*. London, 1972, pp. 79–98.

"The Principles and Practice of Opposition: The Case of Bolingbroke versus Walpole." In Neil McKendrick, ed., *Historical Perspectives: Studies in English Thought and Society in Honour of J. H. Plumb*. London, 1974, pp. 93–128.

The Foundations of Modern Political Thought, vol. I: *The Renaissance*. Cambridge, 1977.

The Foundations of Modern Political Thought, vol. II: *The Age of Reformation*. Cambridge, 1978.

"The State." In Terence Ball et al., eds., *Political Innovation and Conceptual Change*. Cambridge, 1989, pp. 90–131.

Reason and Rhetoric in the Philosophy of Thomas Hobbes. Cambridge, 1996.

Liberty Before Liberalism. Cambridge, 1998.

Smith, David L. "The Idea of the Rule of Law in England and France in the Seventeenth Century." In Ronald G. Asch and Heinz Duchhardte, eds., *Der Absolutismus – ein Mythos? Strukturwandel monarchischer Herrschaft in West- und Mitteleuropa (ca. 1550–1700)*. Cologne, 1996, pp. 167–184.

Sommerville, Johann P. "The Royal Supremacy and Episcopacy '*Jure Divino*' 1603–1640." *JEH* 34 (1983): 548–558.

"History and Theory: the Norman Conquest in Early Stuart Political Thought." *Political Studies* 34 (1986): 249–261.

Politics and Ideology in England, 1603–1640. London, 1986.

"James I and the Divine Right of Kings: English Politics and Continental Theory." In Linda Levy Peck, ed., *The Mental World of the Jacobean Court*. Cambridge, 1991, pp. 55–70.

"English and European Political Ideas in the Early Seventeenth Century: Revisionism and the Case of Absolutism." *JBS* 35 (1996): 168–194.

"The Ancient Constitution Reassessed: The Common Law, the Court and the Languages of Politics in Early Modern England." In Malcolm Smuts, ed., *The Stuart Court and Europe: Essays in Politics and Political Culture*. Cambridge, 1996, pp. 39–64.

Spencer, Lois. "The Printing of Sir George Croke's Reports." *Studies in Bibliography* 11 (1958): 231–246.

Stacy, W. R. "Matter of Fact, Matter of Law, and the Attainder of the Earl of Strafford." *AJLH* 29 (1985): 323–347.

"Richard Roose and the Use of Parliamentary Attainder in the Reign of Henry VIII." *HJ* 29 (1986): 1–15.

Stone, Lawrence. *The Crisis of the Aristocracy, 1558–1641*, abridged edn. Oxford, 1967.

Taylor, Charles. "Interpretation and the Sciences of Man." In *Charles Taylor, Philosophical Papers* 2. Cambridge, 1985, pp. 15–57.

Thorne, S. E. "Praemunire and Sir Edward Coke." *HLQ* 2 (1938–9): 85–88.

English Constitutional Ideas in the Fifteenth Century. New York, 1966.

Thornley, Isobel D. "Treason by Words in the Fifteenth Century." *EHR* 32 (1917): 556–558.

Timmis III, J. H. *Thine is the Kingdom: The Trial for Treason of Thomas Lord Wentworth, Earl of Strafford, First Minister to King Charles I and Last Hope of the English Crown*. Tuscaloosa, Ala., 1974.

"Evidence and 1 *Eliz. I, Cap.* 6: The Basis of The Lords' Decision in the Trial of Strafford." *HJ* 21 (1978): 677–683.

Trevor-Roper, H. R. *Archbishop Laud, 1573–1645*, 3rd edn. London, 1988.

Tubbs, J. W. "Custom, Time and Reason: Early Seventeenth-Century Conceptions of the Common Law." *HPT* 19 (1998): 363–406.

Tuck, Richard. *Natural Rights Theories: Their Origins and Development*. Cambridge, 1979.

Philosophy and Government, 1572–1651. Cambridge, 1993.

Tyacke, Nicholas. "Puritanism, Arminianism and Counter Revolution." In Conrad Russell, ed., *The Origins of the English Civil War*. London, 1973, pp. 119–143.

Anti-Calvinists: The Rise of English Arminianism, c. 1590–1640. Oxford, 1987.

Underdown, David. *Pride's Purge: Politics in the Puritan Revolution*. Oxford, 1971.

Walter, John. "A 'Rising of the People'? The Oxfordshire Rising of 1596." *P&P* 107 (1986): 91–143.

Waugh, W. T. "The Great Statute of Praemunire." *EHR* 37 (1922): 173–205.

Wedgwood, C. V. *Thomas Wentworth First Earl of Strafford, 1593–1641: A Revaluation*. London, 1961.

The Trial of Charles I. Glasgow, 1964; reprinted Harmondsworth, 1983.

Weston, C. C. and Greenberg, Janelle. *Subjects and Sovereigns: The Grand Controversy over Legal Sovereignty in Stuart England*. Cambridge, 1981.

Woolf, D. R. *The Idea of History in Early Stuart England*. Toronto, 1990.

Worden, Blair. *The Rump Parliament 1648–1653*. Cambridge, 1974.

"Classical Republicanism and the Puritan Revolution." In Hugh Lloyd-Jones, Valerie Pearl, and Blair Worden, eds., *History and Imagination: Essays in Honour of H. R. Trevor-Roper*. London, 1981, pp. 182–200.

"English Republicanism." In J. H. Burns and M. Goldie, eds., *The Cambridge History of Political Thought, 1450–1700*. Cambridge, 1991, pp. 443–475.

UNPUBLISHED WORKS

Carter, P. R. N. "Royal Taxation of the English Parish Clergy, 1535–1558." Ph.D. dissertation, University of Cambridge, 1995.

de Sousa, Norberto. "The Idea of a Civil Society and the Roman Tradition of Republicanism." Paper prepared for Pick'n'mix meeting, 16 May 1994, Jesus College, Cambridge.

Muldrew, Craig. "Amputations of the Body Politic: Episodes in the Early Public Life of Oliver St. John 1629–1641." MA dissertation, University of Alberta, 1986.

Orr, D. Alan. "John Lilburne and the Ancient Constitution 1646–1649." MA dissertation, Queen's University, 1993.

"Sovereignty, State and the Law of Treason in England 1641–49." Ph.D. dissertation, University of Cambridge, 1997.

Perkins, Nicola P. "The Judiciary and the Defence of Property in the Law Courts During the Personal Rule of Charles I." Ph.D. dissertation, Cambridge University, 1999.

Stacy, W. R. "The Bill of Attainder in English History." Ph.D. dissertation, University of Wisconsin Madison, 1986.

Ward, Lesley J. "The Law of Treason in the Reign of Elizabeth I." Ph.D. dissertation, University of Cambridge, 1985.

INDEX

Cambridge Studies in Early Modern British History

Titles in the series

*The Common Peace: Participation and the Criminal Law in Seventeenth-Century England**
CYNTHIA B. HERRUP

Politics, Society and Civil War in Warwickshire, 1620–1660
ANN HUGHES

*London Crowds in the Reign of Charles II: Propaganda and Politics from the Restoration to the Exclusion Crisis**
TIM HARRIS

*Criticism and Compliment: The Politics of Literature in the England of Charles I**
KEVIN SHARPE

Central Government and the Localities: Hampshire, 1649–1689
ANDREW COLEBY

John Skelton and the Politics of the 1520s
GREG WALKER

Algernon Sidney and the English Republic, 1623–1677
JONATHAN SCOTT

Thomas Starkey and the Commonweal: Humanist Politics and Religion in the Reign of Henry VIII
THOMAS F. MAYER

*The Blind Devotion of the People: Popular Religion and the English Reformation**
ROBERT WHITING

The Cavalier Parliament and the Reconstruction of the Old Regime, 1661–1667
PAUL SEAWARD

The Blessed Revolution: England Politics and the Coming of War, 1621–1624
THOMAS COGSWELL

Charles I and the Road to Personal Rule
L. J. REEVE

George Lawson's 'Politica' and the English Revolution
CONAL CONDREN

Puritans and Roundheads: The Harleys of Brampton Bryan and the Outbreak of the Civil War
JACQUELINE EALES

An Uncounselled king: Charles I and the Scottish Troubles, 1637–1641
PETER DONALD

*Cheap Print and Popular Piety, 1550–1640**
TESSA WATT

The Pursuit of Stability: Social Relations in Elizabethan London
IAN W. ARCHER

Prosecution and Punishment: Petty Crime and the Law in London and Rural Middlesex, c. 1660–1725
ROBERT B. SHOEMAKER

Algernon Sidney and the Restoration Crisis, 1677–1683
JONATHAN SCOTT

Exile and Kingdom: History and Apocalpyse in the Puritan Migration to America
AVIHU ZAKAI

The Pillars of Priestcraft Shaken: The Church of England and its Enemies, 1660–1730
J. A. I. CHAMPION

Steward, Lords and People: The Estate Steward and his World in Later Stuart England
D. R. HAINSWORTH

Civil War and Restoration in the Three Stuart Kingdoms: The Career of Randal MacDonnell, Marquis of Antrim, 1609–1683
JANE H. OHLMEYER

The Family of Love in English Society, 1550–1630
CHRISTOPHER W. MARSH

*The Bishops' Wars: Charles I's Campaign against Scotland, 1638–1640**
MARK FISSEL

John Locke: Resistance, Religion and Responsibility
JOHN MARSHALL

Constitutional Royalism and the Search for Settlement, c. 1640–1649
DAVID L. SMITH

Intelligence and Espionage in the Reign of Charles II, 1660–1685
ALAN MARSHALL

The Chief Governors: The Rise and Fall of Reform Government in Tudor Ireland, 1536–1588
CIARAN BRADY

Politics and Opinion in Crisis, 1678–1681
MARK KNIGHTS

Catholic and Reformed: The Roman and Protestant Churches in English Protestant Thought, 1604–1640
ANTHONY MILTON

Sir Matthew Hale, 1609–1676: Law, Religion and Natural Philosophy
ALAN CROMARTIE

Henry Parker and the English Civil War: The Political Thought of the Public's 'Privado'
MICHAEL MENDLE

Protestantism and Patriotism: Ideologies and the Making of English Foreign Policy, 1650–1668
STEVEN C. A. PINCUS

Gender in Mystical and Occult Thought: Behmenism and its Development in England
B. J. GIBBONS

William III and the Godly Revolution
TONY CLAYDON

Law-Making and Society in Late Elizabethan England: The Parliament of England, 1584–1601
DAVID DEAN

Conversion, Politics and Religion in England, 1580–1625
MICHAEL C. QUESTIER

Politics, Religion and the British Revolutions: The Mind of Samuel Rutherford
JOHN COFFEY

*King James VI and I and the Reunion of Christendom**
W. B. PATTERSON

The English Reformation and the Laity: Gloucestershire, 1540–1580
CAROLINE LITZENBERGER

Godly Clergy in Early England: The Caroline Puritan Movement, c. 1620–1643
TOM WEBSTER

*Prayer Book and People in Elizabethan and Early Stuart England**
JUDITH MALTBY

Sermons at Court, 1559–1629: Religion and Politics in Elizabethan and Jacobean Preaching
PETER E. MCCULLOUGH

Dismembering the Body Politic: Partisan Politics in England's Towns, 1650–1730
PAUL D. HALLIDAY

Women Waging Law in Elizabethan England
TIMOTHY STRETTON

The Early Elizabethan Polity: William Cecil and the British Succession Crisis, 1558–1569
STEPHEN ALFORD

The Polarisation of Elizabethan Politics: The Political Career of Robert Devereux, 2nd Earl of Essex
PAUL J. HAMMER

The Politics of Social Conflict: The Peak Country, 1520–1770
ANDY WOOD

Crime and Mentalities in Early Modern England
MALCOLM GASKILL

The Church in an Age of Danger: Parsons and Parishioners, 1660–1740
DONALD A. SPAETH

Reading History in Early Modern England
D. R. WOOLF

The Politics of Court Scandal in Early Modern England: News Culture and the Overbury Affair, 1603–1660
ALASTAIR BELLANY

The Politics of Religion in the Age of Mary, Queen of Scots: The Earl of Argyll and the Struggle for Britain and Ireland
JANE E. A. DAWSON

Treason and the State: Law, Politics, and Ideology in the English Civil War
D. ALAN ORR

**Also published as a paperback*

Printed in the United States
76985LV00004B/337-348

9 780521 037334